All best wishes

a. Louise Staman

Loosening Corsets

Rebecca Latimer Felton
First Woman Senator of the United States

Tiger Iron Press
Macon, Georgia, USA

Loosening Corsets

The Heroic Life

of

Georgia's Feisty Mrs. Felton,

First Woman Senator of the United States

A. Louise Staman

Tiger Iron Press

Includes endnotes, index, bibliography, pictures, and questions for book clubs. Printed in the Unites States of America.

ISBN-10: 0-9787263-1-6
ISBN-13: 978-0-9787263-1-7

Search by: 1. Rebecca Latimer Felton. 2. Women Senators. 3. Women journalists – South. 4. Georgia history – women. 5. Suffragists – South. 6. Southern reformers. 8. Title. 9. Author.

Back cover drawing and frontispiece of Rebecca Latimer Felton courtesy of Georgia State Archives. Photographs of Felton home and William Harrell Felton from *My Memoirs of Georgia Politics,* by Rebecca Latimer Felton, 1911. All other illustrations from the Library of Congress Prints and Photographs Online Catalog.

First Edition: November 2006

In loving memory of my mother

Maurine Harmon Lofgren

Contents

Preface

Rebecca Latimer Felton was born in 1835 on a large plantation near what is now Atlanta. Except for the fact that she was better educated than most young women of the times, she was the typical Southern Belle – beautiful and adored. At age eighteen she married a medical doctor and Methodist minister, a widower with one small daughter. They shared a large plantation with his parents. Hers was a traditional southern-plantation life – until the Civil War and General Sherman. Then she lost nearly everything, even her children. Yet she refused to be defeated, constantly working, at first just to find enough food to feed her family, and next to restore her plantation. She also examined her state, still in shambles, and began to work for its betterment, too. By the end of her crusading life, she had become one of the most remarkable women in American history.

Her good friend Margaret Mitchell took many of Rebecca's Civil War and Reconstruction memories and placed them in *Gone with the Wind.* Even the scene in which Scarlett O'Hara, having nothing to wear for an important meeting, tears down the curtains to make her dress, first occurred in Rebecca's real life. Rebecca's dress exists today, bearing slight traces of its earlier curtain existence. A love story is also involved in both works, but each is quite different. History remembers her husband Dr. William H.

Felton as a wonderful orator and honest politician not afraid to stand alone for his beliefs, a man who loved and encouraged his wife. He tended the wounded throughout the Civil War, unlike the hustler Rhett Butler.

Following Reconstruction, Rebecca began to reject the traditional expectations of chivalry regarding women, becoming a reformer, speaking and writing against crooked politicians, the brutal chain gang, and graft, while promoting education and opportunity for all. No Georgian woman before Rebecca had dared speak out or write in opposition to corruption. Amid fierce denunciations from church bishops, pastors, politicians, and even many women, she changed from a traditional southern lady into a crusading politician forty-seven years before she got the vote. She became a full-blown suffragist at the age of eighty, wrote books, owned a newspaper, gave speeches everywhere, and seemed to grow stronger each year. In 1922, at the age of eighty-seven, Rebecca was appointed to take (for only a few weeks) the Senate position left vacant by the death of Senator Tom Watson. During this time period the Senate wasn't even in session. Her Senate appointment was merely a token. Georgia's lame-duck, anti-suffragist governor had appointed her because he wanted that Senate seat for himself – without competition in the upcoming election. Besides, his action might attract new women voters to his side. He had seriously underestimated Rebecca. What happened next is unbelievable.

This story is true. All of the quotations are accurate, with one exception. A farm woman all of her life, Rebecca talked to her animals and loved in particular her dogs, horses, mules, and a chicken that followed her everywhere. On brief occasions Rebecca is quoted talking to Pompey, the real name of her favorite saddle horse, one mule, and that beloved chicken. I believe that these simple quotations give Rebecca more authenticity, even if the exact words are not in archival deposits.

Finally, it seems that nearly all of Georgia has helped me tell the story of this great woman: relatives, archivists, old people who remember her, librarians, professors, curators, courthouse clerks, and many others, making my three years of research on her a joy. I am grateful to them all. Rebecca loved her state, and apparently her state has not forgotten her, as I had once thought. It is fitting that so many Georgians have helped me write the biography of this stubborn, feisty, funny, always-working woman, this national treasure: Rebecca Latimer Felton.

Chapter One

Out of the Embers

In the twilight, he fished in his pocket for another cigar, took it out and sniffed it, bit off the end and struck a match. He watched as the fire sparked and rose in yellow-orange, lit the tobacco, puffing deeply, and once again held up the glowing match, examining it. Only when it reached his fingers did he shake it out, shifting slightly in his saddle. He glanced at all the fires that marked his trail, some still visible a mile away, flames and smoke licking the sky. Burning, such a quick solution to years, sometimes decades of work. They left the house since it appeared to be occupied, and burned the outbuildings. The flames shimmered.

They were burning her plantation now – trampling and looting her home. She had come there as a bride of eighteen. On October 11, 1853, the bright, energetic and fun-loving Rebecca Ann Latimer had married Dr. William Harrell Felton, a solemn, idealistic widower, a physician and Methodist minister twelve years her senior. He took his beautiful young bride to his Cass County plantation, near Cartersville in northwestern Georgia, jointly owned by his father John Felton. Along with William's mother, Rebecca took over the responsibility of rearing William's young daughter, Ann (then age four) and helping to run the plantation. For eleven years Rebecca and William had toiled together to tame the rich land, to have their own children, to prosper. Their six hundred acre cotton plantation, with more than fifty slaves, was fertile and beautiful.

General William T. Sherman, mounted on his small, sturdy horse, watched the flames consume, as he had so often before. He was tired of the killing, weary, determined to end this protracted and hideous struggle – a war that he had never wanted. The Georgia inferno had already begun – ahead of him lay rich Atlanta. Matches, that's what he needed now – matches for his fresh smoke – and all of Georgia if that's what it took to finish the Confederacy.

By the late spring of 1864, nearly everyone guessed that Sherman was planning to march into north Georgia from Tennessee; he was coming with the same certainty as death itself. Along with his 100,000 troops, he had been preparing for weeks. Some Georgians still believed that the Confederate forces could stop his march, maybe even turn him back, while others shared the apocalyptic vision of one journalist for the *Augusta Daily Chronicle and Sentinel*, who predicted the killing, plunder and destruction of everything in Georgia. "No man, woman or child will escape. One universal ruin awaits us all."

Escape! That's what the people of north Georgia needed to do – escape from the path of the Yankees, the fighting, the burning and killing. Which way would lead to safety? Some grimly remained in their houses, waiting, looking toward the north, while others went south to Atlanta, or ran into the woods, counting upon their knowledge of the countryside to hide them from Sherman's massive troops. A few placed as many valuables as they could into their wagons and fled to the homes of friends or relatives who lived in safer places. Others simply moved away, not certain of their final destination even as they hitched their wagons.

William and Rebecca Felton tried to face this looming catastrophe with intelligent deliberation. By 1864 Rebecca had given birth to three children: John Latimer, born in 1854; Mary Eleanor, born in 1856 (who died in infancy); and William Harrell, Jr., born in 1859. There was also Ann Carlton, William's young daughter, named after his first wife. They considered their family, their options, all of which seemed fraught with danger.

Their proximity to the Western and Atlantic Railroad (their home served as a small depot) convinced them of the need to leave. The railroad would become Sherman's lifeline, moving troops and supplies. Even if he didn't use it for his own purposes, he would see that no Confederate could ever use it again. His army had become expert at exploding round houses, stations, locomotives. His troops tore up miles of railroad tracks, piled up the ties, set them afire, and threw the tracks into the flames. When the tracks were molten, they twisted them around tree trunks – Sherman's neckties, they were called. A home so near the railroad would be a Yankee target.

After considerable discussion, they decided to leave their plantation, rent a farm and grow a crop elsewhere until they could safely return. They would divide their slaves, leaving some to care for their Cartersville plantation, and taking others with them to work the rented farm. William soon located and rented the Plant's farm in central Georgia "near the Clinton Road" not far from Macon. Surely General Sherman would not find them there. Rebecca looked out over the rolling hills of their plantation, holding everything within her mind, even the small white chicken in the front yard...already remembering. While William tended to the wagons, Rebecca walked where she had so often gone before – to the top of a beautiful knoll not far from the house, sheltered by enormous ancient pines. She stood silently only for a moment, then turned toward her husband and children, already sitting in the wagon, expectantly watching her. She did not look back or even shed a tear as she climbed into the wagon. They had become refugees within their own state.

As the feared and dreaded Sherman surveyed their plantation that late summer evening in 1864, smoking his cigar, the Feltons were on their rented Macon farm. A kindly neighbor, learning that Sherman had promised not to burn homes that were still occupied, had slipped into the Felton's Cartersville house and lit a lantern, saving it from total destruction. The land the Feltons now worked, on their rented farm, was poor and swampy, the house a mere shack in the midst of a rough pine grove. The rooms were made of unsealed planks, the windows badly shuttered, making the house bug ridden and steamy in summer and damp and freezing in winter, with wind blowing straight through the cracks. While they tried to harvest what they could from the red Georgia clay, Sherman's huge army relentlessly moved on, away from Cartersville and the Felton plantation, heading south now for Atlanta.

Rebecca and William didn't have time to worry about Sherman. A measles epidemic struck their farm. Although they tirelessly nursed black and white children, there was not much they could do but keep them as comfortable as possible…and watch seven of them die. One was their son Willie. Realizing that she had no time to grieve since so many others were desperately ill, she continued her work, vowing that only God would see the depth of her despair and know how much she had loved her son.

A few days after they buried Willie, Rebecca received word that her mother, who lived in Crawfordville, about seventy-five miles north of their Macon farm, was desperately ill and asking for her. Although the trains were still running in central Georgia, no one knew for how long. William did not want his wife to go to Crawfordville. He warned her that Sherman could cut her off from their home in Macon, leaving her stranded God knows where – or that her train might be captured or destroyed. No, that trip was fraught with too much uncertainty – danger. He looked into her eyes, brimming over now. He knew how much she loved her mother, how important this trip was to her. Sadly, he let her go, making her promise to wire him by telegraph whenever she could.

Rebecca reached her destination without incident. She was at her mother's bedside on the night of November 15, 1864 (General Sherman was approximately ninety miles to the west). While Rebecca fed her mother her supper, Sherman, with a roaring fire and a band playing outside, sat at a table in an Atlanta mansion and stuck his fork into a small pile of sweet potatoes. Thin, wiry, of ruddy complexion, he talked, ate, drank coffee, received messages, issued orders, and reached for his ever-present cigar. As the ominous orange outside the windows grew brighter, the band struck up the haunting "Miserere" from Giuseppe Verdi's *Il Trovatore*. He paused briefly, his face somber, to listen to this sad melody, punctuated by violent detonations. He would later explain in his *Memoirs* that one of the nearby torched buildings held ammunition and that the "night was made hideous by the bursting of shells, whose fragments came uncomfortably near Judge Lyon's house, in which I was quartered." Atlanta was burning; towering flames shattered the sky while Sherman ate his simple supper. As one witness observed, "Presently the skeletons of great warehouses stand out in relief against...sheets of roaring, blazing, furious flames...as one fire sinks, another rises...lurid, angry, dreadful to look upon."

Intent upon making certain that Atlanta would never again serve as the supply depot for the Confederate cause, Sherman had already emptied the city of its civilians and sent his own wounded away. The destruction of Atlanta marked another beginning for him, the start of a campaign to "make Georgia howl!" Sherman's infamous March to the Sea began that night with his Atlanta bonfire accompanied by a Massachusetts regimental band. The following morning Sherman and his troops, in four long columns, moved like molten lava from an active volcano, burning, destroying everything that resisted – heading east toward Crawfordville. Reaching the top of a hill, Sherman paused to look back. "Behind us lay Atlanta, smoldering and in ruins, the black smoke rising high in the air, and hanging like a pall over the ruined city." Already another type of destruction was taking place in

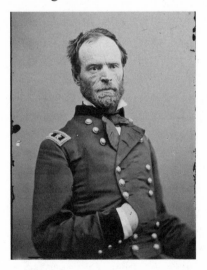

William T. Sherman

that broken city, as human vultures, looters, picked and scraped the remains, taking anything valuable from the wreckage. They even plundered the houses left standing. Following those looters would come another scourge: smallpox. Invasion, fire, theft, then plague.

Not yet knowing that Atlanta lay in ruins and that Sherman was on the march, one can imagine Rebecca greeting her mother with a cup of tea and a small piece of cornbread, sitting with her while she ate her breakfast, then bathing her mother's hands and face and helping her change into a fresh nightgown, fluffing her pillows and straightening the covers.

Sherman urged on his little horse Sam, whose prodigious walk could out trot other steeds. Determined, wrinkled, shabbily dressed, astride his formidable mount, he took full responsibility for his ambitious march. He realized that if he failed, his campaign would be called "the wild adventure of a crazy fool." His troops respected, revered him; the Confederates feared him. Some rebels claimed that this Union General had more fire and brimstone in him than the devil himself...or maybe he *was* the devil himself. Sherman's own troops, especially those who recognized his great tactical skills, said, "Sherman'll never go to hell. He'll flank the devil and make heaven despite the guards."

Rebecca opened the curtains; the sun burst into her mother's room, filling it with colors and warmth. She opened the window and inhaled the fresh air, as fallen leaves gently swirled in the bright yard. She could hear a hound yelping in the distance – must be on the trail of something. Her mother smiled at her beloved, dutiful daughter. She felt better just having Rebecca at her side.

Sherman also enjoyed the beautiful morning, watching the endless columns of men, their "gun-barrels glistening in the sun, the white-topped wagons stretching away to the south;" he noted their quick steady march, "with a cheery look and swinging pace." Again a band began to play, and the troops joined in. Sherman later wrote of that moment saying, "and never before or since have I heard the chorus of 'Glory, glory, hallelujah!' done with more spirit, or in better harmony of time and place."

While Rebecca tended to her household chores that evening, Sherman and his men approached Decatur, about eighty-five miles west of Rebecca's family home in Crawfordville. A young woman anxiously watched their arrival in Decatur. "As far as the eye could reach, the lurid flames of burning buildings lit up the heavens...I could stand out on the verandah and for two or three miles watch them as they came on. I could mark when they reached the residence of each and every friend on the road."

As Sherman approached Conyers, about seventy miles to the west of Crawfordville, one elderly woman told the Yankees, "I've run away from you six times, clear across the south, starting back in Kentucky. I don't care where you go next, I'm done running. I'm going to let you go first, maybe I'll follow."

Where is he now? Nearer, closer, moving, burning, Sherman and his men steadily approached. There was no reliable news of their impending arrival, only the sickening shouts of people who had witnessed their inexorable approach. "They're coming! Headed right this way! Millions of 'em! Look out!" Like a massive tornado in relentless and painful slow motion, the Yankees, still moving in giant columns, cut a 60-mile wide swath of destruction from Atlanta heading southeast.

Realizing that Rebecca could be cut off from her family for months, her mother, claiming to be much better, urged her daughter to return to her family. And her father demanded that she return to her family before it was too late. Reluctantly, she acquiesced. After a tearful parting, Rebecca boarded the train for Macon. At first her trip was uneventful. Then suddenly she was nearly jolted out of her seat as the train came to an unexpected, screeching halt in the middle of a forest. Although no one was hurt, some passengers had to pick themselves up from the floor. Everyone debarked and walked to the front of the locomotive, still billowing black smoke. There they saw a ruined bridge ahead; the one that went over the Oconee River had been burned. After backing up for many miles, the train took a long detour south and east to Savannah. The ride seemed interminable; Rebecca grew restless within the confines of her stifling car, ripe with the foul odor of weary, dirty travelers, slowly grinding toward Sherman's destination. She reached Savannah ahead of the Yankees.

Still she could not go to Macon. She wired her husband that she would take a train instead to Augusta the following day, well to the north and east of her town. Weary, worried, she boarded the train and found a seat for what would again be a long, crowded, dirty trip. Finally, as Rebecca stepped onto the Augusta platform, she spotted a man holding hands with two children, smiling broadly. William, Ann and Johnny had found her. Tearful and relieved, she kissed and hugged them all. At least now they were together. Knowing something of the Yankee advance, William decided to take his family back to Savannah, then head south again toward Florida and try to reach Macon from there. The train was packed, stinking, filthy, and lacking any amenities. Often there was only one seat for the four of them...and no food. They were lucky to obtain even one meal a day, a few stale biscuits, or cold potatoes, or cornbread.

From the window of her train one evening, Rebecca watched in horror as wretched, living broken shadows of men, some skeletal, passed their train. The Confederates, fearful that Sherman might try to free the Yankee prisoners at Andersonville, were moving them to a more secure location. "The night was gloomy and the torch fires made a weird scene as our train rolled along beside passing flat cars on which those Federal prisoners were guarded, with torch lights illuminating the faces of those ragged, smoke-begrimed, haggard and miserably filthy men." Although she had indignantly read about the cruel treatment of Confederate prisoners at Camp Chase and Johnson's Island in the North, "that sight of train-loads of Federal prisoners on that wild night in Southern Georgia, when I could look into their faces within a few feet of the train I became an eyewitness to their enforced degradation, filth and utter destitution, and the sight never could be forgotten." No matter that these ragged prisoners were the enemy; she concluded that "Prison treatment of such men has always been a disgrace to Christianity and civilization."

On the depot platform where their train stopped lay a twitching black man, apparently shot only moments before by one of the Andersonville guards. The victim had allegedly said something 'annoying.' Rebecca could never forget this horror. "The quivers of dying flesh had hardly subsided in his stalwart body as we rolled away."

Rebecca and the children stayed with friends in Quitman, not far from Florida, while William returned to their Macon farm. He arrived to discover that Sherman's rapacious parade had passed them by, marching slightly to the north. Instead of Macon, Sherman headed for Georgia's then state capitol, Milledgeville, there to take and burn the city, then continue marching east. On December 22, 1864, General Sherman took Savannah. The war should have ended at that time. Georgia lay sprawling; the Confederacy was in ruins. William sent a message to Rebecca telling her that it was safe to return. He met his family at the Macon depot. There he told her that some of their slaves had remained with them, refusing to follow the Yankees. But nearly all of their food was gone. He neglected to tell his wife that an injured Confederate soldier lay in their bed. She would find out soon enough.

With little equipment or medical supplies, Dr. Felton tended the wounded in Macon. Often treatment meant amputation, screaming men with little or no anesthetic, swarms of flies, puss, and infection. He saw the blood, suffering, severed limbs, and death of this war firsthand and heard the reports from the soldiers. He knew the Confederate cause was hopeless. But there was no end to the killing, not yet. Southern politicians continued to urge the Confederacy on, claiming, incredibly, that victory would soon be theirs. In February, 1865, President Jefferson Davis came to Macon to give a speech, and William went to hear him. Rebecca waited anxiously for her husband's return. She later reported that when William entered their home after the speech, "I saw little hopefulness in his face. 'The President told us we were doing well and there was no doubt as to our final success.' It was the old, old story, and Sherman had already marched to the sea and Georgia was prostrate."

Not only Yankee troops depended upon the rich harvests of Georgia's farmers for their survival, the Confederates also helped themselves to crops their own people had preserved for the coming winter...and stock and chickens...anything they could eat or use. They emptied corncribs in a matter of minutes, took cured meats, shot yelping dogs and squawking chickens. Rebecca later noted, "When it came to foraging one side was nearly as bad as the other." The troops of Sherman, Wheeler, and Storeman all plundered the Feltons' lands, stripping fruit trees, taking anything that could be used and often trampling what they did not take. Finding enough nourishment to feed her family and the few remaining slaves became Rebecca's all-consuming task. "Our principal diet was corn bread and sorghum syroup [sic] – and not always plentiful at that."

Nearly always hungry and cold, the Felton family survived the winter by hiding the small provisions that remained. And still the fighting continued, this time almost directly to the west of them as Yankee General James Harrison Wilson (a West Point graduate, age twenty-eight) prepared to enter Georgia from Alabama. Finally, on the afternoon of April 9, 1865, the angular, white haired, aristocratic General Robert E. Lee surrendered his Army of Northern Virginia to the stocky, moody Ulysses S. Grant at the home of Wilmer and Virginia McClean at Appomattox Court House. Many histories say that Lee's surrender ended the War of Secession – but it didn't, not in Georgia. There were no telephones, and most telegraph lines had been cut or destroyed during the course of the War.

Unaware that the War had ended, General Wilson mounted his horse and headed east – from Alabama straight for Georgia. On the morning of April 16, the *Daily Sun* of Columbus, Georgia reported, "The public is hereby notified of the rapid approach of the enemy, be assured that the city of Columbus will be defended to the last."

Defended? By whom? By what? Wilson's men attacked Columbus at night. "Charge 'em! Charge em!" "There's a ravine!" "Go to the left." "Look out!" Confederates and Yankees unknowingly passed each other in the darkness, as horses, rebels, bluecoats, artillery wagons, ambulances, rifles, cannon, men blindly pushing, yelling, fighting – ran together all at once in the blackness. It soon became a rout. Two thousand mostly inexperienced men were no match for thirteen thousand seasoned Union troops. Columbus fell. As General Wilson later reported:

> Before leaving Columbus, Gen. Winslow destroyed the rebel ram
> Jackson, nearly ready for sea, mounting six seven-inch guns,

burned fifteen locomotives, two hundred and fifty cars, the railroad bridge and foot bridges, one hundred and fifteen thousand bales of cotton, four cotton factories, the navy yard, foundry, armory, sword and pistol factory, accoutrement shops, three paper mills, over a hundred thousand rounds of artillery ammunition, besides immense stores, of which no account could be taken.

Still no one realized that Lee had surrendered one week earlier. In fact, no one in Georgia knew that only two days before the fall of Columbus, President Lincoln was assassinated while watching a comedy, *Our American Cousin,* at Ford's Theater, leaving to much smaller minds the Reconstruction of the South.

As rumors approached of an impending attack, Rebecca became concerned. Her husband was away from the farm, treating the wounded. She mounted a horse on the morning of April 20, 1865, and set out alone on the cart path that led through deep woods…five miles of huge trees and thick undergrowth…not another soul anywhere. With tree limbs so thick above her, it seemed sometimes as if she were in a tunnel; she urged her horse on. Approaching Macon from the east, she hitched her horse, then walked across the Georgia Central Railroad Bridge, a footbridge over the Ogmulgee River, and into the eerily quiet town.

Passing Wharf Street, then Walnut, she turned right on Mulberry and headed straight for Burke's Book Store. As she came to the store's front door, she noticed a heavy-set man with dark wavy hair, round somber face, sitting on the porch in a split-bottomed chair. "He had on plain clothes, plain hat." His face seemed familiar. Curious, she asked the store owner about that man. "Said Mr. Burke, 'that is Major-General Howell Cobb, commander-in-chief of the military forces of the State of Georgia.'" He was waiting alone to surrender to Wilson. Reports were coming in that the bluecoats were now only about twenty miles away, marching steadily forward.

Hastily, she made her way back to her horse and returned to her farm. She later wrote, "I still wonder that I had the temerity to undertake that lonely ride. It was a deserted road, much of it still in forest growth, and the poor little horse was slow."

When General Wilson began his march to Macon, he intended to destroy everything that could be of use to the South – and, in fact, Macon had a great many factories serving Confederate needs. Yet unlike Columbus, Macon was spared, for there Wilson finally learned of Lee's surrender.

One hot spring evening a few weeks later, William was sitting on the front porch, tired from a long day's work, when suddenly a bullet whished near his ear, embedding itself in the house. He rushed inside, chased by two more bullets, reached for his rifle, and returned the fire out of one of the open front windows. All night the miserable family kept watch. But it was so dark they could see nothing. Upon learning of this incident, the Yankees in Macon sent a guard to their isolated farm for two weeks to protect them against the many hungry, desperate people who now roamed Georgia. "A trooper named Dowling, a youth from Cincinnati, was billeted in my house. He used to read to my boy. They became chums. I treated the Yankee soldier like one of the family." After Dowling ascertained that Rebecca knew how to handle a gun, "he left a loaded musket for my protection when he was not around." In an ironic historical twist, the Yankees protected her – probably from her own southern people – while William continued to aid the wounded in Macon.

Then sturdy, healthy John, age eleven, suddenly didn't feel well one bright June day in 1865. Five hours later he was dead of malaria. The Feltons auctioned off a beautiful carriage, the only thing of value left, to pay for their last son's burial expenses, along with some other debts. Referring to that Macon farm, Rebecca once said, "Oh the horrors I suffered there."

William and Rebecca, too, fell desperately ill with malaria. In fact, Rebecca had two potentially fatal illnesses in close succession, typhoid fever, then malaria, which even upon her return to her Cartersville plantation left her "chilling off and on for months." Their sorrows were enough to drive them both mad. Rebecca later marveled that her "reason was not fatally dethroned."

They remained at their rented farm until August, 1865 – four months after Appomattox – because they needed a good harvest for winter. Gathering what produce they could force from the land, they packed their few belongings and headed back to their Carters-ville plantation…their home. Sherman had pointed the way with countless chimneys, jutting out of the rubble, most blackened with soot, standing starkly against the sky, forlorn reminders of homes (and times) that were no more. As they approached their planta-tion, they became excited for they could see that the house was still standing. Then they noted that all the windows were broken, the outbuildings burned. Rebecca later wrote, "When I reached the gate I picked up the springs that had been a part of my dead child's fine baby carriage, also the arm of a large parlor mahogany chair that had been also burned. Desolation and destruction everywhere, bitter, grinding poverty – slaves all gone, money also." Even the fencing had not survived. Nothing but their barren land, ash piles, and the shell of their ruined home remained.

Sherman's Destruction of the Atlanta Railroad Station

Chapter Two

Starting Over

At first Rebecca did not even try to take in the enormity of the tasks that lay before them now that they were back on their war-ravaged plantation. There was no time for grief; she just started working. Rescuing the house from the elements became her first priority. Since they had no money for new windows, boards or rags would have to do. Sweeping, scrubbing – mucking out as if their once-fine home were now a stable...it may as well have been for all of the damage and filth inside. And food! How would she feed her little family? Ann, now in her teens, tried to help by foraging in the woods, locating berries, or greens, even edible roots to eat, but many others also searched the land for food. Always preoccupied with the next meal, Rebecca struggled to put something, anything, on the table each day...often in those early weeks she didn't succeed. "Without money – with labor disorganized to the point of anarchy in some places – with fields bare of fencing – destroyed by ravaging troops and the camp followers of two armies – it was a hand to mouth struggle to live, to exist."

If they were to survive, they had to grow a crop. Scraping and struggling together, they managed to purchase eight bushels of wheat seed. Desperately, with appalling effort because they lacked the necessary equipment, they worked to prepare the soil and sow the wheat. The rain came, and the weather was right, and patiently they waited. But to their dismay, nothing happened. "Not a grain of that wheat sprouted, because it had somewhere undergone extreme heat, until the seed germ was killed. We bought cotton seed at three dollars a bushel, because lint cotton brought 30 cents per pound – and the ravaging cattle and stock, which were forced to graze at night, to do a scant day's work on the tomorrow – ate up the last stalk of young cotton, after it had been planted and worked over – at enormous expense on borrowed money."

One late morning Rebecca emptied her last sack of cornmeal to make some cornbread – all that they would have for lunch, which would be their only meal that day. She set the piping-plate on the table to cool, then began to straighten the kitchen. But something caught her eye. Trying not to appear too obvious, she turned her head slightly and glanced out the window. Two huge eyes stared back. She was looking at the scrawniest red mule she had ever seen, ribs sticking out, nostrils flaring as the scent of fresh cornbread wafted out the window. She spent the rest of the morning befriending that mule. It wasn't hard; the starving mule came right up to the small bucket of feed she held out. Soon he was in the only pen they had made, eagerly eating. Rebecca liked the looks of this mule, whose big frame impressed her. She promptly named him Zeb.

Zeb, their first mule after the War, would soon have company as William and Rebecca rounded up other mules turned loose by the armies of both sides, now returning home. With those sturdy animals, they managed to grow and harvest their first crops. Rebecca would later say, "But for the abandoned army mules that were turned loose to starve and die, the South would have faced starvation in many places."

Although Zeb was always sweet and gentle with Rebecca, for anybody else he was a terror – running off, bucking a surprised rider from his back, or dragging a wagon with a yelling driver down the wrong road. Rebecca liked his spirit. He would kick anything, man or yelping dog, as quick as lightening – except Rebecca. She could walk behind him anytime. Zeb was always her favorite mule; she liked to brush him, scratching all the itch spots, speaking softly to him: "Zeb, you're such a scoundrel. You must have been a Yankee mule the way you kick."

Even with Zeb and the other mules helping with the farm, William and Rebecca still desperately needed money. Which Felton first suggested it is not clear, but both embraced it with excitement. They decided that in order to make ends meet and restore their farm, they would start a school. In 1866 they established their little school for boys and girls at the Methodist Church in Cartersville, and with their meager earnings they bought seeds and a plow. Together they taught about eighty students. Some parents, unable to pay any money, gave the Feltons fresh eggs, or sometimes a chicken or potatoes.

For Rebecca turning to books, teaching – and children – was the best way to rid herself of her grief. In spite of her losses and sorrow, Rebecca spoke joyfully of her teaching experience. "How I enjoyed that work would take a volume to tell and my diligence in my own school days was a prime factor for success in this strenuous time." She had always loved reading, learning, even from her earliest youth. Her father, Charles Latimer, a central figure of her young days, encouraged her interest in books and music. He often read aloud to her, enjoying her keen interest. He also played the violin, and she learned to accompany him on the piano, or sometimes on the guitar. He enjoyed her exuberance, her enthusiasm, watching with pleasure her activities, especially when she galloped her fat pony across their plantation. "I began to ride at six years old and one of the proudest days of my life came along when my father slackened his firm hold on my pony's bridle and let me go alone to manage for myself." She would love horses all of her life and expertly ride them, even as a grandmother.

Her father's was the hand that held hers on that exciting walk to her first day of school. Charles and his daughter had much in common: great energy with a large capacity for work, curiosity, and a desire to read and learn. It was not long before Rebecca developed a strong, serious interest in politics, just like her father. Her parents' plantation, called Belmont (ten miles from Decatur in DeKalb County), was located on the Decatur-Covington Road. Their home became a stagecoach stop, post office, general store, blacksmith shop, wood shop, mill, hotel and eating establishment (called Latimer's Tavern, famous for its food – especially its waffles and biscuits – and warm hospitality) for those who traveled between Savannah and the south and Nashville and other cities to the north. Rebecca wrote, "I thought then nothing could be grander than to see a great stage coach, with an immense leather boot attached to the rear, drawn by four sleek, well-groomed horses, coming down the big road in a sweeping gallop while all the folks gathered about the store-house door to watch the travelers or wait for the mail bag to be opened." The stagecoach driver would sound his horn about three quarters of a mile away, alerting the plantation to their arrival, and especially the hostlers, who were required to have another four-horse team at the ready.

Rebecca's home was always filled with strangers and friends alike. Her mother, Eleanor (Swift) Latimer, taught Rebecca at an early age the importance of hospitality, southern gentility and the supervision of the home. Rebecca also followed her maternal grandmother, Lucy Talbot Swift, around her vast Georgia plantation, taking an interest in everything that went on, whether it be the geese, the making of starch, soap, the supervision of meals, or sewing. But it was her father and his duties that most intrigued her. Little Rebecca loved to be in the thick of things, eagerly listening to political discussions in the store, sometimes standing on a barrel reading newspapers aloud to others, or walking the aisles, staring in wonder at coffee, tea, spices, lute string ribbon, dress goods, pronella shoes – mysterious boxes, tins, and bottles – brown sugar, dark molasses, and kit mackerel.

One day in 1842, when Rebecca was seven, something miraculous happened at her plantation. Everyone lined the dirt road in front of her house, shouting, smiling and pointing. At first, Rebecca could make out only a small dot in the distance, but as it approached, her eyes grew wide. A team of twenty mules approached their home, pulling a huge flat wagon. On that wagon was a locomotive...the first locomotive ever to be used in the tiny village first named Marthasville, then Terminus – now called Atlanta. The locomotive was followed by another mule team hauling one freight car. The last team carried a small passenger coach.

While the drivers ate at Latimer's Tavern, Rebecca was permitted to enter the passenger coach and to look closely at the freight car and engine. So many mules, such excitement, her first sight of a real train, only one more surprise awaited her. Because the Latimers had helped to house and feed the men who planned and constructed the railroad (to be named the Western & Atlantic), her entire family was invited to ride on the little train's maiden voyage. Rebecca treasured the memory of that first train ride.

As she grew a little older, her interest in the activities of other towns and people increased. As an old woman, she wrote, "I can look backwards, through a long vista, and see a little girl with pantalets and short dresses, as she stood beside her father and listened to the wonderful things going on in the outside, busy world." Politics, newspapers, and books were her major interests even before she reached her teens. "I heard a great deal of discussion among the politicians – and when the Editor of the "Southern Recorder" stopped over with us for several days, I remember walking around him and wondering to myself how such an average-sized man could know so much and write so well!"

Her home was always filled with excitement, activity, music, and great food. When Rebecca was five, her sister Mary was born. In the years to come, Mary would be not just a sister, but a great and life-long friend to Rebecca. Rebecca and Mary loved their childhood so rich in activity in the various parts of the plantation. There seemed to be music and singing everywhere. Even in her old age Rebecca remembered the 'corn-shucking melodies,' sung when she was a child. She once sang them to her own babies. The corn shuckings lasted all night. After the ripe corn was hauled to the barn, word was sent out that there would be a corn shucking on a certain night. All the men on the nearby farms, along with their slaves, would arrive. The women prepared a huge supper. "In the big house there was a bountiful table, in the kitchen another table just as plentiful for the blacks. It was a big time for everybody." And everyone sang until all the corn was shucked and stored; then (usually at daylight) all went home.

The women also had their quilting bees. On the appointed day, all the women of the nearby farms would bring their thimbles and needles and gather together to quilt. The hostess would prepare a huge meal. "Along about midday the husbands began to come, some afoot, others on horseback." Then everyone enjoyed a feast, with tables overflowing with food. Afterwards, the men went back to work and the women, some famous for their sewing skill, finished the quilt. Rebecca, with tiny, quick, exacting stitches, would quilt for most of her life.

Unlike most men of the time, Charles Latimer did not seem to notice or care that his only two living children were female. He enjoyed their spunk and intellect and wanted them educated. He first built a small schoolhouse on his property. As Rebecca and Mary grew older, Charles made several business sacrifices by moving to Decatur so that they could continue their studies.

Rebecca thrived on books and learning. The Methodists (their denomination) had established a female college in Madison, Georgia, and when the time came, Charles Latimer decided that Rebecca should attend. There were twelve girls in her class. At her graduation she first met her future husband. The principal speaker at her commencement in 1852 was the earnest physician and Methodist minister: Dr. William Felton. It was love at first sight.

He was tall, handsome, serious – intelligent, well spoken – and just like Rebecca's father, William had a keen interest in politics. In 1851 he had been elected to the State House of Representatives, demonstrating then his honesty, integrity, and desire to help the common man. He was a populist even before populism had found its voice. Dr. Felton listened intently as Rebecca read her valedictory essay. He watched her as she played the piano and guitar on that commencement day. He smiled at her. She was small, tiny in fact, with large brown eyes and long chestnut hair that framed her beautiful face and smile. She seemed joyful to him, energetic. He met her parents…then was introduced to her.

Later, he asked if she and her mother might accompany him on a buggy ride. He visited her home, talking seriously with her father, but always mindful of Rebecca's whereabouts. They sat together on the front porch. Unlike other suitors, he listened carefully to Rebecca and talked with her of politics and the future of

their beloved state.   Rebecca cherished their conversations.   He
touched her hand.   She was seventeen, he was twenty-nine, with a
small daughter; just a hint of sorrow lingered on his face.   He
talked to her earnestly; he was gentle, kind.   How could she have
dreamed when she was so young that their marriage would last for
fifty-seven years, that they would both know so much sorrow – joy
– achievement?   How could they have found each other?   She married him in a simple ceremony at her home shortly after she turned
eighteen.

Rebecca treasured these happy memories, skipping over
thoughts of Sherman, the Civil War, death and hardship.   Although
she delighted in remembering, she never ceased the work before
her at their little school or on their farm.   William and Rebecca
taught together, worked the farm together, and started to rebuild.
Once again they began to look to the future, to hope.   According to
Rebecca, "Within two years we were able once more to raise our
bread and meat at home, and I went back to the life of a farmer's
wife.   It took the most rigid economy to make ends meet.   The old
bountiful South was gone, and a new South struggled grimly out of
its ashes and poverty."
For Rebecca, her own war sorrows seemed small against the
nation's tragedy.   "The most serious thing about war is the slaugh-
ter of boys," she said.   They must battle in a war they often do not
understand, lose their education, face horrible perils, disease, the
loss of innocence.   "They are the 'seed corn' of any nation and the
crop fails."   They must set in motion the goals of politicians, often
without real knowledge of their purpose.   She couldn't help but
wonder if the Civil War could not have been avoided if the politicians had not been so uncompromising and scalding.   Was the issue of States' rights really the cause of that terrible war?   Or was
its source found within the economics of slavery?
Reconstruction didn't help the situation.   With Lincoln's as-
sassination, lesser men more bent on retribution took charge of
governing the South.   Georgia was not immediately readmitted to
the Union.   Instead, it was occupied, placed under the military rule
of the United States government, a system that lent itself to corrup-

tion and favors, along with Georgian resentment. Aside from reading the newspapers and having discussions, sometimes with friends and neighbors, about the deteriorating political situation, the Feltons had no time to focus on Georgia's political morass.

Then one day Rebecca told her husband that he was going to be a father again. Did it mean another sorrow? Love, so much love and care and hope went with a baby. They did not dwell on this pregnancy; they dared not become too hopeful. In 1869 their third son Howard Erwin was born. He was a sickly baby and constantly worried both of his parents. Rebecca stayed by his tiny crib for hours, just looking at him, as if somehow her presence could keep death away.

Then one last time Rebecca informed her husband that she was pregnant. In 1871 Rebecca gave birth to Paul Aiken, strong and healthy. The robust baby lived for only two years. Then like so many babies of that time, he succumbed to illness. Paul's death caused Rebecca to watch over little Howard with even greater care. Surprisingly, the baby with the weaker constitution survived all the childhood illnesses of the time. Rebecca tended to his every need with grave concern and love, always fearful that he might die as had her four other children. But Howard, the weakest of her offspring, lived and grew.

Georgia, arguably the state that incurred the most destruction as a result of the Civil War, was finally readmitted to the United States on July 15, 1870, the last Confederate state to be returned to the Union. But even the end of military occupation did not result in good government. Georgia's state government lay in shambles, ripe for patronage, outright thieves and plundering. Rebecca and William agreed with Congressman Daniel W. Voorhees' assessment of the political situation in Georgia when he said in 1872:

> Georgia was the fairest and most fertile field that ever excited the hungry cupidity of the political pirate and the official plunderer. She was full of those mighty substances out of which the taxes of a laboring people are always wrung by the grasping hand of power. She was the most splendid quarry in all history for the vultures, the kites and the carrion crows that darken the air at the close of a ter-

rible civil war, and whet their filthy beaks over the fallen; and they speedily settle down on her in devouring flocks and droves.

The North didn't help, providing in addition to carpetbaggers, demands and retribution. Added to Sherman's nearly total destruction of Georgia's rail system (the most advanced in the South before the war), were punitive freight rates, making commercial rebuilding even more difficult.

Yet like most Georgians of the time, William and Rebecca could not turn their attention to politics following the Civil War. Instead, they devoted all of their energies to rebuilding their farm and teaching school. William no longer had the time or constitution to put in the additional long hours of a country doctor. But as the political situation went from bad to worse in Georgia, Rebecca and William began to include politics more and more in their discussions as they rocked on the porch in the darkness, their only time of respite before bed. Following the Federal occupation of Georgia, the South developed into a one-party system: the Democrats ruled, with party rings, bosses, and serious abuses of power. Rebecca and William shared a vision of a new Georgia, with honest government. But the farm, restoring the farm had to be their first priority…along with raising little Howard.

Starting Over

Chapter Three

Politics?

After sweeping the back porch, Rebecca set the broom against the house and walked down the steps past the vegetable garden, stopping briefly to pull a few greens and stuff them into her apron pocket. She went to the barn to pick up an old brush, then lifted the gate and entered the pasture, walking swiftly, head down, taking no notice of the apple trees along the fence, blooming in the warm spring sun. Zeb, who turned out to be the biggest, orneriest, hardest-working mule they ever had, raised his head, pricked up his long ears, and followed her to the shade of a giant crooked pine tree, which had always been their spot. She brushed Zeb, picking a swollen tick off his ear; it was her thinking time, his joy. He nudged her pocket, knowing that she always kept a tasty scrap or two inside. While he chomped her fresh greens, she stroked his huge ears – contemplating Georgia – and its corrupt politics.

She had always held such high hopes for her state. After Sherman stopped his burning...after Appomattox...after Reconstruction's carpetbaggers and scalawags...after five resentful years of military occupation...after Georgia's re-admittance to the Union, things still did not get better, honest men did not take up the reins of government. Georgia's politics were dishonest, ruled by Democratic Party bosses and crony rings out to line their own pockets. The previous day, a small committee of concerned neighbors and local businessmen had met with her husband William and asked him to run for Congress as an Independent Democrat in the Seventh District. William Harrell Felton, a United States Congressman, her husband – the brush moved faster now down Zeb's slick, short hair.

He could make a difference, she knew he could. But could he win? The odds weren't in his favor. The Bourbons, as they were called, were politically entrenched, mean, stop-at-nothing Democrats. They would be his opposition in Georgia's one-party system. It would cost a lot of money, and he was so needed on the farm. She brushed Zeb's back and withers, then stopped and stood erect. But Georgia needs him more, she thought. After caressing her mule's silky muzzle and giving him the last of her greens, she marched back to the house.

William and Rebecca sat on the porch together that same day, rocking in the twilight, discussing political strategy, backing...money. They knew it would be a terrible fight. They knew it might be hopeless. The Bourbons were noted for their voter fraud. They rocked on the porch, silent for a long time. They could hear the longing foghorn calls of bullfrogs from the creek. Rebecca pledged her husband her full support. He told her he could use it. They listened to the night sounds, no longer able to see each other in the darkness. But somehow they could feel each other's presence and enthusiasm. Like a moonflower unfolding its white petals to the stars, their excitement rose about them in the night.

They left the porch arm in arm and prepared to go to bed. She wondered as she slipped on her nightgown – how she could help her husband win this campaign, besides keeping him fed, in clean clothes, and sending him her best wishes. In 1874 a woman in Georgia couldn't vote. She couldn't sit on a jury or hold office; she couldn't give speeches (a lady did not speak in public); she couldn't speak in church; she couldn't participate in a local school election or attend political rallies. In fact, she wasn't supposed to hold or express any political opinion at all. A southern lady did not, could not, participate in civil matters. Tradition and the concept of chivalry precluded such activities.

He kissed her goodnight. They lay together in bed, listening to the extravaganza of bullfrogs and bug sounds reverberating in the darkness. A mockingbird landed in a tree next to their house and joyfully began his nocturnal repertoire. Long after she had fallen asleep, William continued to think of her, breathing softly beside him, his treasured wife. He liked the smell of her, often a puzzling cross between cookies and fresh grass. He thought of her as she worked outside; some creature always followed her, a speckled hound, a plump, clucking chicken – and Zeb. As for her saddle horse, Pompey, William worried that the bay with long white stockings would be too spirited for his small wife. But Pompey and Rebecca thought alike. Both had only one gait in mind and one solution to an obstacle. William could hardly bear to watch as horse and rider soared – over the hedge, down the lane, over the log, and gone, leaving only faint red dust clouds here and there to mark their passage. No one could handle a horse as well as Rebecca Felton…or judge one either. She was a farm wife, after all, possibly the best farm wife in all of Georgia, at least in William's mind. But politics…no woman had ever…he knew she was resourceful. She would help him, he was sure.

The next morning Rebecca decided that she could oversee the farm and serve as William's part-time secretary. She could answer his mail (signing his name to the letters) and make his appointments. She could also keep track of his schedule and make sure that he had everything he needed for his trips to the fourteen counties where he would be campaigning.

As soon as William entered the race, the Bourbons started an attack campaign and heaped personal abuse upon him. Although William was tall, handsome, serious, with dark hair already threaded with gray, he had a raw-boned appearance that made his arms seem somehow too long for his shirts. The Bourbons decided that Felton was a bumpkin, totally lacking in culture, a "self-nominated candidate," "a clerical demagogue," and an "old Democratic Pharisee." They ridiculed his clothes (his "reckless coat and breeches"), and his way of speaking.

Although William ignored these insults, even when they appeared in the local papers, Rebecca became enraged that her husband would be called "Jeans Breeches" or "Old Wool Hat." How dare they? Without really thinking much about it, she fired off two brief unsigned comments to the two local newspapers that supported her husband. His political opponent Colonel Trammell had been associated with several scandals, one concerning railroad bonds. So Rebecca wrote, *"Bonds of iniquity,* those which Col. Trammell received from the Brunswick and Albany Railroad." Then she added, "Why does a certain distinguished lawyer of Rome [GA], who supports Felton, deserve the confidence of the people of the seventh District? Because he is *(W)right."* Her snippets were published…anonymously.

She decided to write an entire letter, just to set the record straight – signing it "Un-Trammelled." The editor of the Cartersville paper published it, and people read it, discussing its points among themselves. One day while shopping in Cartersville, Rebecca saw a friend, a neighbor of long acquaintance who asked her if she had read that article in the paper yesterday supporting her husband. Before she could even respond, the neighbor concluded that it was about time that someone answered the charges of those Bourbon Democrats. About time! Rebecca could not help smiling to herself.

Rebecca began to send anonymous letters to the editors of all the newspapers in the Seventh District, in spite of the fact that only two papers "with limited circulation" favored Dr. Felton. The Bourbons had the other newspapers in their camp, due to their large advertising budget and political clout. Determined to help her husband win an election that both realized would be fixed, in a campaign that would become as hot and hellish as Sherman's fires, Rebecca used the only weapon available to a Southern woman at the time – her pen. She spiced her facts with wit and sarcasm, beginning her own personal anonymous political campaign, and signing her letters, "Fair Play," "Feltonite," and "Eutowah," [named for the Indians of that region]. Several editors realized who was authoring these bellicose, bitingly funny letters that gave such unflattering portraits of Felton's political enemies. Some men loyal to Felton's opposition conveniently 'lost' her missives. But most newspapers published them. Why not? The public loved the amusing and informative anonymous political potshots. Printing Rebecca Felton's letters added zest and cleverness to their newspapers and helped to raise their circulation. Following the unwritten code of the day, the newspapers continued to keep her name secret.

William's opponents didn't know what to make of these anonymous newspaper attacks. Everyone read them. As Rebecca later noted with some satisfaction, "I made it lively for the gentlemen." Lively may have been an understatement. Rebecca was intelligent, well read, a woman who loved politics and soon became an excellent writer and researcher – always uncovering new Bourbon indiscretions. With resounding energy, skill, and determination, "I posted myself and flung hand grenades." She would tend to the house, the family, the meals, keep the books for the farm, then drop into her favorite chair, put a small square board cut for the purpose into her lap and write letters, smiling with satisfaction at her points.

William decided to make his wife his official campaign manager. For the first time in the history of Georgia, a woman became a political campaign manager – and for someone running for the United States Congress. Even if he had had the necessary money to hire someone else, he would not have bothered. Rebecca was the best political campaign manager he could find. He announced it publicly and consulted her on every aspect of his campaign. "From June until the election in November I was in the thick of it. Working night and day, I wrote hundreds of letters and sent them all over 14 counties. I made Dr. Felton's speaking appointments, planned other speakers for him, answered newspaper attacks – in short, did everything a campaign manager does." Still she did not sign her name on most of the letters; she did not appear in public on his behalf; she remained within the confines of her home – diligently working.

Unlike his opponents, William had no free train passes to take him to the fourteen Georgia counties that comprised the Seventh District. Most often he used his horse and buggy to reach his many speaking engagements throughout that simmering hot, humid Georgia summer and fall. Heat and Georgia. Searing, unremitting

heat and humidity *are* Georgia in the summer without air condi-
tioning. As Rebecca later noted, "He perspired tremendously and I
often heard him say that he could feel the perspiration racing down
his limbs during a long speech in a crowded house, until it would
slop about in the heels of his boots." After each speech, he
stripped off his wet clothes, washed, donned new garments and
jumped into his buggy. His suitcases bulged with spare clothing.

When he returned, his campaign manager took care of his
wardrobe, hanging his sweat-soaked clothes on the line until they
could be washed, ironed, and packed once again for new speeches
in hot crowded halls. When she wasn't answering his mail, writing
for newspapers, tending to the duties of the farm in his absence,
taking care of little Howard, and cleaning, mending, and packing
his clothes, she contracted with the printer for campaign materials,
paying for it "out of a scanty pocket book" and set out herself to
distribute them. They even borrowed seven hundred dollars to
continue William's campaign.

Loathing the constant abuse and attacks upon her husband,
she felt obliged to counter every Bourbon assault. As Rebecca
later described, "From a quiet country life in a plain farm house,
with only farm worries and expenses to contend with, I was hurled
into a vortex of excitement, abuse, expense and anxiety that no
words can describe or pen portray." The protracted fierce election
race of 1874 soon became known as the campaign in "The Bloody
Seventh." Both Feltons constantly worked:

> I had a sick boy to nurse, a house to keep, farm matters to manage
> and unlimited writing and correspondence. We had company, I
> was appealed to from all quarters, and still was able to keep a smil-
> ing face for the sake of the cause. But that seemed a small part of
> it compared to the brave soldier who made his way, round after
> round over 14 counties, speaking often three times a day, occa-
> sionally five times, and such speeches as the listeners always re-
> membered and the very woods echoed with their shouts.

Having lost any claim to wealth and power during the Civil War,
William ran his campaign as a simple Georgia farmer, just like his
neighbors and with their same worries. His Bourbon opponents

took aim at this farmer/pastor/former physician…and fired. They decided that Felton was just like those corrupt Yankee ministers, who mixed politics with religion and were, they claimed, largely responsible for the Civil War. As for farming, Felton owned a huge tract of land, a veritable estate, not like his opponent Trammell, a true farmer, a true man of the people. And they soundly rebuked Felton for running as an Independent Democrat and splitting the party. That action just might lead to the worst outcome of all, possibly worse even than death itself: the election of a Republican!

Finally, to polish off this unsuitable pretender to Congress, they questioned his loyalty to Georgia, ignoring his work as physician and surgeon who had tended the Civil War wounded under the worst of conditions. It is impossible to say how many lives he saved because of his skill and insistence that wounds, aides and patients be clean. Overlooking his service to those wounded in battle, the Bourbons decided that Felton hadn't served in the Confederate army as Colonel Trammell had. He would weld no power in Congress, as Colonel Trammell could. Old Parson Felton wasn't even advocating anymore the glorious Lost Cause of the Confederacy, as Trammell was. How unpatriotic! If all that didn't do the old parson in, the Bourbons had one more cannon pointed straight at Felton's chest. They accused him of "soliciting votes from Negroes and Republicans." That should do it!

Yet every Bourbon assault was met with an even bigger counteroffensive – printed in the newspapers. The Bourbons couldn't find anyone in their party who could write as well, as amusingly and promptly as the author of those anonymous letters. It almost seemed as if every cannon they fired at William Felton expanded and bounced back in their faces. While Rebecca kept up her newspaper attacks and tended to everything else, William went out on the campaign trail for days, even weeks at a time. He asked her to write him every day. "I bought stamps, many dollars worth at a time, and whatever else was neglected or went undone, I strove to keep his mind as easy as I could make it, so that he could feel that all was well in the home that he loved as he loved his life."

In an unofficial Bourbon meeting in the back of a barroom, now blue with cigar smoke, the Bourbons contemplated murder. If they killed their opponent, they were sure to win. But such a drastic action bothered some of them. They believed that there must be better ways to win this race than to run against a corpse. After many drinks, much smoking and discussion, they decided that they wouldn't kill him outright. They would just threaten him with death. After all, he was just a parson and would probably scare easily. All smiled at that.

The following day about fifty Bourbon Democrats threatened William's life, claiming that "old Felton" would soon "bite the dust." To their surprise, Felton paid no attention to them, going about his regular campaign business. Even his wife, at first terrified, recognized the threat for what it was – an empty Bourbon bluff. But just the thought of such intimidation incensed Rebecca. WAR! If those Bourbons dared to threaten to kill her husband, Rebecca decided that she would have to declare total war on all of them! From that point on she decided to handle them 'with her gloves off,' an expression she was fond of using. No Bourbon realized at the time that those gloves were small and lacy.

Most people knew that Colonel Trammell had cheated to win his political nomination in the town of Calhoun. And many also knew about the scandal regarding the Brunswick and Albany Railroad and the greasing of political palms – Colonel Trammell's in particular. On September 26, 1874 a long anonymous article mysteriously appeared in the *Atlanta News*. It began: "When the Calhoun Jockey Club led out their *nag* for the coming race, about half their number swore by all that was good and honest that they could never run that animal." The jockey, learning of the nag he was expected to ride, abruptly quit, saying, "The horse that pulled all the *dirt* of the Brunswick and Albany railroad could never run a race for me." Then Bartow [referring to the people of Bartow county, where the Feltons lived] was highly praised as being "an excellent judge of horse flesh." Closely examining this nag in the race, Bartow concluded: "He is not in running order, in the first place; *too fat;* then he is *tricky,* I know that horse; he was run around here in

Radical rings a long time. He might do for a circus, but a straight Democratic race he can't run; no use to try."

Aside from the Bourbons, the people of the Seventh District roared with laughter, loved the article while taking serious note of its accusations. Trammell, *"the nag,"* was becoming a laughing-stock. With Felton's earnest eloquence, his spotless reputation, those infuriating anonymous political potshots constantly in the newspapers, followed by that Calhoun Jockey Club article (equivalent to a massacre!) the Bourbons decided that if they wanted to win the Seventh District, they should replace their nag. In mid-October, only two weeks before election day, the Bourbons, after an unsuccessful attempt to get both candidates to step down, switched horses. Now Colonel William Dabney was their man. By this time William and Rebecca were so immersed in battle, they merely researched Dabney and his past, reloaded and took aim. As Rebecca later said, "Every whipper-snapper that had howled and yelped before, snarled, howled, yelped and slandered us right and left during that fortnight of strenuous endeavor. But the new nominee had a heavy pull on a steep rough road, because the Trammell surrender was strapped to his back...."

The Bourbons, once certain of their victory, grew more concerned each day. An Independent with no political backing, a parson at that, shouldn't be getting so much attention. He wasn't acting like a loser, that's for sure. People came from miles around to see him. He had a deep commanding voice, an impressive presence, and a keen knowledge of the problems that worried his neighbors and district. He knew how to pack a hall and was good at speechifying, great in fact, the Bourbons had to give him that.

He could whip up a crowd and hold them spellbound with his eloquence. "Everywhere in the State good men – liberal men – progressive men – are anxious for a new political regime. Our young men feel that, in following this [Bourbon] organization, they have followed an ignis-fatuus [will-o-the wisp] that only deceives – that dances before them brightly just previous to our National elections, and, when the votes are counted, leaves them stranded upon political blunders and apparent corruption. Georgia is ripe today for revolt." His gestures, impassioned looks, his powerful bass voice profoundly impacted his audience – moved them. No wonder the Bourbons were worried. They especially hated his so-called "hallelujah lick." Whenever he named his opponent, he would raise his hands above his head and loudly clap once. People differed as to the definition of this action. Was he giving his opponent up to God? Or to the devil? Dismissing him with one quick clap? Whatever the precise definition of this act, everyone agreed it worked. No one thought of Dabney anymore without that 'Felton Clap.'

William and Rebecca worked tirelessly, relentlessly together, almost as if they were each participating in an intricate, quick dance, stepping together in their personal, effective war upon the Bourbons. Although she had never worked in politics before, she anticipated her husband's every need, in addition to answering every Bourbon accusation in the newspaper. As Rebecca later noted, "Sometimes I couldn't sleep – then to rest myself, I would get up and write." Whether with sarcasm, wit, or eloquence, they campaigned and conducted their two-person war in apparent unison and with mutual respect.

The Bourbons met again in the back of a bar, uneasily drinking and talking. It wasn't supposed to be working like this. Their new nag, Dabney, should be doing better. Felton's run for Congress was supposed to serve as a little protest, nothing more. He wasn't supposed to be...well, to be so serious and determined about it all. But even so, with all that Bourbon power and money and entrenchment, and tradition, and skill at voter fraud, old Parson Felton really didn't stand a chance. Just the same, he worried them.

By now they realized that they weren't just fighting one Felton – but two, and that his wife's repeated damaging newspaper articles were taking their toll. They complained loudly calling her a busy-body and claiming that someone should show that woman her place. But no one succeeded in stopping her, or keeping her letters out of the newspapers, or forbidding the electorate to read and enjoy her missives. While all the Bourbons agreed that it wasn't right that some female and parson could cause so much trouble, they couldn't decide what to do. Then one of the Bourbon bosses chose a more serious plan, one involving matches and fists.

The following night fifteen men on horseback with torches rode through the countryside. They threw their torches into the haylofts of six farmers (all staunch Felton supporters); the barns were in full blaze by the time anyone got out to them. And for good measure, the next day some Bourbons punched and kicked a few other Felton supporters. But their actions backfired, serving to get the citizens all riled up and to become more determined than ever to rid the Seventh District of their crooked Bourbon politicians.

The parson and his wife continued to work so hard both lost considerable weight, giving them a haggard appearance – maybe even mean. Speaking of her husband, Rebecca said, "He was gaunt as a greyhound, and nothing but skin and bones." Although William and Rebecca were exhausted, they kept a serious, determined look the Bourbons didn't like at all. They resembled scarecrows now, their clothes hanging limply upon them. Although they knew that they really didn't stand a chance, they wouldn't quit or even slow down their campaign.

The day for which they had worked so hard finally came: Election Day. Rebecca later wrote, "Tuesday was a cold, raw November day. I saw him leave home to vote wrapped in a heavy overcoat and neckwear, but I was afraid he would come back with pneumonia, because he was a worn old pilgrim and liable to be prostrated from fatigue no matter how the election went."

Fix the election! That had to be the only way to achieve a Bourbon victory now. But nobody knew just how many extra Bourbon votes were needed to be certain of a win. There is an historical record of the ballot fraud for the Seventh District for the election of 1874. A young telegraph operator from Kingston, Georgia admitted that he had heard, passed over the wires, several Bourbon orders to change the count. "How many have you counted off?" "Take down the figures – Dabney must have it."

William returned to his home around 10:00 P.M. Exhausted, both went to bed. Before he went to sleep, he told his wife, "I can now go to defeat with such a vote as this county has given me.

Bartow has given me 1,782 votes and Col. Dabney 340, a majority of 1,442. Cobb had also given me between five and six hundred majority. Any man could stand erect with such a victory at his own home. We will hear tomorrow, and I want you to be satisfied as I am satisfied that we have done brave, faithful work and have nothing to regret or reproach ourselves for."

He was wrong about one thing: they did not hear the elections results on Wednesday. Instead, they rested and read the newspapers. Rebecca decided that she was happy at least to have gotten rid of Colonel Trammell. Dabney was a better candidate – for a Bourbon. Her husband agreed, his face still buried in the newspaper, looking for election news. Although there were many predictions, no clear winner was announced. All day Thursday they waited again for election results, but even with rampant Bourbon voter tampering, this election was still not clear. On Thursday night they were too tired to discuss politics, or even to read. Besides, there wasn't much more to say. They just sat quietly together in front of their wood fire, the silence only broken by the crackle of wood and the soft jug-blow hoots of a nearby Great Horned Owl. Suddenly, they heard something else – noises, faint shouting coming from the direction of Cartersville. From the window, they saw strange lights too, unusual, eerie. Rushing to the door and opening it, they could hear what seemed at first to be a small vibration, soon changing into the sound of "rapid riding, horse hoofs [sic.] pounding the highway. As the rider and horse rose on the top of a high hill a mile distant we also heard a war-whoop and we then knew the rider to be an old friend who was born in Indian times and who had ridden horse races in the long ago and who was a Felton man to the core and **was bringing news.**" As they ran down to "the front gate, candle in hand, he bore down upon us, his horse drenched with sweat and foam dropping from its mouth." At first their breathless friend was too excited even to speak. But he didn't have to say anything. His huge grin said it all. With Dr. Felton's skill and determination, along with his indomitable campaign manager, he had won by eighty-two votes.

Chapter Four

From the Hills of North Georgia to Washington

Rebecca gently stroked his soft muzzle, speaking in a low voice to him, as she had so often before, while he took the bright red apple from her palm. "Now you be good, Pompey. You'll like it here, I promise." She patted the neck of her saddle horse, now in a neighbor's barn, then turned and walked back to her buggy. Leaving that fine-spirited bay and her big mule Zeb behind was the hardest part of going to Washington. The packing, closing the house, saying good-bye to her friends, helping her little family get ready, all of those chores were easy and exciting. As she climbed into her carriage, Pompey, always ready for a gallop, whinnied after her.

Washington! They were really going to the nation's capitol, and not just as tourists. They were on important business – Georgia's business. Congressman Felton still seemed somehow to have outgrown his clothes – gangly, serious. And his wife, although beautiful, still wore the simple black homespun dresses she had made herself. Exhausted from that turbulent campaign, she had taken to her bed for some weeks following William's win. She had not found the time to "set a stitch," as she called it, to alter her dresses after losing so much weight. They hung shapelessly upon her. If they had had a photograph taken of their departure from

Georgia, it might have been captioned: "Two Country Bumpkins from the South."

According to the dictates of women's style in 1875, hoop skirts were out; the bustle was in, as were tight crepe or silk dresses decorated to the floor with layers of intricate lace, bows, tassels, gold braid, and fringe. Hairdos of the time, done in glorious upsweeps, were as fussy as the dresses, topped with puffs of silk or enormous hats with ornate feathers or jewels. There was not a trace of homespun or a simple straight bun, parted in the middle, anywhere within Washington society. The Feltons had never gone so far away. They said good-bye to their daughter Ann, a grown woman now, soon to be married, and to their many friends who came to see them off, and along with little Howard (age five), excitedly boarded their train. As black smoke billowed from the locomotive, they looked out the window, noting everything they saw on the way, pointing, exclaiming, and smiling as they listened to the clickity-clack of the train that took them farther and farther away from their north Georgia home.

As they got off their train in the nation's capitol, they gawked at everything, mouths open, exclaiming – looking more like shabbily dressed tourists fresh from the countryside than part of Congress. Their new residence would be room 120, two bedrooms complete with a parlor, in the famed five-story National Hotel (decked out with huge flags on high poles at the end of each angle of the roof). Conveniently located on the corner of Pennsylvania Avenue and Sixth Street, the hotel was home to many politicians – even Henry Clay once resided there. The Feltons stood on the street in front of their hotel, grinning and pointing at the Capitol Building just down the street, an

The National Hotel

easy walk away. They would also take their meals at their hotel. Within the Felton papers at the University of Georgia archives is a bill from the National, "For 1 Month and 1 Days Board: $206.67; Baggage 50 cents; Ex. Dinner $1.00; Medicine 75 cents: $208.92." The always-frugal Rebecca must have frowned at such extravagance.

Even at such 'high' prices, the Feltons were delighted to be in Washington – finally in a position to do something positive for Georgia. Both realized how lucky they were. She later said, "Dr. Felton's election was a miracle in Georgia politics. They [the Bourbons] all hated him as the 'D---l hates holy water.' He was always in their way."

Rebecca did not run out to buy bustles and lace…she didn't have the money for such expenses. While she had slightly more elegant attire for parties and receptions, she clung to her homespun dress for every day, finally taking in the waist for a better fit. As for hats with feathers and jewels, a simple bonnet would due quite nicely and went well with her plain bun. She was not a ringlets-and-curls upsweep kind of woman. Her husband was, after all, representing one of the poorest states in the nation. Sparkling garments were not on their agenda.

While her husband's domain was the House of Representatives, she set up her own little fiefdom in her parlor. There she received anyone who knocked at her door – constituents from Georgia, Washington friends, or people from other states. Rebecca welcomed everyone alike, whether elegant and well connected, simple tourists, or passing travelers. With her warm southern hospitality, she took an interest in her visitors and listened to what they had to say. It was not long before Georgia women began to seek out the advice, not of Dr. Felton, but of his kindly, sympathetic wife. She later admitted that she believed that she represented Georgia's women.

At the time, Congressmen had to pay for their own clerical help. With so little money, and a willing, capable wife, Dr. Felton made a natural decision: Rebecca would become his secretary. "I learned how to draft my husband's bills, and I kept track of the House calendars, the committees and all legislation in which he was particularly interested." And then, of course, there were all those letters from constituents, friends, politicians. Rebecca answered them all. Although she didn't put her name on most of these letters, occasionally she did sign "Mrs. William H. Felton" to a letter. Dr. Felton didn't seem to mind. And sometimes she wrote an article to a newspaper back home, and signed her own name to it.

In her free time, she loved to go to the Capitol and sit in the gallery of the Senate, or more often the House of Representatives – watching, learning. Most of all, she loved to hear her husband speak – as did nearly everyone else. When Congressman Felton took the floor, seats soon filled, people came in from the corridors, reporters took note. His speeches were compared to those of that great orator, Henry Clay. One day Rebecca took her son with her to the House gallery to hear his father speak. Rebecca later wrote that the speech was so moving, "I found myself leaning over the seat in front of me, the great glad tears coursing down my cheeks, and my little boy clinging to me, crying 'What is it, mother?'" All the reporters present at Dr. Felton's speech were impressed. The Associated Press called his speech "masterly and eloquent beyond all expectation." It soon became clear to everyone that Dr. Felton would be an influential Congressman.

Rebecca Latimer Felton just plain loved politics, was fascinated by it, and soon began to understand, even better than most men, its inner workings. Continuing to wear simple clothes and hairdo, she decided that she had been a farmer's wife and mother for too long to try to put on airs. She simply was who she was. And now she was meeting Washington's upper crust, shaking hands and speaking with Presidents, Supreme Court Justices, Senators, wealthy and learned people of society. And most of them liked her. She was gregarious, knowledgeable, sympathetic, and good at conversation – a woman who appealed to simple uneducated people and high-brows alike.

It was not long before she met suffragists, real suffragists from the North – Yankees who before the Civil War had frequently been Abolitionists as well. Many felt great distain for southern women, particularly those, like Rebecca, who had once owned slaves. Yet Rebecca later wrote, "I became well acquainted with Lucy Stone, Susan B. Anthony and the other pioneers in the suffrage movement and in later years I knew their successors, Dr. Anna Howard Shaw and Mrs. Carrie Chapman Catt. They were deeply interesting women, who left an impress on their times." Although their eyebrows may have arched, their eyes widened in surprise when they first heard Rebecca's deep southern accent, once they began to converse with her, they came to appreciate her intelligence and conviction.

Yet Rebecca did not become a suffragist at that time. Obtaining the vote for women was not her main concern. Instead, she worried about a number of problems within her state, especially a new kind of slavery that was rapidly evolving: the convict-lease system. When slavery ended in Georgia, there were not enough people to work the land, and certainly not enough money in Georgia to pay for such workers. Sherman, Wilson, and other Yankee soldiers had decimated much of the state. In fact, Sherman had even burned Georgia's state penitentiary in Milledgeville. Instead of rebuilding the penitentiary, a new type of punishment was soon considered. On May 11, 1868, General Thomas H. Ruger (then serving as Provisional Reconstructionist Governor of occupied Georgia, signed the first convict lease, granting William A. Fort 100 convicts to work on the Georgia and Alabama Railroad for one year in return for $2,500. For a small price, and with little supervision, Georgians could replace their slaves with convicts. And even a small infraction of the rules, alleged by his master, could keep a good worker within the system indefinitely.

In their early years in Washington, Rebecca and her husband opposed the convict lease. But progress was slow, and abuses continued to pile up. In her research on this subject, Rebecca discovered that black men and women were sometimes chained together during the day and even at night. Prisoners could be punished, sometimes beaten to death for minor infractions, such as cursing or working too slowly. Often lessees couldn't account for all of their prisoners. Bullet-ridden, bloody prisoner clothing was occasionally found in nearby brush and forests. Those who tried to escape were often shot and killed. And worse, those who had served their time in the convict-lease system were generally given no new clothes upon their release. Dirty, recently released, rough-looking men roaming the countryside in striped prisoner uniforms often led to mistakes, shootings by farmers and others who believed they were capturing or killing escaped convicts. Rebecca decided that something should be done about this unfair system. In addition to abuses within the political and penal systems, education, health, and so many other things required serious attention. It was not long before several Georgia newspapers regularly received and published letters and articles from this keen and sometimes witty observer of the Georgia and Washington political scene.

From the beginning, it became apparent that Dr. William Felton was an honest, diligent, hard-working Congressman. The Feltons were serving Georgia well. They returned to Cartersville on August 17, 1876, to begin another election campaign. As they drew into the station, Rebecca could see crowds of people and many personal friends smiling and waving at the train. She was touched by this display. She hadn't yet noticed the band, which began to play triumphantly as they exited the train. And this time it was not just to Dr. Felton that these accolades were given, but to both of them. William gave a rousing speech at the Bartow House amid cheers and applause. Later the Cartersville *Standard and Express,* which had not been friendly toward this political couple, referred to Rebecca as Cartersville's "second representative."

Not all people appreciated Rebecca's efforts, however, and her opponents were not only Felton enemies within the Bourbon democratic ranks. Important men and women began to look askance at this woman who found the dirty, sometimes dangerous field of politics so fascinating, and worse, who helped her husband with his political agendas. Members of the clergy, businessmen, and many ladies, even members of high society took a dim view of the notion of a woman politician. After all, many believed that the Bible says that God has a plan for man and a different design for woman, and woe to the person who strays from God's divine purpose. Many espoused the idea that God gave woman the greatest role of all – that of wife and mother. As for man, God gave him dominion over everything else. Therefore, it is man's duty, his divine purpose, to serve and protect his wife and children. Some people believed that in these "modern days," some uppity women had unsexed themselves and tried to imitate the man. Some have even ventured into the realm of politics – clearly and always a man's domain, far too complex and even downright dirty for a lady. For many, the idea of a female politician was most unbecoming, like a squealing sow among the lilies of fair womanhood.

Throughout the late nineteenth century and well into the twentieth, the following notions were held by many regarding a woman in the political arena:

"The insistence on a right of participation in active political life is undoubtedly calculated to rob woman of all that is amiable and gentle, tender and attractive; to rob her of her innate grace of character, and give her nothing in return but masculine boldness and effrontery." Rev. O. B. Frothingham.

"Woman is queen indeed, but her empire is the domestic kingdom." J. Card. Gibbons, Archbishop of Baltimore.

"The best way for women to approach politics is to let them entirely alone." Jennie June, President of the New York Women's Press Club.

"Women must bear and nurse children, and if they do this, it is impossible that they should compete with men in occupations which demand complete devotion as well as superior strength of muscle and brain." Goldwin Smith, D.C.I.

"There is full scope for woman's patience, power, purity, and prayers without attempting to override that divine arrangement which never fitted her to be a soldier, a sailor, a civil engineer, a juryman, a magistrate, a policeman, a politician." Rev. Theodore L. Cuyler, D. D.

"If women achieve the feministic ideal and live as men do, they would incur the risk of 25 per cent. more insanity than they have now." Dr. Charles L. Dana, "eminent" neurologist.

"The rough contests of the political world are not suited to the dignity and the delicacy of your sex." Daniel Webster.

With the exception of quilting bees, southern women did not have their own social or civic organizations where they might speak among themselves. But in the North a new woman's move-

ment was taking form that would soon spread inexorably, wor-
shipfully, and spiritedly to claim some of the South's most able
women. It began with gatherings of groups of women, like those
prayerful, determined, and somewhat frightened ladies who as-
sembled in Ohio at the Hillsboro Presbyterian Church on a cold
December morning in 1873. Seventy women came together, fal-
ling to their knees on the hard church floor. Although some trem-
bled as they arose together, none turned back. "Walking two by
two, the smaller ones in the front and the taller coming after, they
sang more or less confidently, 'Give to the Winds Thy Fears' as
they marched together straight for the town's saloons, there to
kneel and pray together, pleading for an end to Demon Rum and
drunkenness." And with such female demonstrations, the
Women's Christian Temperance Union was born, officially in
1874, and soon became the largest women's movement of the
nineteenth century.

Most historians of this movement have only recently noted
the profound impact it had on women, women's rights, the improvement of their status, and general reform, in addition to their
temperance crusade. This organization addressed what had actually become a serious problem in the nineteenth century: drunkenness. With impure water becoming more common, and bacteria
often found in milk, many men turned to liquor to quench their
thirst. Spirits were even touted as promoting health, and often became an essential part of custom and tradition. Since divorce was
practically impossible, marriage to men who later became alcohol-
ics was common, often serving as a life sentence for the wife. The
WCTU had what many people considered to be a just and serious
cause. And to serve that crusade, this organization, under the
watchful eye of its founder, Frances E. Willard, actually organized
women and taught them about politics, rules of order, how to run
meetings…and eventually how to lobby state and national legislatures. But even more important, the WCTU encouraged women to
speak, to speak out in public, even in church – and to write. Their
speeches were not limited to temperance. They were encouraged
to look closely at their community, state, and nation, and to speak

out about possible reforms. Even more unusual, for the first time ever in their lives, women were praised for their words.

It was not easy, of course. But in the South the fight for temperance seemed more serious and altruistic than the struggle for women's rights and suffrage. The temperance movement may have come in by the front door with the WCTU, but women's rights also came in through the back, from the windows, and through every crack and crevice in that organization. "The WCTU was itself a celebration of women, dedicated to improving the image of and conditions for women. Only women could be voting members." Southern ladies began to organize – speaking, writing, working together, no longer the silent blossoms of chivalry. And few men could fault their cause.

Frances Willard
Founder of the WCTU

Determined opponents soon sought to stop them. They pushed these women, spat upon them, doused them with filthy water, paint, beer, whipped them, threw rotten eggs, stones, and dragged them through the streets. Husbands ordered their wives to quit this organization; mobs rushed them; the press denounced and ridiculed them (especially their "screeching voices" and "ugly sexless demeanor"). The WCTU responded by glorifying their ill-treated demonstrators, turning them into heroines, and citing other such brave women within history and the Bible.

No one had ever commended women for their courage, their ideas, their determination before; those characteristics formed no part of woman's chivalric descriptions. Heroes praised on the Fourth of

July and at other such holidays had always been men. In rhetoric and writing, WCTU women, such as Mary Torrans Lathrop, successfully changed the idea of the role of women "by carefully crafting an image of WCTU women as patriotic 'warriors' in the service of their country – not victims, but victors, 'a force in the Nation's life' – by showing the respect and admiration they had won."

The WCTU adopted a simple, at first seemingly innocent motto: "For God, and Home, and Native Land." Few outsiders at the time realized just what that final addition, "and Native Land," would mean. It helped to open the door for women to considerations of their nation. In fact, the WCTU considered it woman's duty to be concerned not just with God and home, but with the entire country and its government as well. As high-ranking WCTU member, Cornelia B. Forbes stated, women have "awakened." Her future holds no bounds. "Because of her there is today in place of the timid and retiring, or frivolous, vain, helpless species of woman kind, a vast army of energetic, educated, self-reliant and self-supporting women." The WCTU opened its doors to such strong-minded women as Rebecca Latimer Felton and her younger sister, Mary Latimer McClendon. No longer was social reform left in the hands of the men of the nation, but of their women too.

The WCTU provided both Mary and Rebecca with a network of intelligent women, trained in the workings of meetings and politics, who knew how to get things done and were willing to work to that end. Without the political training of the women, particularly of the South, learned at the WCTU, Rebecca and her sister would not have been able to locate the support that they needed for their reform movements.

In addition to its temperance work, the WCTU attempted all sorts of societal reforms, especially those involving women. The union women worked to try to reform prostitutes; they assisted young girls and unwed mothers; and they attempted to provide women of all classes and races with more civil rights. They resolved in 1889, "[t]hat we as women will use our utmost efforts to encourage and strengthen our sisters of every name and profession – that their sorrows shall be our sorrows. If they have strayed we shall try to reclaim them; if they are oppressed we will seek redress, and whenever we find the law of the State unjust towards any, we will by petition and agitation endeavor to change the same."

Many WCTU members noted that men were quick to give advice regarding the women's sphere and their deportment; they had even concluded that women might be physically harmed if they used the full power of their intellect. But these same men ignored the deleterious effects of tobacco and whiskey upon their families. Many women, including Rebecca, praised this organization for opening new vistas for womankind. Some even claimed that the WCTU taught them to abandon their passive roles within society and to take action and give serious consideration to events and activities outside the home – for the first time in their lives. As Frances Willard noted, "the WCTU is doing no more important work than reconstructing the ideal of womanhood."

WCTU women learned about suffrage, lobbying, peaceful protest, petitioning their legislatures, speaking, writing effective pamphlets, and persuading. Many women later claimed that their experience with the WCTU was one of the most enriching and rewarding experiences of their lives. It took nine years for the WCTU to reach the women of Georgia, established in that state in 1883. Its impact upon Georgian women would be profound. Rebecca officially joined the movement three years later – but she had championed the WCTU right from the start.

Chapter Five

Into the Battle Again

While the WCTU was spreading throughout the northern states, Rebecca was concentrating on her husband's second campaign for Congress. In this election contest, Rebecca began to take further steps out of the traditional southern roles for women. In addition to supporting her husband with shrewd anonymous letters sent to the press as she had done in his first campaign, Rebecca dared to go where no respectable Georgia woman had ever gone before. Accompanied by another lady, Mrs. Felton attended one of her husband's political rallies. As soon as the two women entered the hall, a hush fell over the crowd. Everyone stared at them in disbelief as they quietly took their seats. Then as the speeches began, the crowd resumed its usual uproar. In its next edition the local newspaper denounced Rebecca's attendance and sternly rebuked her, saying she had no business at such a "rough and tumble" rally.

Instead of responding directly to this newspaper attack, Rebecca asked the son of the woman who had accompanied her that night to write a letter to the press. And of course, Rebecca would be glad to help him write it. The son wrote, "Dastardly beyond expression is the personal attack on a lady visitor, an invited guest whose only offense was her presence and her quiet unobtrusive demeanor." Several "anonymous letters" sent to the newspapers fully supported Mrs. Felton and her friend and at the same time attacked the Bourbons.

By now everyone knew that the Felton name was linked not once, but twice, to politics. Denunciations of Rebecca were only beginning. "I was called a 'petticoat reformer' and subjected to plenty of ridicule, in public and private." William was also harshly criticized for allowing his wife so much latitude. The *Milledgeville Union Recorder* circulated the following rhyme about the Feltons:

> Some parsons hide behind their coats
> To save their precious life.
> But Parson Felton beats them all
> He hides behind his wife.

Ignoring customs and criticisms, William showed no inclination to attempt to curtail his wife's political activities. Before long she started "electioneering" for prohibition. "Probably I was the first woman in Georgia to 'electioneer' in county prohibition contests. By that, I do not mean lectures at meetings but public appeals on the eve of elections – talks on the street or anywhere I could collect a few voters." The first political campaign manager in Georgia, the first woman to attend a political rally in Georgia, and now the first Georgia woman electioneer – Rebecca was only warming up.

She began to speak up, to stand as her husband's political representative. She loved it. Later, she wrote that when her husband "…was worn down with speaking and sought a little rest and quiet, I met his friends in hotel parlors or piazzas, and between us we managed to see as many voters as was possible in these frequent trips. It was fatiguing, arduous work – there was no let-up, day in or day out – Sunday or Monday – but it was far from unpleasant."

Sometimes in her political battles she even managed to turn entrenched chivalric traditions to her own advantage. She could attack her political opponents at will, and did. But if one of her enemies dared to attack her personally, she would promptly remind him that she was, after all, a lady, and a southern lady at that! Rebecca enjoyed her ability to use chivalry to her own purposes – turn it upside down for a change, while outwardly keeping her look of shock and disdain. She was, after all, an attractive southern woman, a wife and mother with all the traditions of the South behind her. She played her part well – and to her advantage, leaving more than one politician speechless, humbled and embarrassed. Somehow her opponents thought she wasn't playing fair, but how to stop her, shut her up, just wasn't clear.

Unlike her activity in her husband's first bid for Congress, Rebecca also refused to remain at home while her husband campaigned – another first. "We had a roomy buggy, made to order, in which we could stow away some baggage and find room for a little boy of six – whose delicate health was much benefited by change of water, etc." And those long rides over all of the fourteen counties comprising the Seventh District did nothing to damage Rebecca's health and enthusiasm either. "We made hundreds of friends as we visited them in their homes, and I became strong and vigorous in health when I was out and going."

With Rebecca and her straightforward husband, making friends was as easy as making enemies of their political opponents. One observer of the times later remembered Rebecca as a "tiny figure of a demure little woman who sat in the buggy while the Doctor spoke, and carried around a 'scrap book' that was 'a veritable nightmare to the host of the organized.'" Scrapbooks. Apparently she started keeping them during William's first campaign. Whenever she found what she considered to be important information, or stories of political graft or corruption, she clipped it from the newspaper or journal and pasted it in a scrapbook. When William faced an opponent, his wife brought along the scrapbooks that were pertinent to the occasion. When William needed the precise information against his opponent, all he had to do was ask his wife to locate 'the dirt,' and she would take a scrapbook from her lap, turn it to the proper page, and hand it to her husband. How those Bourbons hated Rebecca Felton's scrapbooks! She always had the goods on them, neatly pasted in a nearby book. By the end of her life, she had countless scrapbooks, giving invaluable testimony to the issues of the day.

Working together, the Feltons gained new supporters. Even the *Atlanta Constitution*, which had never favored the Feltons, grudgingly had to admit their popularity. One evening the Feltons returned by train to their home in Cartersville where they were met by a cheering, waving crowd, eager to see them both. As the *Consitiution* reported, "It was amusing to hear the stalwart, gallant men of Bartow pledging her their support. 'We all are for you.' 'You have no lack of support here.' 'We are going to send you back,' etc., etc., were the enthusiastic utterances which they poured into the ears of the astonished lady."

But politics could be nasty, particularly in Georgia. Fights and name calling sometimes broke out at rallies and elsewhere. Once while Rebecca was at home, a mob stormed her husband's train, entering his car, yelling and screaming, cursing, calling William a "damned old hospital rat," and other more vulgar names. Instead of warning his wife to stay away from his next speech, he sent a telegram asking her to meet him at Marietta. "We were met at the depot by an immense crowd, a carriage drawn by four white horses, and they drove us all around, even in front of Judge Lester's office [Lester was Dr. Felton's political opponent], as a stinging rebuke to the dastardly persons who met the train on the previous Friday night." They were a brave couple, those Feltons.

The Feltons were also denounced by anonymous letters in the newspapers. For example, "Citizen" stated in the *Atlanta Constitution,* "You, Dr. Felton, march down into the mire and filth of the political arena, thrusting before you into the besmirching foulness – a **woman, your wife.**" This barrage was followed by an editorial in that same newspaper excoriating both Feltons. Years later Rebecca admitted, "Time has mellowed my feelings, but I am willing to say it took a good deal of God's grace to be friendly with such people in later life." Her admission was an understatement; Rebecca rarely forgave or forgot, especially when her husband was attacked.

But shrink away, run and hide when politics got rough? Never! Neither Felton withdrew when situations got dangerous.

In her writings Rebecca describes political bosses, boss rings, corruption, and sometimes even Georgia's representatives engaged in fist fights, slapping and punching each other within the hallowed halls of State. Threats to life and limb were not uncommon. Rebecca sometimes carried an umbrella with a sharp point at the end, and not just for the weather. A potential voter for the other side could deftly fly across her path at any time, airborne by the opposition. Again the Feltons won their seat in Congress in 1876.

From the beginning of William's first term in Congress, husband and wife continuously fought the leasing of convicts to private persons, who worked them on farms, railroads, or factories, without pay and with no governmental supervision – the infamous convict lease. In his second term they once again joined in common purpose to try to rid their state of this dark plague. They battled against its abuses and corruption with newspaper articles, legislative bills, and William's speeches. Although several other crusaders, both black and white, joined their cause, none was more single-minded, more devoted to the destruction of the convict lease than Colonel Robert A. Alston, who would become Georgia's Chairman of the State House of Representatives' Penitentiary Committee. It was by reading Alston's thorough investigations of this system that the Feltons learned the full measure of its evil. Robert and his wife Mary Charlotte soon became close Felton friends, meeting often together to plan their next offenses against the convict lease.

Reading Alston's and others' investigations into the convict-lease system is haunting, harrowing. Page after page of unremitting horror is recorded there, safely kept now within Rebecca's papers:

     Q. – What position was he in when whipped?
     A. – Standing up.
     Q. – Did he die right then?
     A. – He did not; he walked out of the cut and lay down in
         the shade of a tree.
     Q. – For what was he whipped?
     A. – For not working, I think.

Q. – Did they send for a physician?
A. – Not until after he had died.

Of southern aristocratic lineage Colonel Alston had distinguished himself as a cavalry officer in the Confederate army. He was gentle, intelligent, a lawyer and owner from the early 1870s until 1876 of a newspaper, *The Atlanta Herald,* in which he promoted many of the causes that the Feltons also championed: education reform, prohibition, and especially a more humane treatment of Georgia's prisoners. The Feltons and Alstons worked together to try to effect reform, if not the outright abolition of the convict lease, which would come up before the state legislature for a twenty-year renewal on April 1, 1879. With his accurate reports (some spilling into northern newspapers) of the brutal and deplorable conditions of Georgia's convict-lease prisoners, Colonel Robert A. Alston was becoming more than just a nuisance to the Bourbons, many of whom were getting rich by renting out convicts. His reforms could kill their money flow.

With the Feltons attacking the convict lease from Washington and Alston fighting for its defeat within the state legislature, people began to take notice. Even the *New York Times* joined in the battle to rid Georgia of the brutal convict lease, citing parts of Alston's investigations along with the support of other Georgia crusaders. In early March, 1879, Colonel Alston once again visited the Felton's parlor in the National Hotel where he admitted that his entire family had been harassed for more than a year and that his wife was so distraught, she was having fearful premonitions. "Of course, she's just overly worried about me," he said. But he, too, was upset. He would sit and read the newspapers and talk, then rise and pace back and forth, his hands clasped together, his face in a slight frozen smile. Even William's strong, gentle words of reassurance could not console him.

Alston returned to Atlanta to put the finishing touches on his last convict-lease report to the legislature before that April 1 deadline. It was scathing in its denunciations, particularly of Georgia politicians who lined their pockets from leasing prisoners. On March 11, 1879, at about noon, Alston was walking near the Atlanta Capitol when he noticed a man following him. No, maybe not… Perhaps they just happened to be walking the same way. Not wanting to be obvious and turn around, Alston quickly turned left, then right, then right again – and so did the man. Alston walked faster, nearly running now – the man kept up. Quickly, he entered the crowded Dougherty Hutchens barbershop…and so did that man.

It was Cox! Captain Edward Cox – Alston knew him, had known him for a long time. Although Cox was a Bourbon crony and a convict sub-lessee, they had been friends in spite of their political differences. But this day Cox did not look friendly at all. His face was drawn, menacing, his hands clenched, eyes narrow, staring now at Alston. His voice was louder than it should have been when he asked (no, demanded!) that Alston join him in the back room for a talk. Had he been drinking? Solemn, quiet, Alston followed him to that room. Everyone in the barbershop could hear Cox's shouting and cursing, along with Alston's softer more conciliatory tones. It had something to do with that convict lease, and Cox was boiling mad. "I'm going to cut your God-damned throat," Cox shouted. Someone in the barbershop had seen he had a knife, but no one made a move to try to stop the quarrel. The crowd in the barbershop listened.

"I'm unarmed, Cox," Alston replied. "I have no quarrel with you."

"Go get a gun!" Cox shouted. Alston then opened the back-room door and, without a word to anyone, walked through the barbershop and out the door. Cox soon entered the main room of the barbershop – shouting now – heaping strings of epithets and curses upon the absent Alston. No one in the barbershop moved or said a word. Cox stormed out the door and headed straight for the nearby Saloon of Mr. Pause, there to get another drink or two and meet with several Bourbon friends. As he drank and shouted about that "bastard Alston," he got madder still. Finally he said, "Can anybody loan me a gun? I'm going to kill that son-of-a-bitch!" But no one there would loan him a gun. Furious, Cox left the saloon, heading straight for the Heinz & Berkele gun store on Whitehall Street, in search of a pistol "a damned good one and well loaded."

After examining all of the pistols in the shop, he purchased "a new nickel-plated revolver, of the 'Swamp Angel' pattern...carefully loaded by the vendor." Then he turned back to Marietta Street to look for Alston.

Robert A. Alston disapproved of duels – he didn't even like guns. Now here was this madman after him. Alston was a gentleman in all respects. "Oh God, I don't want this," he muttered aloud. Reluctantly, he borrowed a pistol from one of his friends.

"Surely, this won't come to guns," his friend told him. "Surely, you can stop this thing." But Alston, tucking the gun into his belt, slowly shook his head.

"I don't know," Alston replied. "I just don't know."

Armed now, he walked to the State Capitol, opened the heavy main door, walked down the hall, then entered the state treasurer's office where he found several more of his friends. After relating to them the events of the day, he told them he intended to leave the Capitol and locate Cox.

"No, no, you shouldn't do that," one man told him. "He's probably just had too much to drink. Give him some time. He'll cool off."

It seemed like a good idea to Alston. He didn't want a fight. At that point a messenger, a man named Sams, employed by Cox, arrived seeking Alston. "Captain Cox sent me to tell you he is ready and waiting for you, and that you should go to him and fight it out like a man!"

Alston looked sadly at Sams. "Has he been drinking?" he asked.

"I don't know, Sir, but he's mighty excited."

"Then go back and tell Cox that I'm not coming. I want no difficulty here. Tell him to attend to his own business, and I will attend to mine." And so the messenger left.

A few minutes later, Alston also left the State Capitol, in search of his friend Governor Colquitt, whom he knew to be at dinner. He met Colquitt on Forsythe Street, on his way back to the Capitol and told him what had happened. After Colquitt tried to reassure Alston, they returned to the Capitol where the Governor sent Captain Nelms, the main keeper of the penitentiary, to go find

Cox and calm him down. Nelms found Cox in the "Girl of the Period" saloon and tried to call him out, but Cox refused to talk with him. Nelms returned to the Governor and reported what had transpired. Annoyed, the Governor sent him back to try again. But he was too late. Cox, still furious and excited, with his hand close to his pistol, entered the Capitol. He located Alston, still sitting in the treasurer's office, talking with Treasurer Renfroe and a tax collector. Immediately, Cox began to threaten and abuse Alston, repeatedly cursing him.

But Alston wouldn't play his game. "Mr. Cox, I do not want to have any difficulty with you about this matter, and there is no need for it. Let us drop it now. It will do you no good to kill me, and do me no good to kill you – not a bit in the world." Then Captain Nelms also entered this fairly small office and tried to calm things down.

Fearing that guns could be drawn right there, Renfroe tried to ease the two men outside – to no avail. Cox abruptly turned, unhooked the office door held open by a latch on the wall, and closed it. In this office there were two large desks, two tables, one long sofa, one large vault, several chairs, and five men, two of whom had pistols.

All the witnesses said they fired almost simultaneously while the three unarmed men dove for cover. Alston's first bullet found Cox's jaw. They were standing so close together, the victim's face was pocked with powder grains. Two molars flew from his mouth, found later in a pool of blood on the floor. Now engaged in their mortal dance, both men moved to the right. Cox, weaving and dipping, continually tried to fire, but was having trouble with his new gun. Then another bullet grazed his hand spurting streams of blood. Cox was flying now, ducking, spinning, while Alston continued to fire. Blue smoke rose everywhere as Cox got off his second shot. Then they heard it: click, click. In the melee, Alston had emptied his gun. Click, click.

Making no further attempts to duck or weave, Alston stood perfectly still, erect. He turned his head and smiled at his horrified friend Nelms. Cox slowly rose from his crouched position, stared at Alston, aimed his gun and fired a bullet into Alston's temple.

For two full seconds Alston did not move, then he dropped his head. Everyone watched as Alston's body, as if in slow motion, slid down the safe door to the floor.

Cox then shouted to Treasurer Renfroe, "We are both of us killed!" He turned, walked to the sofa, and lay down.

Nearly everyone in the state capitol heard the shots and ran to the treasurer's office. There they looked in horror at a scene that even the newspaper admitted defied description. Blood continued to pour from both men. "The floor of the room was slippery with pools of blood and yet the faint blue smoke from the pistols was creeping along the ceiling in search of an outlet."

The Atlanta newspapers tried to explain the reasons for this tragedy. It had resulted from a personal dispute between Alston and Cox about a particular lease in that convict-lease system. But the *New York Times* took a broader view. "The killing of Colonel Alston is not only a fresh illustration of the slight value which the violent men of the south place upon human life, but also a striking example of the terrible risks which are run by those who attempt to correct abuses in that section of the country." According to this newspaper, the reasons for the dispute, cited by those Atlanta newspapers, were merely "superficial." Then it concluded, "Of the causes which really led to it no mention is made, but it is, nevertheless, well known to those who have watched the course of recent political events in Georgia, that the killing of Colonel Alston was directly the result of his laudable effort to reform the penitentiary system of that state, a system which has long been a disgrace, not only to the commonwealth, but to humanity."

Other newspapers, including the *Wesleyan Christian Advocate,* and *The Nation,* joined the *New York Times* in their condemnation. Although it seemed that everyone in Georgia attended Alston's funeral, no one in the state legislature dared take up his cause. The convict-lease system was renewed without significant change on April 1, 1879 – for another twenty years.

Rebecca later wrote, "Who can forget poor Alston who drew such a graphic picture of the horrors of the convict system and who can forget that the poor fellow lost his life because he dared to interfere with such a system so deeply imbedded in Georgia politics?

Is anybody's life safe who attacks it?" Yet if anything, Alston's murder only served to increase the Feltons' resolve to attempt to end the convict lease. If they felt fear or intimidation, they failed to show it or change their ways.

Cox's murder trial took eight days and resulted in a guilty verdict with a recommendation for mercy. Someone in Georgia had written legislation forbidding capital punishment for murder convictions where juries recommended mercy: Colonel Robert A. Alston, himself. Even though Cox was sentenced to prison, he never served the prisoner's part of that convict lease. Instead he was required to do office work for the Dade County Coal Mines, owned by his friend and one-time political boss, General John B. Gordon, a particular Felton enemy. In fact, Cox had been one of Gordon's convict sub-lessees. His life sentence was quietly commuted, and he was granted a full pardon right after the 1882 political elections. His special treatment within the prison system and untimely release caused northern newspapers and the Feltons to suspect that Cox's whole role in Alston's murder had been a political set-up, designed to rid the Bourbons of their opposition.

Rebecca would later say that Alston "appealed to the governor; he appealed to the State treasurer, and told them Mr. Cox was armed and hunting him down, but nobody seemed interested enough to inform the police authorities. I did also hear that a policeman who knew something about this armed pursuit was dismissed from the force." If it hadn't been a set-up, why didn't anyone help him, try to protect him from the stalking, murderous Cox? "Dastardly," she muttered. The whole convict lease, the murder and its aftermath, General John B. Gordon along with Cox – all were dastardly beyond all understanding.

Chapter Six

Defeats...and Wins

The profound difficulties in every aspect of life in Georgia following the Civil War help to explain why issues such as civil rights and woman suffrage, hot and rampant in other parts of the nation, were hardly a consideration in the South, even in the early 1880s. There were so many other problems...survival for one. William and Rebecca recognized the problems and poverty of their state. End the convict lease and educate: these became Felton suggestions, mottos, goals for the betterment of Georgia. Along with the brutalities of the chain gang, it is not surprising that Rebecca would turn the plight of impoverished, illiterate southern women, and the need for education, particularly technical education for young blacks and young white girls into her reform crusades. Little girls put to work in cotton mills, growing up there with no chance at education or improvement; hillbilly girls, trapped by ignorance and poverty, often making moonshine to subsist; and black children sentenced to the chain gang for stealing vegetables to eat; issues such as these particularly concerned her.

Even when the Feltons became well known, their Cartersville home remained a warm and hospitable place for travelers, strangers and friends. Rebecca recalled a visit from a "good woman" from the mountains of northeast Georgia who spent a few days with them while on her way to a nearby city. "She had been raised up in those primitive regions – where apples, cabbage and moonshine Whiskey composed the staple commodities of her native section." This woman described in some detail her wonder at seeing her first locomotive on this trip, but Rebecca hastened to add that although the woman was inexperienced, she had "a lot of strong hard common sense stored away in her active brain and robust anatomy." The mountain woman had thirteen brothers and chewed tobacco with as much enthusiasm and accurate spitting as any of them. Rebecca wrote:

> One day as we sat cozily on the back piazza after dinner, she pulled a good sized twist of tobacco from her dress pocket, that had been grown and pressed at home and offered me a chew. Declining as modestly as the case permitted, she ejaculated, "You'd better take a chaw, you never seed no home-made 'backer that kin beat this hyar twis'." ... "Do all the mountain women chew?" I inquired. "Do the mountain wimmin chaw? – did I hyar yer ax.? – Bless your soul honey – de men, wimmin and chilluns chaw – I hab actually seen ebry mother's son in brother Mat's fambly of thirteen a chawins at one time – from Mat down to de sucking baby."

> I suppose I must have expressed some unusual surprise at the last statement, for my loquacious visitor added with a hilarious laugh, "Oh! Yuins need'nt open yer big black eyes so wide at dat, fer de babies do love 'backer. I hav seen em quit dey mothers' breast many er time, to git de quid outen her mouth inter thern."

Rebecca knew the women who worked in those cotton mills, too – entering into dead-end jobs as mere children, often staying for lifetimes, working long, exhausting hours for little pay, then buying their supplies at "pluck me" company stores. She would defend them from anyone who said that they were "no accounts," who did not deserve more than what they already had. Educate! These mill girls and women had no future without an education, especially technical education which would lead them to better jobs and living conditions.

Also a diligent fighter, William worked constantly in Congress for reforms that would allow his constituency better opportunities and more humane treatment. From March 1875 until March 1881, he ably represented the Seventh District in Congress, with Rebecca standing staunchly beside him. But his opposition was formidable; many Georgia politicians loathed this honest Con-

William Harrell Felton in 1880

gressman and his 'interfering' wife. After considerable discussion, the Bourbons decided upon a new strategy for the election of 1880. There would be no big issues in the next race – not a thing to raise Rebecca's writing fervor, no debates, nothing that could start a fight. Instead of being full of brimstone, as William's other campaigns had been, the election of 1880 would be as uncontroversial as a glass of warm milk. William ran his campaign on many of the same issues that he had in his earlier elections: the abolishment of the convict lease, better education for all Georgians, an end to child labor, an independent railroad commission, and the need for prohibition. Both Feltons urged all Democrats, including blacks, to vote for William. He felt that blacks should elect government officials who wanted to ensure their rights. Unlike many who opposed him, William respected the rights of everyone, black or white, male or female.

Yet William had crusaded for all of these issues before. With no new issues to inspire grand speeches or fire-branding letters to the newspapers, and with some apparent ballot fraud, William lost the election of 1880. They would be farmers once again. Although William and Rebecca kept up with their political contacts, wrote letters, attempted to influence Georgia politics, it was not the same as being "in the thick of it," as Rebecca liked to describe her experience in Washington.

Rebecca, always busy, soon turned her attention to their farm. She took a particular interest in poultry and horses, and one hen in particular took a great interest in Rebecca and became her special pet, Tippy. Wherever Rebecca was, Tippy followed. The hen was not particularly beautiful, no wondrous Barred Plymouth Rock or multi-colored strutting Bantam. She was a simple white chicken, noted only for her devotion to the busy woman of the farm. Rebecca loved that hen.

Tippy kept close watch on Rebecca as she hoed the vegetable garden. Whenever she turned over a fat, juicy grub or worm, the big hen helped herself. Wherever she worked outside, Tippy proudly followed her...loudly clucking. Sometimes when she sat reading the paper on the front porch, the chicken attacked her shoelaces, pulling them untied.

"Stop that, Tippy," she said, not too sternly. She kicked her shoe, and Tippy jumped again for that dark lace. When Rebecca noticed an article on Georgia politics that particularly intrigued her, she took a small pair of scissors from her apron pocket and began to cut it for another of her many political scrapbooks. Tippy darted once again for those shoelaces. Rebecca gave her tail feathers a little pull. The old hen squawked and darted off the porch…but soon was back again, roosting with contentment on the arm of Rebecca's chair. Life was certainly different now. A fat old hen had become her close companion, instead of all the tumult, friends and foes in Washington.

Rebecca tended to household duties; she rode fine horses across the countryside; she quilted; checked the accounts; paid the bills; complained of the taxes; she sewed; made soap, and brushed and petted Zeb, who was now too old to work. She also read long articles on animal husbandry and breeding; she tended to the vegetable garden, canning mounds of produce; she gathered eggs; she slopped the pigs; she purchased a fine broodmare; she read the papers and wrote articles to the editors, still attempting to influence politics; and sometimes she talked to friends, and also to her devoted hen. When the next election came, William and Rebecca were still too angry and annoyed with politics to run.

Even out of politics, Rebecca continued her crusades, particularly regarding the need for prison reform. In 1881 she read an article in Atlanta's *Constitution.* "During the recent criminal trials in the superior court one Adeline Maddox, a colored girl, was convicted of robbing a negro child of fifty cents, and was sentenced to five years in the penitentiary." Also within that article was a story about Willis McAfee, who had served ten years on a prior conviction and now had been convicted again on a charge of burglary. He was sentenced to four years.

Incensed about the treatment of that black girl, Rebecca wrote letters to the editor: "Now, can you explain to me why Willis McAfee, '**The Notorious Criminal,**' was only sentenced for four years, while the fifty cents highway robber was sent up for five?" She remembered the lenient treatment of Alston's convicted murderer and was once again outraged. She had already looked into what happens to young female prisoners in Georgia and decided, "it would have been kinder to her and her future if they had taken her out and shot her!"

In 1884 Rebecca's father died, the able man who had encouraged her, helped to form her thoughts, and saw to it that she was educated. She felt she hadn't seen enough of him these past few years, but knew he realized how much she loved him. From her father she received a significant inheritance – assets in money and deeds to lands rich in mineral deposits. She had always been an excellent businesswoman. Now she had her own money to buy and sell properties and perhaps to put into effect all those articles she had read about breeding. Horses, yes, her love and knowledge of horses could have a bigger outlet now. She was astute, an able accountant, knowing where every penny went. Her small fortune began to multiply.

In 1885 the Feltons also purchased a small newspaper which Rebecca ran, becoming one of the first women in Georgia, if not the first, to own and run her own newspaper. They named it the *Cartersville Courant*. In addition to providing the current news, Rebecca sometimes used the newspaper as her bully pulpit, advancing Felton causes and exposing political corruption within the Seventh District and the state. Yet like many small Georgia newspapers of the time, the *Cartersville Courant* did not prosper, and Rebecca, shrewd businesswoman that she was, soon recognized it as a financial liability and got out of the newspaper business.

Rebecca had more than enough to keep her busy with her farm work, her housekeeping, and writing articles for other newspapers. In addition, she was an avid reader, reading everything that came her way – especially anything to do with politics. Yet still there was something missing. Even while dusting or hoeing, always within her active mind lingered thoughts of politics. She continued to tell herself that William and she were much too old to think of taking any active political role. After all, she would soon be fifty, her husband sixty-two, ancient in those times. She didn't want William to run for any election anywhere. It would be much too hard on him. He was not well. He shouldn't undertake any other work except the overseeing of their farm, which was difficult enough. But still she could not keep her mind from drifting into Georgia's legislature and Washington's Congress.

One bright summer day as she sat reading in the shade of the front porch, with Tippy perched on the nearby rail, she spotted a buggy coming down the road – followed by another buggy, then two more – all headed for their farm. She got up and walked to the barn where William had been mending harnesses and pointed to their visitors. The buggies were closer now, each containing two or three men – important men – Rebecca soon discerned. William and Rebecca watched them as they stopped before the gate and tied their horses. The men looked serious as the Feltons walked down to greet them and invite them into the house.

They had not come to speak of crops or weather. They had come to speak of politics to Dr. Felton. "They told him that a crisis was upon the State right then, and the need of safe and honest leadership in the legislature was apparent," Rebecca later wrote. This time it was not just the convict lease that was a problem, but also the attempted weakening of the Georgia railroad commission, so that the lessees and their crooked lobbyists would have more power. They asked William to run for the state legislature. Regarding the goals of Georgia's lessees, Rebecca concluded, "If these people had their way and could carry out their will, railroad syndicates as well as State road lessees and convict lessees would be absolute masters of the State of Georgia." The men now sitting in their parlor expressed their confidence in Dr. Felton's ability and integrity. They asked him to see that the lessees of Georgia did not get their way.

After their unexpected guests had left, Rebecca and William discussed at length the possibility of his running for state office. At first Rebecca tried to dissuade her husband. As she later said, "We understood that he would be a target for venom, that they could pay purchasable men to write newspaper articles over other signatures than their own, as had been done in his congressional campaigns, to injure him in the State." In addition, William's health was not as good as it once was, and great time and effort would be required, not to mention the expense.

After Rebecca had expressed her serious reservations, William had some other thoughts to share. In addition to the convict lease, and the possible weakening of the railroad commission, the prohibition movement was not doing well. And furthermore, the Methodists and Baptists wanted to reduce the appropriations for the University of Georgia (William's *alma mater*). He could be useful in the state legislature (he knew how to stir his wife). Soon both agreed. Rebecca wrote, "To enter into a political furnace, already heated seven times seven, was a daring deed for even such a courageous man as Dr. Felton, and we were prepared to expect trouble at the hands of men who had made a business of paying for lobby work, before the state legislature, and who did not scruple at buying and bartering for even a seat in the United States Senate." She could not help but think again of their friend Robert Alston, murdered in the state capitol – and here was her husband preparing to enter the state legislature to fight the same battles as Alston had – with many of the same politicians.

One politician in particular galled Rebecca. Even his name evoked outrage in this tiny woman: John B. Gordon. How she hated him! Also from North Georgia, Gordon was six feet tall, with soldier-straight posture, slender, wiry, a Lieutenant-General in the Civil War – a hero, three years younger than Rebecca. In Rebecca's eyes he was not a hero. In fact, she considered him to be a failure at just about everything: a brilliant student at the University of Georgia who quit school before receiving his degree; an unsuccessful lawyer; a failure as a businessman (in the lumber business, publishing, and insurance); a man always in some sort of financial difficulty – a politician. Rebecca suspected him of taking money in return for political favors…bribes.

Most of all she hated him because he had consistently and fervently opposed her husband right from the start of his campaign for Congress in 1874. And Gordon was a formidable opponent; he was an excellent speaker and had been elected United States Senator from Georgia in 1873. He had lied to her – she had the untruth in his own handwriting. When she wrote to him asking if he planned to campaign for her husband's opposition in William's first election to Congress, he had replied evasively, suggesting that he would be in South Georgia and was unsure just when he would return. Yet only one week later, there he was, in the Seventh District speaking before a giant rally for Dabney. Beside Gordon's letter in the Felton archives is a brief statement from Rebecca: "This consummate liar was in Rome [GA] the next Saturday – abusing and reviling Dr. Felton."

She got madder still at Gordon during her husband's second political campaign for Congress. William was running against a war hero who had lost an arm in service to the Confederacy, Judge George N. Lester. Gordon, whose face had been scarred by a Yankee bayonet, and the one-armed Lester tried to turn that campaign into a noble Confederate pageant, with William serving as the enemy, or at the least the shirker. Lester would speak, rousing the crowd with his enthusiastic endorsement of the "Glorious Lost Cause," soon waving his stump in the air amid cheers and applause. Then Lester would denounce Rebecca's husband; he was a Radical; a disgrace to the ministry; a liar, a traitor; a man who left "no tracks at Manassas or Chickamauga."

When Lester had warmed up the crowd, out came that 'noble,' battle-scarred hero, General John B. Gordon (Rebecca had witnessed this show many times), and the crowd would rise in ovation for this gallant old Confederate officer. He would smile at the people, bow his head slightly in mock humility, then walk over to Lester and reverently raise his armless sleeve, waving it gently. The crowd would erupt in rebel yells and cheering for these two ageing warriors, Lester and Gordon. Rebecca sat in silent gloom as this show replayed in fields and halls across the Seventh District.

Rebecca remembered the many soldiers William had treated in that war, the suffering, men sick and dying, the dysentery, the screams, the lack of medicine. And the surgeries William had to perform – most of them amputations, some done without chloroform because that sole Civil War anesthetic was in such short supply. William had worked to have the Macon hospital cleaned and the men bathed in an attempt to stave off rampant infections. She wondered how many men were alive today because of the heroic efforts of her husband. Even before they fled to Macon, they had both climbed into fetid, bloody boxcars to tend the wounded near their Cartersville plantation. She would never forget feeding anguished men – some without arms or legs – slumped against the sides of the boxcars – dying. Her husband...her valiant, steadfast husband had saved so many of the Civil War wounded. Now here was Gordon, smiling and waving, his whole demeanor and speech designed to discredit William – to imply that he had been a Civil War slacker. She decided that Gordon was 'dastardly.'

Then came the Alston murder. John B. Gordon and Alston's murderer, Edward Cox, were "thick as thieves." Everyone knew that in the convict lease Cox was Gordon's sub-lessee. Every time Rebecca thought of Gordon, the little blue vein near her temple began to bulge. John B. Gordon represented the Old South and, at least in Rebecca's mind, the corruption of a political system out of touch with the true needs of her state.

Gordon had had a hand in Felton's loss in the 1880 election, too. This fact galled Rebecca beyond all measure. The Atlanta *Constitution,* unfriendly toward the Feltons, dared to gloat at her in their defeat. It stated that following her husband's election loss, there was no woman "who didn't feel happier than Mrs. Felton." She read the article to her husband, who shook with rage. She then wrote a letter to the *Constitution* quoting from the author of the offending article, Colonel Styles, then saying, "I will tell Colonel Styles I have a proper appreciation of his interest in my unhappiness, but I prefer to interview Mrs. Styles (a lady in every sense of the word, I understand) before it is decided who is the unhappiest woman in Georgia."

Gordon, Styles, the *Constitution,* politicians leasing prisoners and selling their leases, the whole Bourbon political ring, would there be no end to it? If only to rid Georgia of such men as Gordon, Rebecca agreed that William Felton needed to run for the state legislature, no matter what the political or personal fallout might be. In fact, he ran unopposed. From 1884-1890 William served Georgia as a member of the State House of Representatives. In that position William helped to see to it that the railroad commission was not weakened. He pushed for the same reforms as he had in the past: reform of the prison system and the convict lease; the advancement of the cause of prohibition; and better education for all Georgians. He also championed the University of Georgia. According to Rebecca, he "did more to protect the University of Georgia from well-planned schemes of emasculation and destruction than any man in Georgia." William and Rebecca stood as contradictions and impediments to the Bourbon Democrats, annoying them whenever possible, and struggling to loosen their control upon the state.

Child Spinning Cotton in Georgia Mill

Chapter Seven

Battles and Humiliations

In 1886 at the age of fifty-one, Rebecca became one of the first women ever to speak publicly in Georgia, addressing the Macon convention of the Women's Christian Temperance Union, where she had recently become a member. Those kind ladies told her she could discuss any topic. Terrified yet gleeful, she approached the podium, set her papers down with trembling hands and looked out at a sea of faces, all women, all quietly attentive, most smiling back at her, encouraging. The oldest members had the biggest smiles, remembering that sometimes women's knees gave way, or they fainted to the floor as they began to speak for the first time in their lives. All speakers were cherished, praised while given smelling salts. Although the WCTU had provided the Southern woman with her first chance to give a public speech, no one denied that it was a scary prospect. Every woman present knew how hard it was to stand up after a lifetime of sitting down.

Rebecca cleared her throat, looked sternly at her audience and began, not lecturing on temperance, but rather on her passion, the need for prison reform...in a desperate, urgent plea to these voteless women to end the convict lease. Was it then that it first occurred to her, that the thought became concrete? If they could only vote.... Although faltering a bit at first, it was not long before

Rebecca found her voice – somber and full, eloquent, filled with information and passion.

In the tightly corseted realm of Southern womanhood, certain subjects were taboo: rape, for one. No true Southern Belle should ever hear of that. Rebecca tiptoed to that subject. She stated that in a legislative report of 1879, written for the General Assembly by Robert Alston, it was accurately reported that "twenty-five little children, under three years of age, were then in camp, along with their convict mothers, little helpless innocents, born on the chain

The chain gang = Thomasville - Georgia

gang, in the lowest depths of degraded humanity. These children, according to the report, who were born from convict mothers were also the offspring of the guards (employed by the lessees to punish all offenders), who had basely used their authority to compel these women to submit to their carnal desires." Rebecca spared these genteel women nothing. Throughout her impassioned speech, there was not a sound in that entire hall except for her voice, ringing with its powerful message. For a few moments after she had concluded, the audience remained silent, stunned – then ripples of applause began, soon rushing, fierce, and all at once they stood for her in reverent ovation, fervently applauding.

Horrified by what they heard, the WCTU members resolved to do something about prison reform. The temperance women authorized Rebecca to introduce a resolution to the Georgia legislature advocating, in the name of the entire membership of the Georgia WCTU, the reform of the convict lease. In addition, Rebecca got the editor of the *Wesleyan Christian Advocate,* Reverend J. H. Potter, to endorse their proposition. She wrote scathing articles to the newspapers, condemning the lessees; and she spoke, she lectured, she was asked to lecture nearly everywhere now that her beautiful voice, so full of energy and facts, had been discovered. In addition, "**The Forum** invited an article from my pen and I do not suppose there were ever 3,000 words, freighted with more meaning or **fuller of 'ginger,'** than that arraignment of our convict lessees in Georgia, who were filling the highest offices in the State."

The following year Rebecca boarded a train in Cartersville to go to Atlanta to hear her husband speak to the state legislature. Still a State Representative from Bartow County, he was going to introduce his bill, which she had helped to draft, for a reformatory prison, one that would finally separate the sexes and remove the young from hardened offenders. Although he had attempted prison reform many times before, this time William and Rebecca believed there was a chance. But the train that she had taken arrived late. She hurried to the State Capitol, that hated Bourbon citadel. Passing the Office of the State Treasurer, where her friend Bob Alston had been murdered, she grimaced. In her mind she could see him – alive, vibrant, an earnest aristocratic gentleman – not sprawled and bleeding on the state office floor – a bullet in his head. All to silence him, to keep his mouth shut forever about the convict-lease system, the wretched form of convict slavery used to line the pockets of the Bourbons. Bob Alston, "murdered by a sub-lessee …his life-blood spattering the very walls of the strong-box of Georgia as he fell to the floor." Her husband had taken up Alston's banner, stepped into his shoes, and she was helping him. Was she handing the Bourbons the nails for her husband's coffin? She hurried past the office where the murder had occurred, not even glancing at the door. She hadn't time to think of bullets or murders now.

She had not stopped to consider the dangers to herself, that hot, humid day of August 7, 1887. Even more than they hated William, the Bourbon Democrats loathed Rebecca, whom they considered to be that always-sniping beast in woman's petticoats. More than one Bourbon politician would have loved to see her busy brains spilled out. Yet no one had the stomach for it, to pull the trigger on a Southern woman, that was too unseemly even for the worst of them. Perhaps there was another way. Public humiliation, yes, right in the State Capitol, in front of everyone – someone to denounce her, ridicule her and her whole family for that matter, but cleverly – yes, that might work. But who? Certainly not someone from her region; she had the goods on all of them, and besides, she fought so roughly, no north Georgia Bourbon wanted any part of this scheme.

A young ambitious Representative from Sumter, Georgia, in the southern part of the state, volunteered to put that woman in her place...and possibly gain some notoriety in the process. E. G. Simmons was their man. He was pudgy with sagging alabaster skin, a large oval head, brown hair parted on the right, long nose, bushy eyebrows and a brown mustache that drooped around his large fleshy lips, then joined his neatly trimmed beard, ending at a point at his collar. He had addressed the legislature before, but never for anything as momentous as this. Although his Bourbon bosses cheered him, urged him on, they warned him that his attack must be done with caution, in a veiled manner, just in case it should backfire. God forbid that anyone dare accuse a Bourbon of eschewing chivalric tradition by publicly dropping a southern lady to her knees.

Simmons, his ambush in hand, tapped his pen on his desk while waiting for Representative Felton to finish his arguments for penitentiary reform. Rebecca entered the gallery and found a seat. She loved to hear her husband speak and listened attentively as once again he discussed their favorite topic. "Take that little white boy, or black boy, I care not which. He is a Georgian. You are his guardian. In the sight of God and all men you are his keeper if he is sentenced by the courts to the chain-gangs of Georgia. ... The legislature of Georgia is responsible for him." But the legislature of Georgia was not really paying much attention to this impassioned old Congressman.

After Felton concluded his remarks, E. G. Simmons, somehow seeming even plumper, all puffed up, strutted to the rostrum, shuffled and tapped his papers, cleared his throat and smiled. Rebecca later wrote, "From my seat in the gallery I had a good view of his face. I noted the delight that was expressed in the faces of the men that I knew favored the lease, and were opposing Dr. Felton's reformatory bill." Simmons began his speech with a sing-song dramatic eloquence, deeply edged with sarcasm, comparing Felton's proposed reformatory to a wonderful college campus, with every amenity, ivy-covered buildings, a courtyard, and even a statue to Dr. Felton himself, bearing the inscription, "The John Howard of Georgia." And just in case anyone was not familiar with this English reformer, Simmons would be glad to explain the similarities. You see, Howard had this strong, commanding wife, a writer, "a woman not much to be regarded." Like Felton, he also had an only son. Howard sorely neglected him; the son became "a jail bird." Ultimately Howard went insane with his reform ideas. In fact the whole family was a failure, a bunch of crazy fanatics. The crowd snickered.

Nearly all eyes in the room darted first to Representative Felton, then to his wife, whom most had seen enter the gallery, then back again to the still-smiling Simmons. Some took out their opera glasses to get a better look. Simmons was just warming up. "He made sport of Dr. Felton's palsy, his infirmity, and made merry over his trembling limbs and aged, tottering frame." Rebecca could see that Simmons "enjoyed the notoriety, he spread himself." As for Rebecca, "I felt the hot blood surge in my veins. I would have given considerable money for the privilege of answering him then and there, and nothing was plainer than the employment of a willing legislator to do what no one of his political owners was willing to undertake." Yet she kept her seat, erect, hands folded in her lap, staring solemnly and dry-eyed at the speaker.

It was a long speech, nearly unendurable...lavishly punctuated with humiliation for the entire Felton family. E. G. Simmons approached his intended *coup de grâce* for Rebecca Latimer Felton. How he relished this moment! His entire speech was poised for his last thrust. Disguising his own glee with a stern pout, he referred to Rebecca as "The political She of Georgia." Looking at that phrase with the eyes of someone in the twenty-first century, there seems to be nothing wrong with it. After all, she really was "the political She of Georgia," if one assumes its literal interpretation. A closer examination quickly reveals the horror of that denunciation from the viewpoint of all of those sitting in that room in the nineteenth century.

Nearly everyone present that day had either read or knew about a recently published scandalous erotic British novel, *She,* by H. Rider Haggard. Its story had made all of the Atlanta newspapers and was frequently discussed. The "She" in this work was a witch, a female monster, the Devil's consort, who had despised and preyed upon men for two thousand years. Simmons' thinly veiled comparison implied that the "the political She of Georgia" was out to destroy both family and state with her talk of prison reform and prohibition, always out to dominate, demanding complete obedience...or else she would destroy! It was not until after two thousand years of tormenting men that this "She" fell into the fire, there writhing and shriveling until she became no more than a foolish monkey. E. G. Simmons may as well have slapped Rebecca soundly in the face. Still tearless, somber, she sat stiffly as everyone now stared at her...some even whispering and furtively pointing. Simmons was proud, triumphant as he strode past the hollow-eyed and sallow Dr. Felton, back to his seat. No one had ever tried to put Rebecca in her place like this! With the legislative meeting adjourned for the weekend, everyone in Atlanta talked about little else than that grand speech given by the "Gentleman from Sumter."

Atlantans realized that Simmons' speech marked only the first act to this huge drama playing out in the State Capitol, with the weekend serving as an intermission. "What will the Feltons do?" was the question of the day. Rebecca and William did not see each other for the rest of that Friday until they met for dinner at the Talmadge House (where William had rented rooms while the legislature was in session). The Honorable William Hamilton Felton (William's cousin) also ate with them, only three at the table. Although William was reluctant to show the full extent of his outrage in a public restaurant, they all shared their belief that it was a "put-up-job." William then said, "I'll take care of him in due time."

"Due time" came the following Wednesday. All of Atlanta and most of the state knew that was the appointed day for Dr. William Felton's response to E.G. Simmons – all the newspapers had announced it. Rebecca had not seen his speech. He had not wanted her help. This time the old lion intended to defend his mate and den himself. Rebecca took the earliest train from Cartersville to Atlanta on Wednesday morning, thinking she would have plenty of time to arrive and get a seat before her husband's speech. But the train was delayed. Usually constantly at work, Rebecca could not concentrate on the letter she was attempting to compose on the train. Finally, she put her pen and papers back into her purse and looked out the window. After what seemed like an interminable ride, she arrived, rushed to the Capitol and opened the door to the House of Representatives. The entire room was "packed floor and gallery – every seat on the floor occupied – the aisles packed, the lobbies crowded, eager faces peering in the doorways – the galleries thronged with ladies and gentlemen, the ushers whispering, 'Standing room only.'" Dr. Felton was already speaking. An usher spotted Rebecca, the star of this extravaganza, and showed her to the best seat in the house, especially reserved for her – front and center in the gallery – for all to see. It seemed this time that everyone had opera glasses, all now trained upon her. She felt hot, flushed.

At first it was hard for her to adjust to the scene. There was her beloved husband in the midst of this storm of people, who altered between hushed silence and roaring applause and stomping. His figure bent, his hands trembling, his white hair framing his pale face, his eyes blazing, he poured out his wrath and scorn against "the man from Sumter." The *Journal* summed up the Felton speech in one sentence: "It was as frightful as a murder."

Dr. Felton compared Simmons to a yapping, snapping, pug twisting to reveal "his hinder parts." He also said, "I do not know and do not think that man (pointing to Mr. Simmons) has sensibilities enough to rise above the gutters and slews and scum of a ward politician.

> Mr. Simmons – I protest that --
> Mr. Felton – Not a word, not a word from that source
> Mr. Simmons – Very well then, I will speak later.
> Mr. Felton – Every dog has his day. (Great applause
> and laughter.)"

The Honorable Mr. Simmons was now twisting in his seat, pale, nervous, trying vainly to object. But William was just getting warmed up. "May my right hand and my tongue forget their cunning and their powers before I avail myself of the privileges of a member on this floor to ridicule the family of another." Once again Simmons tried to interrupt, nearly whimpering now, but the Doctor put him down. Then Felton said that he had married "one of the noblest and purest and most intellectual women of Georgia." As for his son, he ably defended himself; no, there was no neglect of his "only son, now living, all the others crowned gloriously with the Father in Heaven." Those who still trained their opera glasses upon Rebecca noted that while she sat erect and motionless, her cheeks were shiny – wet, as tears ran unchecked down her face, dripping onto her crisply ironed dress. Still she did not move and emitted no sound.

As Dr. Felton continued, his speech growing more passionate and powerful with each sentence, some opera glasses began to turn toward the speaker:

> There is that little country home, a little way-side home, a home where I and my companion have lived for the last forty years, and, thank God, whatever may be its surroundings the heart is there. Whatever may be its surroundings all that I love on God's green earth is there. And then the rude hand of the ruffian prompted by the hope of reward probably, attempts to try to ridicule it in the hope of future reward, I will hurl it back at him, and as long as I have the strength I will protect her. It is true that I am old. It is true that my old form is bent as the man from Sumter said the other

day, and it is true my locks are white, and it is true that my nerves
are shattered, and it is true that there are ten thousand indications
that I am on the verge of the grave; but as long as God gives me
strength I will protect the innocent and speak for the prosperity of
Georgia until God takes me from this world.

There was a roar of applause from the gallery and some clapping
on the floor. Rebecca was forgotten as all eyes and glasses fo-
cused on the speaker whose oratory profoundly moved them. Rebecca, motionless, barely able to see through the torrents of unchecked tears streaming from her face – smiled at her valiant husband so bent on her defense…that weak old man who spoke for
her. It was almost as if there were only two people in that
crowded, tumultuous room…only Rebecca and William together
amid this political spectacle, this whirlwind of noise and shouting
and applause. Even the Bourbons were awed by his words. The
crowd cheered wildly at his conclusion, as he said, "Hate him?
Despise him? No, sir, no, sir. I simply turn him over to the intelligence and virtue of Georgia. That is the worst fate that can befall
him." The audience rose as one in ovation, stomping, clapping,
roaring. And Mrs. Felton still sat erect, smiling down at her husband, not even moving to retrieve a handkerchief.

It was not long before even the Yankee newspapers took notice of the prolonged drama within Atlanta's State Capitol. The
New York Sun reported: "There does not seem to have been much
left of Dr. Felton's assailant when the two hours' speech was finished. … The appeal to the chivalry of the Georgian heart was irre-
sistible. Men cheered wildly, hats and handkerchiefs went up into
the air, and parliamentary restraints were forgotten in the enthusiasm of Dr. Felton's remarkable oratory. We congratulate him
upon his triumph."

Not as many came to see the third act of this spectacle, which
took place the following day, most having been fully satisfied by
the power of the second. E. G. Simmons slithered up to the podium intent on setting things straight. In another long speech, he
said that "that creature from Bartow," (throughout his speech he
refused to name his opponent) had simply misunderstood. He had
never intended to disparage his wife. Then Simmons proceeded to

preach his own little sermon on the proper role of women. Referring to women in politics, he said, "Oh, noble woman, such is not thy sphere, such is not thy home. If the creature from Bartow drags woman into it nature revolts, decency protests, the lady herself shrinks. Thy home is by the fireside...." Throughout Simmons' speech Dr. Felton pointedly ignored him. In fact, he acted as if there were no speech at all, sitting at his desk, deeply engrossed in reading a newspaper. He never even bothered to look up.

There was a fourth act, and it should have been the most important of all: the vote for the passage of that reformatory bill. Those Bourbons, still firmly in control, once again nullified any reform of their lucrative convict lease, turning the Felton/Simmons spectacle into a tragedy, and causing even more northern newspapers to point to Georgia with disgust. While this drama took place publicly, another story unfolded in a little country courthouse. A small black boy, age ten, in a little Georgia town stole three potatoes. Condemned to serve five years on a chain gang, he would soon become intimately acquainted with the lowest circle of hell on earth. Now an anonymous cog in that convict-lease system, he had a huge iron collar put around his neck as he was led away in chains, stumbling, wide-eyed, never to be seen again. Just another term for slavery? No – far worse. It was really "nothing less than capital punishment with slow torture added."

There were so many other histories of those (almost all blacks) ensnared within the convict lease for minor offenses that William and Rebecca were nearly blinded by outrage. A woman given "one hundred and sixteen lashes for cursing," a man brutally beaten to death for tossing his hot coffee at a dog, women routinely raped by guards, no medical or religious care, no governmental supervision, illegitimate children forced to run with the gangs, convicts beaten to death for lagging behind or working too slowly – such were the routine abuses of the barbaric convict lease. And the Bourbon politicians were getting rich off of it, leasing out prisoners to the railroads, to companies and farms, and taking the money themselves. The convict-lease system was, as William often called it, an "Epitomized Hell.

"An Epitomized Hell"

Chapter Eight

Feminine Awakening

Near Atlanta's State Capitol building is a statue and small fountain erected in honor of the "Mother of Suffrage" in Georgia. The sentiment of such a memorial would be touching, except for the fact that it is dedicated to the wrong woman. The real "Mother of Suffrage" in Georgia...well, Georgia had some problems with her.

Georgia's true "Mother of Suffrage," Helen Augusta Howard, came from one of the most prominent families in the state. She had endured years of unbearable and unspeakable teasing and torment for being a 'crazy' spinster, for advocating woman suffrage, for bringing Susan B. Anthony to Georgia, and for entertaining her and other northern suffragists in her own home. On May 20, 1920 she allegedly shot a boy with an "old style 33-calibre Smith and Wesson Revolver" in a magnolia tree on her property and nearly killed him. Allegedly, he was picking flowers from the tree. Although the actual court records have disappeared, with only brief summaries remaining, any casual reading of the many and lurid newspaper accounts of this incident leads to the suspicion that at the most, it was an accident, and that the boy who was shot was lying about what really happened. Nevertheless, Augusta, as she liked to be called, was found guilty by an all-male jury, and after several appeals, was sentenced to "not less than one year or more than two years ...on the State Farm" As sometimes happened within the Georgia judicial system of the 1920s, there was an 'intervention' in this case, allegedly by one of Augusta's brothers. According to Augusta's descendents, who do not wish to be mentioned by name, a deal was struck between Augusta's brother and a judge. If Augusta would leave the state of Georgia and not return during the course of her life, no one would pursue her.

Augusta spent the rest of her life in a boarding house in New York City, returning to her native state in a coffin. In a cemetery in Columbus, Georgia her remains rest under a tablet, giving her name, birth and death dates, along with one other word: "MARTYRED," in much greater letters than her name. It is alleged that to make certain that she would not return to Columbus, her mansion was torn down. Her life-story should be the topic of a book.

It all began in the late 1880s, and although she has been nearly forgotten, there can be no doubt that Helen Augusta Howard was truly the founder of the suffrage movement in Georgia, and that it did not begin in Atlanta, as nearly everyone assumes. While William and Rebecca were fighting for reforms within the state legislature in the late 1880s, woman suffrage became a real issue (if only a tiny one) in Columbus, a cotton mill town along the Chattahoochee in west Georgia – which General Wilson nearly destroyed after Appomattox. About two miles from that town, located on the Stage-Coach Road, was a driveway that gently curved through cedars, ancient live oaks, huge magnolias, interspersed with more refined, exotic plantings – "crepe myrtles, gardenias, scarlet pomegranates, boxwoods, yaupons, and other rare shrubs." It was like a park, growing more lush and beautiful as one neared the house, located about one-quarter mile from the road. On top of a gently rising knoll was the mansion, Sherwood Hall. The driveway made a large circle right before the house. Inside that circle were flowers, thousands of them, blooming – fragile pinks, reds and yellows.

Sherwood Hall, named for Sherwood Lindsay, the grandfather of Augusta, the real "Mother of Suffrage" in Georgia, was built in the Greek Revival style by Matthew Evans in 1830. Even

Margaret Mitchell's fictional Tara and Twelve Oaks would have paled alongside the grandeur of this house. It boasted huge white Ionic columns not just in the front, but all around the house, twenty-four in all. Its interior was palatial, leaving more than one guest's mouth agape upon first entering, with some also gasping at the beauty of the striking solid mahogany spiral staircase and rotunda. The ornate and massive mahogany woodwork throughout the house was accented with heavy silver. The fourteen-inch walls, smoothed with white Plaster-of-Paris, were set off by the deeply polished reds, oranges, yellows, and sometimes even blues of the heart pine floors. Damask curtains framed the windows, and ornate mirrors reflected the exquisite, antique English furniture, gleaming china, and broad fireplaces with elegant mantles of Italian and Egyptian marble that graced this home.

In this mansion lived a beautiful, tempestuous woman, Helen Augusta Howard. And she read a great deal, all sorts of books, including a copy of Georgia's Constitution, in which she learned who, according to law, was not permitted to vote within her state: lunatics, felons, traitors, children, and women. The twelfth and last child of Augustus Howard, who died when she was only two, the spirited Augusta decided that she would have to do something about that Georgia suffrage law.

Following her father's death, Augusta's mother, Ann, and all of her children moved into Sherwood Hall to live with Augusta's grandfather, Sherwood Lindsay. When Augusta was in her early teens, her loving grandfather died, and Ann inherited the mansion. But the rest of Sherwood's wealth was divided among his eleven other children. Sherwood Hall was now owned by a woman, and she had no way to earn a living, no means with which to pay the exorbitant taxes on the property each year, or keep the mansion up. Although at first there was enough to cover the expenses that such a household demanded, with each passing year the financial situation of the Howard family became more desperate. "Taxation without representation" took on real meaning for this family.

Augusta read the works on women's rights by Herbert Spencer and John Stuart Mill with rapt attention. She was particularly intrigued by Mill's, *On Liberty*. Although the first part was a general essay on that subject, carefully tucked at the back of the book was a much more precise essay, *On the Subjection of Women.* Augusta soon discovered that here was a writer – a man – who had given the subject of women's place in society considerably more thought and attention than she had ever dreamed. She could not put the book down.

Methodically, dispassionately, Mill described men's total domination over women in all facets of life: socially, politically, and legally. In fact, he noted that from early childhood the female was groomed for her subordinate position. "All women are brought up from the very earliest years in the belief that their ideal of character is the very opposite to that of men; not self-will, and government by self-control, but submission, and yielding to the control of others."

In fact, Mill compared marriage for a woman to a master/slave relationship. "I am far from pretending that wives are in general no better treated than slaves; but no slave is a slave to the same lengths, and in so full a sense of the word, as a wife is." She swore obedience to her husband when she married, and that husband had nearly total control over her until he or she died. Divorce was usually out of the question. "The vilest malefactor has some wretched woman tied to him, against whom he can commit any atrocity except killing her, and, if tolerably cautious, can do that without much danger of the legal penalty." Even sex was her duty, to be freely given whenever her spouse desired.

Mill suggested that the subjugation of women was not the natural order of things, but was rather the result of history, religion, and custom. He further claimed that male domination might actually harm society's advancement by holding back half of its people. He favored woman suffrage, noting that his own country, England, had been ably ruled by women. "When, to queens and empresses, we add regents, and vice-roys of provinces, the list of women who have been eminent rulers of mankind swells to a great length." According to John Stuart Mill, to give women suffrage, to give them their freedom, would ultimately enrich mankind.

Augusta agreed with Mill's reasoning, and especially his conclusions. Avidly, she sought the works of other writers who echoed Mill's thoughts. And right there that night in 1888 after reading Georgia's Constitution, Augusta Howard decided that she must form a group to study women's rights. The initial members of this group were solely members of the Howard family: H. Augusta, her mother Ann Lindsay Howard, and four of her sisters, Antoinette Rutherford Howard, Alice E. Howard, Claudia Howard Maxwell and Miriam Howard Dubose. Membership was extended to both men and women. Anyone was free to join who believed in "the justice of women's demand to be raised about [sic. above] the political level of minors, lunatics, felons, and traitors, with whom they...[were] classed by the Constitution of Georgia." They began their suffrage work on a small scale, mostly studying the writings and methods of other suffragists and discussing what they might do to further women's rights in Georgia. They spent two years (1888-1890) unorganized, busily reading and working independently. Then in July 1890 under Augusta's leadership, these women formally organized and founded the Georgia Woman Suffrage Association, the first official suffragist organization in the state of Georgia. The date of the formation of this association is only four years after Rebecca even dared to give a speech, let alone vote, in Georgia.

Augusta formulated a thoughtful protest to the Constitution of her state. She wrote, "Youth outgrows his political disability; the lunatic may be restored to reason; the felon, however low his crime, pardoned and restored to his full rights as a sovereign voter; the one unpardonable crime under the Constitution of Georgia is being born a woman." Meetings were held once a month at Sherwood Hall; dues were one dollar per year. Furthermore, anyone in the entire State of Georgia who wanted to hear about woman suffrage would be provided a GWSA speaker for free. The Howard women began their suffrage movement in great high spirits, fully expecting that other women – and men – would soon join their cause.

If Rebecca heard of the formation of this tiny suffrage movement south of Cartersville, she took no notice of it. She had more urgent problems to consider. Although her husband had initially announced his retirement from politics, he had been unable to resist another attempt to win his old Congressional seat in Congress, this time determined that he could help the farmers of his state. Although Rebecca believed his opposition to be too strong and attempted to dissuade him, he decided that he would run. Rebecca did everything she could think of to help her husband win the election, but her efforts proved futile. As she had foreseen, he badly lost the election of 1890, not even carrying his own county. As had happened in nearly every other election that William had entered, there were serious reports of rampant election fraud.

Four years later, also against Rebecca's advice, William ran again for Congress, and again went down in defeat amid many assertions of election fraud. Rebecca later noted, "The elections in Richmond County, like Rome's elections were a disgrace to the Commonwealth of Georgia." Many concerned citizens wrote to the Feltons urging them to contest the election. Rebecca believed that such continued election frauds were destroying Georgia's civil liberties. She maintained that her husband had been robbed of elected positions on more than one occasion. Although she was reliably informed that contesting an election would be quite costly, and that the chances of success were slim, Rebecca decided it was worth the effort, and William agreed.

They were required to hire both Georgia and Washington lawyers. Rebecca noted that in Georgia, "we had difficulty in finding a lawyer to conduct for us the contest. They were afraid of political desperadoes clothed with judicial authority." In addition, they needed the testimony of countless witnesses. The process was not only costly but seemingly unending, becoming more turbulent with each passing week. Rebecca and William, whose health was becoming even more fragile, decided that she would testify before a congressional committee. The *Rome Tribune* of Georgia stated that no woman had "ever before invaded the precincts of an election committee hearing in that way...." The entire article disparaged Rebecca and concluded that "Judge Maddox, whose seat Mrs. Felton wants for her husband, much prefers that Mrs. Felton should prattle to the committee than that the lawyers should argue for her husband."

The courtrooms in Georgia in which the election contests were held resembled barroom battles more than sober deliberations. In Rome one of the Felton witnesses soundly slapped the presiding Judge for calling him a liar...and got away with it. As part of her defense in Georgia, Rebecca, the only woman in the courtroom, read aloud to the court a scathing article concerning the election frauds, taken from the *Rome Tribune,* that she had borrowed from the editor that morning. Opposing counsel demanded to be given the paper from Mrs. Felton, implying that she had misread the article. Rebecca clutched the paper, while her lawyer, Mr. Davis said, **"I'd like to see you make Mrs. Felton give it up."** There was laughter in the courtroom.

Rebecca later stated, "I made up my mind to wear out my silk umbrella on whoever attempted to relieve me of the paper."

While Rebecca was contemplating the use of her umbrella as a weapon, William was also attending an election contest in Cartersville. There, one of the opposing attorneys pulled a knife on one of Felton's witnesses, attacking and abusing him. Another battle erupted within the courtroom. Although the election contest in Washington was conducted with more decorum and decency, the result was the same. William and Rebecca lost their contest, along with a great deal of money, in spite of the fact that Congress reimbursed them for a portion. The abuse that followed them after their court loss was almost overwhelming. Rebecca was even accused of falsifying evidence. She hotly defended herself. Both heard accusations, some public, that they did not pay their bills. William provided ample evidence to the contrary. After this exhausting and expensive humiliation, William and Rebecca both agreed; it was time for him to retire.

At the same time that Rebecca was engaged in her husband's attempts at re-election, Congress decided to select Chicago as the site of the Columbian Exposition, a World's Fair to take place in 1892 in order to commemorate the four-hundredth anniversary of Christopher Columbus's discovery of America. Unlike previous expositions, women would be invited to participate – to celebrate women's work and contributions to society. Two women would

be selected from each state and territory to serve on the Board of
Lady Managers. They would even be paid! World's Fair Com-
missioner, General Lafayette McLaws (from Augusta), asked Rebecca to represent her state. She would go alone to Chicago for the
first meeting of the Lady Managers on November 19, 1890.

She was astonished by the cold of the Windy City, often writing home about how it nearly froze her southern bones. But her
work, that was important from the start. At the first meeting of the
Lady Managers, Rebecca, to her astonishment, was elected Temporary Chairman. "I was quickly elected to the position and had
barely time to scribble down a few words of grateful thanks for the
honor, until I was escorted to the platform and the gavel placed in
my hand." She had no experience presiding over a large organization; she had no book of parliamentary procedure; she wasn't sure
what to do. But there she was, standing before some of the most
prominent women in the nation – and she was now expected to
give a speech. By this time in her life, Rebecca knew how to
speak. Many women long remembered what she said that day.

After expressing some concerns regarding her inexperience
as a Chairman, Rebecca said, "My heart is full of kindness to every
one of you. I know no South, no North, no East, no West. We are
all dear sisters engaged in a work of loyalty and patriotism, under
the grand old flag in the home of our fathers." The ladies in the
room listened with rapt attention as Rebecca continued. Her words
set the tone of their organization. She said, "It is the first time in
the history of the Republic that the female sex has been recognized
as competent to attend to any sort of public business for the National Government. It is the very first recognition of woman's services as a citizen and a tax-payer by Congress." She asked the
group to proceed with great deliberation, to use wisely the authority entrusted to them. "Let us take no step forward, that we shall
regret afterward. Let us remember we are on trial before this great
nation."

The experience of the Lady Managers of this great exposition
was unparalled in American history. Educated and renowned
women from every state in the nation were working together now
to demonstrate and display women's contributions to the nation. It

is difficult even to imagine Rebecca, simply dressed, fresh from the Georgia countryside, meeting and working with the head of the Board of Lady Managers: the high-born, wealthy, and regal Bertha Honoré Palmer, the statuesque, poised, and beautiful Queen of Chicago Society. The epitome of well-tailored savoir faire, hair exquisitely billowing above her patrician face, her diamond and platinum choker sparkling, she warmly greeted Rebecca and the other Lady Managers.

Palmer Residence in Chicago

Bertha and her wealthy husband Potter Palmer lived at 1350 North Lake Shore Drive, a Gothic castle that they built in 1885.

Felton Home in Cartersville

She loved art, particularly the Impressionists, and one of her favorite rooms within the castle was a 75-foot gallery adjacent to their rooftop ballroom, where they often entertained. Monet, Renoir, Degas, Mary Cassatt, Pissaro and others (now part of the Art Institute of Chicago) served to decorate this space. Some of her guests came specifically to see her paintings. The Palmers entertained the most prominent people of the nation and abroad, even President McKinley.

Although at first it might seem that Rebecca Latimer Felton and Bertha Honoré Palmer would have little in common, both women had similar attributes and interests. They were both keen intellects and observers of society; they were also shrewd and able businesswomen; both were strong exponents (and members) of women's clubs; and both were deeply concerned about the rights of women and children. In addition, neither was content to do things half-way. Bertha and Rebecca liked each other right away.

The commissioners who offered Bertha the position as head of the Board of Lady Managers underestimated the power and determination of this grande dame of Chicago. They tried to assure her that her position would be mostly ceremonial, that she would not be required to do much. In fact, the commissioners did not want her to do much of anything. But Bertha had other ideas.

She traveled the nation and world, gaining support for her exposition. She used her clout in many women's groups to organize and donate to "Columbus societies" for the women's division of this great fair. She obtained donations from the United States Congress that far exceeded anyone's dreams, and did the same to the commissioners of the fair. No one ever seemed to know how to say "No" to Bertha Honoré Palmer, not even her loving and devoted husband. The

Woman's Building of the Columbian Exposition in Chicago, 1892

woman's division of the Chicago Columbian Exposition was going to be a smashing success – and it was. The first woman graduate of the School of Architecture at M.I.T., Sophia G. Hayden, designed the mammoth and beautiful building that would house the expositions of women from all over the world. Bertha became the hostess of the entire Columbian Exposition, entertaining royalty, diplomats and presidents at her castle on Lake Shore Drive. She was determined that the first time American women had ever been invited to present their contributions to mankind would certainly not be the last.

Only a few months later, on a much smaller scale, and with scarcely any attention, the Georgia Woman Suffrage Association held its first official meeting in July, 1890. But no one except the Howard sisters and their mother attended. Then came August's meeting, again with high expectations. And again no one came. At their September meeting, they quietly waited about fifteen minutes, talking softly among themselves while listening for a knock at the door. This time, in addition to telling all of their friends and posting notices around the town, they had printed a small announcement in the newspaper. But just as in the previous meetings, no one came.

It had already occurred to Augusta that their little organization was really doing battle with one of the strongest-held traditions of the entire South: the concept of chivalry. Some southern women, the Howards included, began to realize that chivalry as it was practiced in the South served to restrain women, rather than to liberate them. At first glance it might seem strange that chivalry, which supposedly honored women, even placed them on a pedestal, would adamantly oppose more rights for the fairer sex. In fact, chivalry served to shackle women in a strange and uniquely southern fashion. An outgrowth of the antebellum plantation aristocracy, early southern chivalry was not unlike a medieval feudal system, with slaves at the bottom, instead of serfs. Plantation owners followed a code of chivalry that found expression in "dress, literature, excessive politeness to women, the holding of imitative tournaments, florid oratory, and a quixotic ideal of personal honor and of the honor of their region." Ideally, the entire plantation would be ruled by 'patriarchal benevolence' toward both slaves and women. From a very early age, young girls were taught their role within this system: polite obedience, profound respect for parents, modesty and manners at all times, and an "abhorrence of the conduct of the 'strong-minded' women of the North who advocated women's rights."

In a strange way, women formed the centerpiece of chivalric philosophy – not women personally, but rather the concept of the ideal woman – or more specifically, the southern white aristocratic woman. In the realm of chivalry, this woman "embodied beauty, grace, purity, goodness and love." She became a stylized version of glamour, modesty, and innocence. The chivalric gentleman protected this woman, was profoundly courteous to her, praised her, and sometimes even worshipped her very being. She was not unlike a priceless, rare flower. As such, chivalrous men reasoned that woman should be protected from the cares and tribulations of the world; she should glorify the home, make it her husband's paradise while valiantly teaching her own sons to be gentlemen. Home was the center of woman's universe, and her kind, sweet influence in that home would help in some small way to smooth the jagged edges of mankind. It was a lovely story.

But there were some qualities this perfect woman did not possess. While she was modest, she was not perceived to be intelligent. Although she was goodness personified, she was not thought courageous. And most of all, while she represented love itself, she was not free. "Intelligence, Courage, and Freedom. These were reserved for her worshippers." In addition, she possessed a narrow version of honor. To defend a woman's honor, under the code of chivalry, meant almost exclusively to defend her chastity.

Following the Civil War, although the feudal plantation system was destroyed, the chivalric code continued, hemming women in with pink ribbons and magnolias, giving them little opportunity in business or education and few civil rights. While women in the West and North were making progress, some even getting the right to vote, the women of the South remained politely restrained. Most southerners believed that higher education should be reserved exclusively for men. Many chivalrous southern gentlemen when asked about the education of women echoed this thought: "Let women and negroes alone, and instead of quacking with them, physic your own diseases. Leave them in their humility, their grateful affection, their self-renouncing loyalty, their subordination of the heart...." Women were supposed to be innocent, so innocent, in fact, as to appear ignorant. They were even expected not to notice or realize why mulatto children sometimes appeared within their households. Such questions were simply not asked. Yet miscegenation, even following the Civil War, was rampant.

Other factors also served to limit southern women. They tended to bear more children than women in the rest of the nation. In 1860 the average woman nationwide bore five children, while the average woman in the South bore eight. And, of course, modesty dictated that clearly pregnant women remain out of the public view as much as possible. Eight children on average, practically no civil rights, virtually no economic independence, and almost no opportunity for a career or an education, such was the status of the southern woman.

Since many northern suffragists had also embraced the abolitionist cause, southerners hotly decried their beliefs. These northern "agitators" were perceived to be unwomanly home-wreckers who were attempting to destroy the goodness and purity of the South's women. Organized religion in the South ranted against woman suffrage, declaring it to be contrary to the commands of the Bible, just as it had once claimed that the Bible sanctioned, even encouraged, slavery. The reasons for both assertions were similar. The belief was that slaves were innately inferior and deeply in need of the 'guidance and protection' that slavery provided. In addition, according to the tenets of chivalry, white women also needed protecting; these fragile creatures needed to be carefully shielded from the worries and cares of the world.

Southern literature also provided ample romantic descriptions of woman joyfully in her realm, the queen of domesticity. Several novels extolled the virtues of educating women entirely in the home, therefore ensuring that they would never be exposed to the world's harsh realities. There was also the "domestic novel," which became quite popular and lauded the virtues of women's role as keeper of the home, family, hearth. Most scholars of Southern chivalry agree with historian William R. Taylor when he says, "Nonetheless, it is impossible to read widely in the literature of the South without gaining the impression that Southern women in a certain sense were being bought off, offered half the loaf in the hope they would not demand more." And with few exceptions southern women did not demand more. Augusta Howard knew the drawbacks to chivalry and discussed them freely with her mother and sisters. They knew that theirs would be an arduous and un-popular battle.

For their October meeting Augusta again put a small article about their group in the newspaper, explaining their goals and in-viting others to join them at Sherwood Hall. On the appointed day, the Howard women sat expectantly. And this time the front door was thrust open, and fast heavy footsteps approached the library where the suffragists were sitting. It was not a future suffragist, but one of their brothers, and he was angry. Holding the newspaper containing their little article, he stormed into the room, pointed the paper at Augusta and told her she was making him the laughing stock of this whole town. He ordered her to disband her little group of suffragists and stop advertising it in the newspaper.

Of course, Augusta refused. She later wrote about this inci-dent in an article, "Progress of the Woman Suffrage Movement in Georgia:"

> Editors from whom space has been obtained have always been more than willing to publish the matter supplied, expressing their gratification editorially or personally, but several editors afterward withdrew space. In one instance a brother of the suffragist who supplied the matter approached the editor, asking him to discon-tinue its publication. His request being refused, he set vigorously to work to injure the journal's business, and succeeded sufficiently to induce the editor's compliance with his request.

In preparation for the November meeting of the GWSA, the Howards had been busily reading. Among the suffragist material they located was an article written in 1874, edited by Abba Wool-son, entitled "Dress Reform," and listing five suggestions to make women's wear more practical and comfortable. They wondered if they dared give the town of Columbus any more fodder for gossip. They remembered the derision of Amelia Bloomer, and others, even of Susan B. Anthony herself when they changed their clothing. Augusta had even seen an article from a New York newspaper in 1853. It described a speech given by Susan B. Anthony, using such words as "very unfavorable opinion of this *Miss* Anthony ... inexpressibly disgusted ... impudence ... impiety ... hatred ... untruthful and pernicious advice..." At the end it said, "Miss Anthony concluded with a flourish of trumpets, that the woman's rights question could not be put down, that women's souls were beginning to expand, etc., after which she gathered her short skirts about her tight pants, sat down and wiped her spectacles."

Although they did not want to wear Amelia Bloomer's bloomers or Susan B. Anthony's pants, they decided to shorten their dresses ever so slightly...just two or three inches, making them much more practical. Surely the residents of their fair city would not mind that. In fact, for months few people in the town could talk of anything else.

Yet in spite of all of their difficulties, other people slowly began to attend this tiny suffragist organization. Among the first visitors to the Howard home was a smiling, attractive lady with warm brown eyes. She had come all the way from Atlanta to attend a GWSA meeting. Her name? Mary Latimer McLendon, the woman wrongly listed as the Mother of Suffrage in Georgia on that Atlanta statue --Rebecca Latimer Felton's only living sibling.

Chapter Nine

New Obstructions

Rebecca's younger sister was now a married woman: Mary Latimer McLendon. At the age of twenty, she had married Nicholas McLendon, an Atlanta wholesale grocer and wine importer, in 1860. Unlike the Feltons, they owned few slaves before the Civil War, only a few house slaves plus one slave to clean the McLendon business establishment, "Jones and McLendon Wholesale Groceries, Liquors and Cigars" on Peachtree Street. William Felton represented Georgia's farming communities, while Nicholas McLendon was an Atlanta merchant, enjoying city life. Both families were grievously hurt by the Civil War (Sherman burned their town, and probably their business and home).

The social consciousness of both sisters was similar. Mary's interests turned to prohibition (in spite of her husband's business) and woman suffrage, while Rebecca, also a prohibitionist, turned to politics as a means of reform. Following the Civil War, Mary's husband, Nicholas, stopped selling liquor (possibly because of his wife's strong prohibition stand) and became more interested in the civic affairs of his city. In 1871 he was elected to Atlanta's City Council and became involved in the city's booming real estate business. He also served as superintendent of Joel Hurt's Atlanta

Street Railway, promoting streetcars as an effective means of city transportation.

Mary and Rebecca were close sisters, enjoying each other and sharing their lives and thoughts together. When Mary started to attend the Georgia Woman Suffrage Association in Columbus, she discussed what she had learned at those meetings with her sister. Both Mary and Rebecca believed that women's votes were needed to pass a law for prohibition in Georgia.

Following her first Columbus GWSA meeting, Mary began giving away Augusta Howard's suffragist literature at the Atlanta WCTU meetings...and started writing some of her own. On March 21, 1894 Mary L. McLendon founded the second Georgia Woman Suffrage Association at the Marietta Street Methodist Episcopal Church in Atlanta. The following week this group moved to that city's Unitarian Church, where it quickly grew to forty members.

Now there were two GWSA organizations within the state of Georgia. They worked together to pass out information and advertise their cause. But the Howard sisters still had the worst of it, becoming the topic of gossip, ridicule and even public denunciations in the town, not to mention the growing opposition and resentment of their brothers. Many Georgia preachers summed up in a few short questions and one simple answer their sentiments on woman suffrage:

1. What would soon lead to the utter destruction of the American home?
2. What would destroy America's moral code?
3. What would lead to the 'unsexing' of women?
4. And finally, what would ultimately destroy our great American government?

One thing, and one thing only: WOMAN SUFFRAGE. As for the suffragists, they are the evil, screeching helpers of Satan!

At their GWSA meetings the Howard suffragists discussed new ways to get their message out now that the newspapers were not publishing anything they wrote. They decided that some mottos might be useful. They had some stationary printed up with their organization's name on it, and then put different slogans on the paper. When they wrote to someone, they would also receive the GWSA's own private slogan – just like an advertisement. All agreed that was a good idea. They selected three slogans, each one to go on a single piece of stationary:

Taxation without representation is tyranny –
WOMEN ARE TAXED.

Governments derive their just powers from the
consent of the governed – **WOMEN ARE GOVERNED.**

Political power inheres in the people –
WOMEN ARE PEOPLE.

They also decided to write and issue pamphlets to explain their stand, and mail them along with a personal note – on their new stationary, of course. Mr. and Mrs. D. M. Allen came all the way from Douglasville just to hear what the GWSA had to say. And they proved to be sympathetic to their cause…both of them. Slowly, ever so slowly, other people from Columbus and other parts of the state began to knock at the Howard door each month. Mary Latimer McLendon started publishing her own leaflets, too, passing them out along with the Howard literature. Their cause was moving forward. Prohibition and woman suffrage were advancing hand in hand. In other areas women were also starting to get their voice. The new farmers' Grange allowed its women an active role, becoming a place where farm wives and daughters could speak, learn and share ideas.

At about the same time that Augusta Howard first read Georgia's Constitution (1888), Emory College, a small Methodist institution of higher education in Oxford, Georgia (it would later move to Atlanta), welcomed its new president, one of its alumnae, Dr. Warren Aiken Candler. He was short, stout, with a large square head and a pugnacious face – a regular bulldog of a man – with strong opinions about how everything should be in this world. It might have been much better for Candler if he had been born earlier than 1857 – decades earlier. Things were so much simpler then. Warren Aiken Candler was a good man, pious, learned, a true representative of the nineteenth century, espousing its values and traditions, even representing them. He loved the simple, absolute truths and customs into which he was born and cast a wary eye at the strange rumblings within his state as the new century inexorably approached.

In Candler's mind, bigness was anathema: big cities, big business, big government, big labor, huge industries, all worried him. He much preferred the old traditions with everything neatly in its place, the sanctity of family, the orderliness of social life in which man and woman had their separate, but equally important roles. He believed the age-old rules regarding family, church, and state should not be modified. He had a happy marriage – deeply loved his Nettie, and 'protected' her from bills and any money of her own. For Warren Candler, blacks had their place, as did women, and of course, white men – it was all ordained by God.

Perhaps it was inevitable that his peaceful, well-ordered world would be disrupted by a tiny woman, just as pious and determined as Candler about how things ought to be: Rebecca Latimer Felton. Theirs would be a battle, no, perhaps a war, lasting decades. Both were intelligent, staunch Methodists, and both could write and speak. Both had a sense of humor, wit and sarcasm, a stubbornness – and both believed that God was on their side. In another time or place they might have liked each other – but not at this time, not with the winding down of the nineteenth century and with it the collapse of Candler's ordered world.

Warren's wife Nettie had many qualities associated with a Georgia Southern Belle. She was a pretty woman, not intellectual, did not care much for books, tended to be light hearted, pleasant, with a slightly frail quality about her. Although she was often ill, sometimes in bed with female monthly complaints, she was a good mother, giving birth to five children, three of whom would live to be adults. Her pleasant attitude softened her husband's frequent bouts of anger. One day as he stormed and grouched around the house, his wife took him in hand. She gave him two little pills, told him to take them, that they would improve his mood. Without thinking, her grumpy husband took the pills.

Only after swallowing them did he ask her what they were. She told him they were Lydia E. Pinkham's Pills for Female Disorders. At this her husband looked at her, astounded, then burst out laughing. "What's going to happen to me? I don't have any place for them to go!"

She pleased him in so many ways. He liked her to be near him, wrote her daily letters when they were apart, sometimes described his love for her in rhyme. His Nettie loved him back, serving as his stabilizer. She was a nearly perfect helpmate for her busy husband, doing the tasks he had no time for, raising the children, and tending to the home. Like many Georgia women of the time, Nettie knew how to handle a gun and was a crack shot. One night while Warren was away, she heard strange noises at the door. Fumbling sounds. Nettie got her pistol, opened the door in a rush, and shouted, "What the devil are you doing there!" The would-be intruder, who had been attempting to open the lock on the door, jumped, grimaced when he saw her gun, and ran away.

Although he was often serious, with weighty church and college decisions, Warren Candler could laugh, sometimes even at himself. On one occasion he was preaching at a pulpit that was too tall for him:

> The pulpit was a high box, with a board on it for short preachers to stand on in order to make them see the congregation; and that board was none too wide or too strong. It was a little limber for a man of my avoirdupois, and on one occasion, while trying to preach I stepped off of it and disappeared from view for a season. It seemed to me that I should never be able to get on it again, and that the congregation would never cease laughing at my mishap.

Warren Candler had strong opinions about most everything. Dances were sinful as was any form of theater or circus. He disapproved of anything that might distract man from his duties to God and home and nation. His students may have said it best. Referring affectionately to their president, minister, and teacher behind his back as "Shorty," they said, "Shorty did not make the earth, but was put there to run it. That Shorty is sorry for those that disagree with him, for they are wrong."

The Felton/Candler war began over two issues: prohibition and the funding of higher education. But behind each of these disagreements was a third and possibly even bigger point of debate: the rights of women in church and state and education as the new century approached. Warren Aiken Candler believed that women should never be ordained, should not be permitted to speak in church, or any other public place for that matter, should not be afforded much if anything in higher education, and should never, never be allowed to vote or enter politics. Already Candler viewed the WCTU with suspicion. Although he did not fault their stand on prohibition – their way of going about obtaining it was just not right.

Even before the Felton/Candler war began, Warren had had some problems with his own faculty regarding the matter of the WCTU. The most notable of these concerned Emory's professor of Greek, Henry A. Scomp, whose wife was president of the local chapter of the WCTU. In 1891 Professor Scomp presented a resolution at the state temperance alliance meeting supporting the right of the WCTU women to speak publicly on temperance or other matters – "wherever God might call her to labor." The temperance alliance passed the resolution.

Warren believed this act to be outrageous. He stormed his protests to his colleagues, and even to Nettie that night at supper, firmly maintaining that women had no right to speak in public – anywhere! Nettie smiled at him and passed him the potatoes, and talked about one of the many students who was rooming with them. She told her husband that this student was without funds and asked him if he could help, as he had done with so many other students at Emory. Only half listening, Warren decided that he would not read any more of those WCTU announcements from the pulpit.

Warren found his poverty-stricken roomer some employment and steadfastly refused to read aloud one single announcement from that 'devious' WCTU. Then he went farther. He withdrew all funding for that organization not only from his own family (some of whom had considerable wealth), but also from the entire Methodist Church South in Georgia. That should give those uppity women some pause, he thought. His withdrawal of funds certainly caused Rebecca Felton to blink. Now her own church wasn't supporting the WCTU's temperance movement! And all because of Pastor Warren Aiken Candler! Rebecca decided that she would have to do something about all this.

The rift was started – between Candler and the WCTU and between Candler and Professor Scomp (ultimately resulting in the latter's resignation after eighteen years of loyal service to the college), and between Candler and the Feltons, in spite of the fact that their relations had once been cordial. To further fan the flames, Candler announced his views on public versus private higher education.

As President of the Methodist Emory College, Candler's views on higher education were predictable. He had already articulated his educational ideas a few years earlier in the *Christian Advocate* of Nashville, Tennessee. According to Candler, denominational education was far superior to state education for several reasons. In his view most parents who wanted to see their children educated were religious and would naturally prefer a denominational college that espoused their views. This religious education gave parents more control and protection of their offspring. In addition, science (then raging with Darwinist and other "radical" considerations) should be taught strictly within the guidelines of religion. The state university tended to support the rich with free tuition, paid for by the taxes of the poor. In addition, denominational schools were more attuned to the average person, unlike state universities whose "atmosphere...is for the most part stimulating to aristocratic pretensions and extravagance." No, no, religious institutions were far better than anything the state could provide. In fact, the state should not even be allowed to found public colleges or universities, at least in Candler's mind. He believed that state colleges were in direct and unfair competition with denominational colleges.

In addition to his duties as state representative, William Felton was also at this time serving as a trustee for the state-at-large for the University of Georgia. His views on the virtues and need for public higher education were well known – as were his wife's. A clash between Candler and the Feltons was probably inevitable.

Other women (and sometimes men) also began to disrupt the organized world of Warren Akin Candler. It may have all begun with that outspoken actress a few years earlier when Candler was residing in Tennessee. There he gave an anti-theater sermon that was also circulated in pamphlet form. He said the theater led to sin and worldliness. While ancient Greek and Latin plays were bad, contemporary theater was even worse, containing filth and degradation that could lead man to ruin.

The Sunday morning that Candler delivered his sermon, there was an actress (who was performing in Nashville) in the congregation: Emma Abbott, who also sang opera. And she didn't like what she was hearing at all. When Candler began denouncing actors and actresses as wicked and sinful, she could take no more. She rose from her pew and, to Candler's horror, began to speak in church! Not only that, she was denouncing him...him!...the pastor! What was this world coming to? A woman (certainly not a lady) had dared to speak in church – and furthermore had tried to contradict him before his entire congregation!

Warren Aiken Candler's hands clenched the pulpit; he raised his head, silent, nearly frozen. As a robed and titled, ordained minister of the church – a distinguished reverend – he would have no part of this disgrace. He stiffened, stood ram-rod straight, looked sternly at the cause of this disruption, then resorted to the code of chivalry of the time. "I decline to reply," he said. After all, Emma Abbott was a woman, and gentlemen did not debate women. Then, staring directly at the actress, he gave her a parting shot, saying "but such a performance is more suited to the theater than in the house of God." Newspapers in several states picked up the story, even as far away as New York. The battle continued in the press, with Candler leading the fight. No woman had the right to speak in church, and certainly not a miscreant actress! As for the sinfulness of the theater and dancing, Candler's views remained unchanged. If anything, his beliefs hardened regarding diversions, women's roles, and everything else in society that was slowly becoming unhinged.

Of course, the lines were drawn between Warren and Rebecca. There was no doubt as to where these adversaries stood on public education, women's rights, and the WCTU. But their lengthy battle and exchange of words, often in the newspapers, took a strange detour, and all because of Jay Gould, or more specifically, Gould's death. In the days of Candler's pastorate, it was common practice to denounce wayward parishioners from the pulpit – and sometimes if they did not mend their ways, even oust them from the church. Such public chastisement served to keep a pastor's flock in line. Candler himself strongly believed in such methods. In fact, he had frequently resorted to them. By this time Rebecca had been the recipient of several denunciations from the pulpit for her work in politics. Although she had never spoken up, as that actress had done in Tennessee, and although such denunciations had never actually stopped her, she disapproved of such tactics – especially in light of the fact that the women who were denounced were forbidden to defend themselves in church.

Then Jay Gould, railroad tycoon and so-called robber baron, falsely rumored to be Jewish, died of tuberculosis in December 1892. From the pulpit, Candler promptly consigned him to hell. Dr. Hawthorne, of the First Baptist Church in Atlanta, did the same. Rebecca was outraged. Referring to Hawthorne and Candler, she wrote, "Both were merciless in their criticisms. It demonstrated to my mind what I had long believed: namely – that you must give your loose change to denominational enterprises, if you do not want them to grill your poor bones in eternal torment, as quick as they can get to the pulpit to do it – a place 'where one fellow can talk, and the other fellow is not allowed to answer.'"

Using an assumed name, Rebecca sent a very short statement to the *Atlanta Consitiution.* Referring to Hawthorne and Candler, she said, "Are these divines certain as to Jay Gould's wherabouts? If so, will they kindly inform the anxious public as to how they got their information – and who brought it to them."

The editor of the *Atlanta Constitution* asked Rebecca to write more on this topic and sign her name. Soon an article appeared that was, as Rebecca was fond of saying, "full of ginger," entitled "Jay Gould's Whereabouts." After the article appeared, Rebecca noted, "Then the fun began. They [pastors Candler and Hawthorne] left poor old man Jay where they said he was, and took after the old Methodist sister, whose whereabouts could be more easily located."

Dr. Hawthorn promptly and loudly denounced her – once again – from the pulpit. He called her a "termagant" [a violent, turbulent, brawling woman – an infidel], and decided that while men should be held accountable for their behavior, "such a monstrosity [i.e. Rebecca] should be held for nothing." The Hawthorne, Candler, Felton brawl began in earnest, with the *Atlanta Constitution* serving as a sounding board for all, and the Baptist and Methodist pulpits providing extra ballast for the men. Jay Gould was soon forgotten in the melee, as the real issues surfaced: the WCTU, prohibition, the rights of women to express themselves in church, and secular versus denominational funding for higher education. Soon all of Atlanta heatedly discussed the Felton/Candler/Hawthorn points. Although no one in this public battle emerged unscathed, the *Constitution* concluded that "everywhere it was the general impression that Mrs. Felton had decidedly the best of it." Her words were eloquent and well aimed. Speaking of Hawthorne, she said, "He rushes to the pulpit on Sunday mornings to strike at his critics where no reply is permitted and no rebuttal allowed." As for Candler, "Let the Woman's Temperance Union in Georgia remember who inflicted a wanton wound upon their heaven-blessed work for rescuing the perishing." And she further excoriated him on his attempts to reduce funding for the University of Georgia.

Warren Candler may have lost to Rebecca Felton in the newspapers, but he had more aces up his sleeve. When his relative, the Honorable Allan G. Candler was elected Governor, suddenly and without warning, Dr. Felton was removed from his position as trustee at large for the state university. Warren Candler silently smiled at this ousting. As Rebecca quoted, "There are more ways of choking a dog than with a hot sweet dumpling." She realized that, "It is risky to offend the 'powers that be.' Those headlights in the ministry were only human, and they knew how to 'work the racket' in politics as well as religion."

But Warren Aiken Candler would not have long to savor his victory. He first read it in the newspaper. He began to breathe heavily, rolled the paper up and threw it in a ball. He raged about the house like a ferocious bull. Not this! This was too much! What was this world coming too? Those brazen Howard sisters and the GWSA had done it now! They were bringing down to the genteel South – to speak and to oversee a huge woman suffrage convention in Atlanta– the one woman in nearly all the world that Georgian men (and some women) most despised – that noxious, noisy agitator, that former abolitionist busybody Yankee female: Susan B. Anthony.

Susan B. Anthony

Chapter 10

Susan B. Anthony's March Through Georgia

Susan B. Anthony was no happier to be coming to Atlanta than Warren A. Candler was when he read of her destination. She hated the South, particularly Georgia. And she certainly didn't want to hold a woman suffrage convention in Atlanta. In her mind, Washington was the only logical place for such a meeting. For nearly all of her adult life, Susan B. Anthony had been a crusader; her causes included battles for temperance, the abolition of slavery, and broader civil rights for women. One of her first causes was temperance. She had a great deal to say about that. But in the early 1850s she was refused permission to speak at a temperance rally because she was a woman. Susan B. Anthony was outraged! She believed that refusing half the population the right to give public speeches was just not right. By 1852 she had become a member of a fledgling movement seeking women's rights to own their own property and to control their own wages. By 1872, she was advocating that women have the same civil and political rights as men. Along with other women, most notably Elizabeth Cady Stanton and Amelia Bloomer, Susan B. Anthony worked tirelessly for women's rights. And to achieve her goals, Susan B. Anthony believed that women needed to obtain the vote. Suffrage – woman

suffrage – that and only that would pave the way for the improvement of women's condition. From 1869 to 1887 Anthony was a
key leader in the National Woman Suffrage Association, which
advocated the passage of a federal amendment granting woman
suffrage.

In 1869 the woman suffrage movement split into two major
groups: one advocating woman suffrage through state legislation
while the other continued to fight for a federal amendment to the
Constitution granting woman suffrage in every state. Anthony remained steadfastly with the latter group and vigorously campaigned throughout most of the nation, but particularly in the West.
She maintained that "...we have neither the women nor the money
to make the canvasses of the thirty-eight States...to educate each
individual man out of the old belief that woman was created to be
his subject." She also asserted that "if the negro had never had the
ballot until the majority of white men...had voted 'yes,' he would
have gone without it until the crack of doom."

The two suffrage groups merged again in 1887, becoming the
National American Woman Suffrage Association. Anthony became its President in 1892. Beginning in 1869 Susan B. Anthony
appeared before Congress every year to ask for the passage of an
amendment for woman suffrage. In 1877 she even presented a
woman suffrage petition to Congress, signed by 10,000 people
from twenty-six states. She knew how to lobby in Washington,
had significant contacts there, and was respected and well known.
There was no thought in her mind of changing the location of her
annual convention. Washington D.C. was almost like her second
home.

But there were other events at the time that served to thwart
Anthony's desires. The suffragist group that had advocated obtaining woman suffrage on a state-by-state basis, which was now
merged with those seeking an amendment to the Constitution,
balked at the idea of always holding their suffrage conventions in
Washington D.C. It was unfair – so far away from those in the
West and even the Midwest. At the convention of 1893 Alice
Stone Blackwell proposed removing the annual convention from
the nation's Capitol. Anthony was astonished at this motion – hor-

rified, in fact, but others supported Blackwell: New England and the West, even some Midwestern suffragists. As one Ohio woman said, "It seems better to sow the seed of suffrage throughout the country by means of our national convention."

These women failed to take into consideration the political support in Washington that Susan had so long and carefully nurtured. She made an impassioned speech from the floor opposing the removal of the convention from Washington. At the close of her oration, she said, "I shall feel it a grave mistake if you vote in favor of a movable convention. It will lessen our influence and our power. But come what may, I shall abide by the decision of the majority." Then Rachel Avery proposed a compromise. She proposed that the convention meet in Washington with the opening of each new Congress (every two years), and in other locations on alternate years. Her resolution, which apparently pleased almost no one, was finally adopted. Susan B. Anthony was greatly displeased. She continued to maintain that any plan that removed her from the seat of power in Washington was not a good idea and could do great damage to the suffrage movement.

Although Anthony had campaigned internationally for woman suffrage and had given impassioned speeches throughout most of the United States, she had assiduously avoided the South. She was outraged by the newspaper accounts she often read of southern lynchings and the artificial and sometimes violent methods used to keep blacks from voting in the South. In the South Anthony embodied all that many southern men and women abhorred about the North. It didn't occur to Susan that her convention could possibly be held in the town that Sherman had once burned. Even moving her convention from Washington D.C. to, say, Philadelphia was a dismal prospect. Little did she realize as the train carrying Augusta Howard and her sisters, Miriam, and Claudia, approached the nation's Capitol, that the 1895 convention might have its location just this side (at least in Anthony's mind) of hell.

The Columbus Georgia Woman Suffrage Association, which was affiliated with the National American Woman Suffrage Association, had decided to be daring and send three delegates to the annual convention in Washington of the National American

Woman Suffrage Association in 1894. H. Augusta Howard, Miriam Howard Dubose, and Claudia Howard Maxwell were elected to represent the group. All three were terribly excited, never having done anything like this before. They spent hours, days, weeks working together, planning what they might say and do. Then finally the time came to pack their bags. Old Tom, who had once been their slave and had remained in their service after the Civil War, carefully cleaned the buggy, harnessed the horses and drove them into town to catch the train for Washington D. C. Excited, determined, expectant, the three Howard sisters boarded the train that would take them from their home to the nation's capitol. Augusta, Miriam, and Claudia were the first delegates from Georgia ever to attend this convention.

For most of the convention the three sisters sat quietly together, listening attentively to the speeches of some of the most distinguished and famous suffragists of the day, experienced, knowledgeable women, passionate in their cause. When the suffragists of the 1894 convention broached the question of the location of its next convention, there were many suggestions. Cincinnati might be a good choice, since it had a more central location and "was on the border between the North and the South." Others liked the possibility of Detroit, while Anthony and others continued to insist that the only real choice was the center of political power and influence: Washington D.C. Then Augusta slowly raised her hand, and when she was recognized, she rose and suggested Atlanta, Georgia. Susan B. Anthony swallowed hard and looked sternly at this unknown delegate. But H. Augusta Howard had more to say; she asked permission to address the convention. This southern woman whom nobody knew wanted to speak before all of these seasoned and highly experienced suffragists. H. Augusta Howard was brave. After they granted her permission to speak, the convention would soon learn that she was also intelligent and eloquent. She rose quietly, wearing her slightly shortened dress, and walked to the podium. And there she said:

> You might hold a thousand conventions in Kansas or any other place above Mason and Dixon's line and you will never hear any-

thing of it in the South. The Georgia papers and the far Southern papers still insist that women do not want the ballot. Until you hold a convention in the South and prove to them that this is not so, they will keep on saying it is. In Atlanta, if the convention should go there, there can be no doubt that the Grand Opera House, which is one of the largest auditoriums in the United States could be secured and it could be packed from ceiling to pit. While a great many of them would come to laugh, many of them would go away with N.A. W. S. A. membership tickets in their pockets. I can assure you that Georgia Congressmen do not influence their constituents, they are influenced by their constituency, and if we ever hope to influence the Georgia delegation in Congress, we shall have to influence the people of that state. I believe that an effort would be made by Atlanta and the prominent business men, as well as the Georgia Woman Suffrage Association, to make the next convention a successful one. While Atlanta is not in sympathy with the movement, she is always ready to help Atlanta.

Susan B. Anthony sat back in dour astonishment. How could this be happening? There was discussion, of course. But it was clear from the start that Augusta had made an impression upon these suffragists. And Claudia Howard Maxwell rose to back up her sister. She said, "In the South , a convention of women is regarded by Southern people as a curiosity, and the newspapers of the whole South would publish articles about it, just to give the people news." To Susan's dismay, veteran suffragist Anna Howard Shaw liked the idea, and further noted the tiny representation from the South at their conventions. Perhaps a convention in Atlanta might serve to increase their membership. Then Emily B. Ketcham, who at first favored Detroit, said, "[Let's carry the] battle right into the enemy's quarters and make the Solid South a friend to woman suffrage." Several other women agreed. After some further discussion, it was time to vote on the matter:

Detroit: seven votes
Washington D.C.: thirty-seven votes
Cincinnati: fifty-seven votes
Atlanta: sixty-seven votes.

Then the delegates from New York and Michigan decided to switch their votes to Atlanta, giving that city a considerable majority with ninety-four votes. It was decided: the Twenty-Seventh Annual Convention of the National American Woman Suffrage Association would be held in Atlanta, Georgia – Dixie! Susan B. Anthony was stunned, possibly even more astonished than Warren Aiken Candler had been when he read the announcement in an Atlanta newspaper. For once the pious Methodist President of Emory and the New York Quaker suffragist agreed: Atlanta was no place for a suffragist convention!

While the Howard Sisters were at the 1894 convention, two of them gave speeches. On February 17, during the evening session, the program included an address by Miriam Howard Dubose: "Some Georgia Curiosities." Although she had almost no experience with public speaking, Miriam excelled at the task. One of the "curiosities" she discussed was the southern concept of chivalry, and the southern gentlemen "whose delicate sensibilities would not survive the shocking sight of women at the polls, but whose delicate sensibilities are not shocked that all women are taxed, legislated for, and governed by the indifferent and vicious without their consent." In fact, she decided that one of Georgia's most significant curiosities was "men who love their women too deeply to accord them justice, and women who are taken in with such affection." Another amazing Georgia curiosity included the profound disapproval faced by "women who resent taxation without representation; women who claim that mothers should have equal rights with fathers to the control and guardianship of their children; and who demand a voice in the laws by which they are governed – a right accorded illiterate vagabonds and pardoned criminals." Her speech was a resounding success. The ladies of the convention vigorously applauded this southern woman from the heart of Dixie.

Augusta also made a strong and positive impression upon the suffrage delegates. She was even appointed to speak before members of the United States House of Representatives, addressing the sub-committee of the Judiciary Committee. And like her sister, she spoke well for the cause of woman suffrage, comporting herself with an assurance and dignity that belied her inexperience.

The trip was a total triumph. The Howard sisters returned to Columbus rejuvenated, filled with new ideas, goals, and expectations. In Atlanta, Mary Latimer McLendon and her small group of suffragists rejoiced. There was so much work to do. Susan B. Anthony! Even Susan B. Anthony would be coming to Atlanta in less than one year, along with the entire convention of the National American Woman Suffrage Association. For the first time in its entire history this convention would not be held in Washington D.C.

Although Susan B. Anthony was appalled by the decision, she began to work immediately for the success of the 1895 convention. She issued a printed circular announcing the Atlanta Convention of the NAWSA. In it she said, "Though twenty-six States have granted some slight concessions to women citizens, in no States of the Union, save Wyoming and Colorado, are women yet admitted to the dignity of equal rights in citizenship. In only six States of the Union are mothers conceded to be legal owners of their own children." Anthony and others were determined to obtain the vote for women along with equal rights, even if she had to march into a state so staunchly against civil rights for women as Georgia. In fact, in an interview she gave to the *New York Sun,* she said, "A story is always repeating itself. There is going to be a second 'Marching through Georgia' but this time it will be women on a mission of peace, and not men in the smoke and suffering of war."

Rebecca Latimer Felton was not a part of all of this suffrage excitement and activity. In addition to her involvement in the politics of her husband, she was busy preparing to participate in yet another huge exposition also to be held in 1895: the Atlanta Cotton States and International Exposition. She had been appointed the business manager for the Woman's Division. Her duties would include locating and placing the women's exhibits, along with keeping a keen eye on her division's finances, a responsibility in which Rebecca already excelled.

Although Rebecca gives no evidence in her writings that she knew the source of the creation of the Board of Lady Managers, she probably knew. The inclusion and recognition of women in these exhibitions, beginning with the Columbian Exhibition in Chicago, was not due to a change of heart on the part of male officials. Instead it happened because of the ardent work behind the scenes of a tall, determined old lady with small rimless spectacles, piercing eyes, gray hair twisted into a bun, long patrician nose, and a passion that somehow belied her age. Although many other women acted on her behalf (Mrs. Upton, Mrs. Spofford, and other close friends), the idea originated with her. And most of the work to create the Board of Lady Managers was also hers, although she continued to work behind the scenes. The creation of the idea and final implementation of the Board of Lady Managers at the Columbian Exhibition in Chicago, on which Rebecca Latimer Felton so proudly served, was due to the inspiration and work in Washington D.C. of Susan B. Anthony.

The Solid South was changing, almost in spite of itself. Women were participating in the WCTU and in the Grange; suffragists were coming to town; and for the first time women had a significant role in the Atlanta Cotton States and International Exposition, speaking, controlling their finances, and ably running their part of the show. Speaking of that exposition, Rebecca said, "Nothing that Northern and Western women advocated was palatable to our politicians and preachers. There was not a woman's club in Georgia, until after that world's fair, when one was inaugurated in Atlanta, during the Cotton States and International Exposition, which opened in the year 1895."

With these and other exposition experiences, Rebecca became bolder regarding women's rights. At one such exposition she was made chairman of a committee on agriculture. "We made diligent search for the percentage of woman's work among farm exhibits, but everything was submerged in men's work." Women were not noticed anywhere or recognized for their achievements. Rebecca then concluded, "The Bible saying: 'A man and his wife are one,' read correctly for the man was the only one." She was at the time 60 years old. In a speech she gave not long after, Rebecca said:

I might consider myself an "ice breaker" in this Southern country of ours. I must have had crude but novel ideas not familiar to Southern latitude, but as I survey the "new woman's" field of action at the close of the nineteenth century, I find that I have been "breaking the ice" for the last quarter of a century, and although I was forced to stem the current with my rude bark, I find the tide is floating in a convoy of elegant and cultured women who are becoming leaders of thought and public opinion.

Susan B. Anthony kept a small diary, *Excelsior Diary: 1895,* in which she recorded her trip throughout the South, the many speeches she made, and the people she met. On Wednesday, January 30, 1895 Anthony met with "H. Augusta, Claudia and Miriam Howard there – with everything in order for us – conef [conference] room with bright fire. The following day, Susan noted in her diary that the conference "opened with a splendid audience."

The only difficulty occurred on Sunday, February 3, 1895.

Dr. A. Howard Shaw and Mrs. C.C. Catt

With the house packed with suffragists, Dr. Hawthorne, who, along with Bishop Candler, was one of Rebecca's chief nemeses, walked to the podium and proceeded to denounce them all. Susan B. Anthony wrote about this incident in her little diary. "Dr. Hawthorne had preached against us in the morn [ing] – Baptist – which stirred Anna [Howard Shaw] to greater power." This Baptist preacher went so far as to declare that "the husbands of suffragists were all feeble-minded men." Hawthorne's fierce denunciation of the suffragists seated before him backfired, stirring them to greater resolve and embarrassing many in Atlanta, resulting in more sympathy for the cause of women's rights among Atlanta's citizenry.

Following the successful convention, Susan accompanied Augusta to spend a few days in her home in Columbus. Susan described the elegance and beauty of Sherwood Hall, but was disturbed by its history, pronouncing it to be "a veritable old slaveholders [sic] mansion." She noted also that while the mansion was elegant, there was frugality within the house. Many rooms were heated solely by fireplaces and as they sat as honored guests within the Howard parlor, "our frozen breaths formed as if out side." Then she hastened to add, "but the hearts of the Howards are great, gave us a cordial welcome."

By Friday, Susan had taken the measure of the Howard household. "Over this dear conscientious family hangs a heavy cloud – a sadness reigns over the house – the other two daughters at home are Ruth and Alice – then there are three other girls married – and two sons all opposed to W. Rights and all the reforms that the mother & five home girls have espoused – they have Old Tom. & old ___ 80 years old who were Ms. H's father's Linsly's [sic.] slaves – " There was another sadness that Susan B. Anthony might have guessed, but could not have known for certain. Augusta Howard had paid for much of the convention costs herself, money that she couldn't possibly have afforded, in order to bring the cause of woman suffrage to light. The convention was her first – and last – success. Although she continued to support the cause of suffrage, she left to others the leadership of woman suffrage in Georgia. Two of those other women were sisters: Mary Latimer McLendon and Rebecca Latimer Felton.

Chapter Eleven

The Pros vs. the Antis

In the fall of 1895 Rebecca was asked to address the joint committee of the Georgia House and Senate regarding a prohibition bill. It was the first time a woman had ever addressed such a body, less than a decade after Rebecca had first given a public speech. Rebecca came before this committee not as a noted dignitary or a crusading female (which is how the legislators viewed the suffragists), but as a wife and mother. She described with eloquence the plight of the wives of drunkards, the destructiveness of drunkenness to marriage, home, and children. "I will only ask you to go home with the drunkard and stay one night with the mother and her children who are shut up within four walls and compelled to watch and wait upon the debauchee until he gets off into a drunken stupor or makes night hideous to his frightened wife and children. You can get away from him, but that long suffering woman must live with and endure him." She concluded her oration with an appeal: "Shall we lean upon you as our protectors or will you leave us defenseless." Although the bill did not pass, Rebecca, unfazed as always, continued her campaign.

The life and battles of Rebecca Felton are contained within the pages of three books that she authored: *Country Life in Georgia in the Days of My Youth* (1919); *The Romantic Story of Geor-*

gia's Women (1930)*; and *My Memoirs of Georgia Politics* (1911). These works provide significant and quite different portraits of this complicated woman. The first two books depict the life of a caring, passionate woman, a loving wife and mother, perhaps even a grandmotherly sort of woman reminiscing about her exciting, adventurous life. In these works she is a keen observer, kind and sensitive, feminine in every respect.

But *My Memoirs of Georgia Politics* shows another side of Rebecca, who was an intelligent political fighter and astute reformer of her times. She could be just as tough and unyielding as her male opponents, not hesitating to fight "with her gloves off," as she was fond of saying. She proved more discerning and intelligent than most of her opponents. In this work one sees a woman who loved political battles and wanted to be in the midst of it all, to sling mud with the best of them, to win. She often refers to her battles in warlike terms – sniping, shooting, taking pot shots, and throwing grenades, if only with her pen and voice. She gives piercing, sometimes withering, descriptions of her opponents. Writing of her time in Washington, she concludes, "I had a full view of what politicians could do in high office, and my disgust has continued through life." She cites the criticism and disparaging remarks her husband received for permitting his wife to help him with his political duties. She attacked her many political enemies with a fierceness not expected in a woman. No one stirred her ire more deeply than her nemesis, John B. Gordon. She once said of him, "When a United States Senator can run a camp of convicts which

John B. Gordon of Georgia

is a 'disgrace to civilization' for **money,** when he can manipulate a **Southern Insurance Company** and a **Southern Publishing Company,** not to speak of other circumlocution enterprises where the **money** of the subscribers disappears forever, when he could borrow the **money** of a **Southern bishop,** and the bishop sold the collaterals for only one dollar in the hundred, you need not feel surprise that he could attack the wife of a political opponent."

Like a true warrior, she refused to weep over her wounds, often not even acknowledging them. No matter how serious the charges were against her, how ugly the words, Rebecca always rose to fight again. Within her papers, written in her own handwriting is the following:

> I know what unfriendly criticism means. I know how hard it is to bear—It is a common thing to sneer at men and women who are brave enough to speak up when right and justice are endangered, and it is a hard place to fill to step forward and volunteer to do work that will provoke sneers, that will provoke criticism – that will cause people to say –"she is out of her place" – "she had better mind her home affairs" – "she should let men's business alone" – and all such expressions as are showered every day upon people who interfere with a business by which money is made at the expense of the happiness and success of those who suffer by it.

Looking carefully at the life of Rebecca Latimer Felton, one begins to realize that she ably defines the scope of her own crusades in the last line of the above quote. Nearly all of her causes involved the interference "with a business by which money is made at the expense of the happiness and success of those who suffer by it." The convict lease; insurance, tax, and railroad frauds; crooked politicians and fixed elections; inferior schooling; the liquor business and drunkenness; all needed (in Rebecca's mind) interference…her interference. It didn't matter to her if the injured were black or white, young or old, male or female – justice was needed to relieve the oppressed.

She continued her battles alone now. Her husband, whose palsy and poor health hindered him, remained at home to look after their farm while Rebecca traveled to expositions, gave speeches everywhere, and remained as active politically as a woman could who was not permitted to vote or be elected. Rebecca was sixty-five in 1900, antique by the standards of her time. Yet in many ways she was only beginning. What history seems to have overlooked in this woman, what it failed to recognize was that her thoughts and beliefs did not remain fixed, but moved along a continuum. For example, as a former slave holder, she would later state, "As I look back on that time of eager slave buying, I am amazed at the lack of foresight in a business way. Every nation that was civilized had abandoned domestic slavery except Brazil, when our people were apparently confident that it was a permanent thing, commanded by the Bible and ordained of God." She did not deny the abuses of slavery, noting in particular that "mulattoes [were] as common as blackberries." She further noted that, "When white men were willing to put their own offspring in the kitchen and corn field and allowed them to be sold into bondage as slaves and degraded them as another man's slave, the retribution of wrath was hanging over this country and the South paid penance in four years of bloody war."

Rebecca's thinking moved from condoning slavery (and owning slaves), to deciding that slavery was wrong, both from a business and a moral standpoint. It became, in her opinion, a curse upon the South. For her the entire reason for the Civil War was the issue of slavery. "Getting into war as we did to preserve the institution of domestic slavery, we risked everything and lost everything by the venture, and we also lost the sympathy of the outside world because of our slavery contention." Therefore, as her mind progressed, the Glorious Lost Cause of the Civil War became the Glorious Wrong Cause. "The children of the Southern States are being unwisely taught by Southern agitators, women as well as men, that the political issues of the Civil War are still germane and worthy of adoration. They are instructed to call the Lost Cause a glorious cause." Not only was this idea wrong, according to Rebecca, it furthered the hatred between North and South. It was time to heal the breach.

At the beginning of the new century, Rebecca addressed the United Daughters of Confederacy in Augusta, Georgia. In addition to praising white Southern women in her speech she lauded the loyalty and contributions of the "colored women" in the South during the Civil War. Almost no one had ever praised or hardly even noticed them before. In a long account of the contributions of the "colored woman" to the South, Rebecca says:

> I shall tell you something about a class of women who lived in plantation homes and who belonged there, and who raised families and whose work in the fields and the kitchen, in the loom-house and the dwelling that we occupied in the Southern States, and who richly deserve honorable mention, and who contributed mightily to the maintenance of the struggling Confederacy during four years of bloody warfare.

> I allude to the colored women, who were the cooks, the nurses, and the main reliance of the white women in their arduous duties and unremitting struggle of the early 60s, where numbers were to be fed and clothed, nursed and protected, both black and white.

Much of Rebecca's education between 1890 and 1910 was heightened not just by her constant reading, but also because of her active participation in the great expositions in America during those times. There she met dignitaries from both the North and South and learned first-hand of new advances in technology and agriculture. She often went to Chicago between 1890 and 1894 to tend to her duties in the World Columbian Exposition. She sometimes complained to her family. She wrote to her husband that she had to have one fire in her room at the Palmer House every day. "I expect my fires will cost me considerable, but I felt that I must have them. The Northern women do not seem to feel the cold at all – have no fires." In early spring she wrote:

> Chicago has not grasped the transportation problem – it can't take care of the crowd here – not the ones to come. Mud, slush – everything nasty – cars [streetcars] crowded to overflowing.

> I am more & more satisfied that Howard is out of it – this is the roughest crowd I ever saw in a civilized country.

Howard, her only living offspring, was a man now, and a medical doctor, but still she was glad that he did not have to experience the hardships she was experiencing. Sometimes she seemed to feel tougher than anyone. She was always frugal, always worried about money, and sometimes embarrassed about her lack of elegant attire. "A few of the ladies made much of the opportunity to exhibit their fine clothes and graces – but I had nothing to do – took a back seat.... As usual mediocrity made its way to the front." In another letter she wrote, "Mrs. Palmer had on a dress the other day – that she wore all last winter – so I need not feel very cheap in my last year's clothes. Indeed I don't care a snap. Brains make the final count, not clothes."

In spite of such difficulties, she met women from all sections of the United States, intelligent and well educated, and able men as well. In her work with other prominent women, she listened intently to their views on suffrage, politics, temperance…and even that topic that was taboo in the South: birth control. Rebecca liked these women, and they liked her and appreciated the fact that a Southern woman held the beliefs that Rebecca expressed. Bertha Palmer, President of the Board of Lady Managers and wife of the millionaire, became her good friend. For Christmas 1893, Rebecca sent her "a Xmas gift of a quilt – large and every stitch with my own fingers – over 3000 pieces." Mrs. Parker wrote Rebecca:

> Be assured, my dear Mrs. Felton, that I shall always prize it, not only as a manifestation of the manifold capabilities of one of the able women of our own time, and of our own Board, but as an evidence of your friendship and kindly feeling. I have displayed the quilt to many visitors, all of whom have considered it most remarkable that so elaborate and painstaking work was done by any women of the present generation.

Prestige, communication with other knowledgeable and articulate people of both sexes, introductions to the newest advances – and a salary plus expenses – that is what Rebecca received as a result of her experiences with expositions. She was actively involved in the Chicago exposition, the Cotton States and International Exposition in Atlanta, the Tennessee Centennial, and the St. Louis Exposition of 1904. William encouraged her to go to these events, then missed her and sometimes asked that she return to their home. Once she gave up her coveted place on the Chicago Expositions Jury of Awards so that she could return home as William wanted.

When she was at their farm in Cartersville, she did not take time to rest – there was so much to do. She purchased extra farm land, using the inheritance money from her father. She kept the books, oversaw tenants and sharecroppers, and did not hesitate to sue them if she thought they had tried to cheat her, or to fight the tax collector for every penny owed. She continued to write for newspapers, became an agent for an insurance company in Atlanta, and more and more looked after William's affairs. She sold the iron and mineral rights to some of her lands, developing a new source of revenue. And when William decided to sell some of the land in his name at what she considered to be too low a price, she purchased it, ultimately making a tidy profit when she later sold it at a much higher price. Rebecca became shrewder than most businessmen in her dealings. Like Scarlett O'Hara, the memory of hunger and deprivation in the Civil War made her determined never to be without food – or money – again.

It is curious to note that with all of her energy, crusades, and business acumen, she still did not advocate woman suffrage as so many other women in the nation did. In 1886 she said she did not need or want to vote. In 1897 she declared, "I have never joined a suffrage association and have never made a public appeal for the right to vote...." With her sister Mary Latimer McLendon so actively involved in woman suffrage, and considering the many causes for the betterment of women that Rebecca espoused, some have found it difficult to understand why she did not pick up the suffrage banner. Her biographer John E. Tallmadge provides the following answer: "Perhaps she was content for a time to be almost the only woman in Georgia to participate, even without the vote, in the man's world of politics." Such an answer seems unlikely, given the many women's causes that Rebecca championed.

A more plausible explanation might be that if Rebecca had become a suffragist at that time, she may have damaged her other crusades. The anti-suffrage movement in Georgia at the turn of the century was so powerful that the granting of the vote to women seemed to be as hopeless as pasting wings on horses and expecting them to fly. Almost no one in Georgia, male or female, took the possibility of woman suffrage seriously. Politicians opposed it; the church preached against it, claiming that woman suffrage was contrary to the tenets of the Bible; the United Daughters of the Confederacy actively fought it; and nearly all Georgia newspapers of the time viewed woman suffrage as anathema and did not hesitate to say so.

In her work, *Women Against Women: American Anti-Suffragism, 1880-1920,* Jane Jerome Camhi provides the philosophy behind the anti-suffragist movement in America. According to the Antis, man ruled (supposedly benevolently) and was responsible for the care and support of the family. If there should be a problem, child custody, along with any other issues concerning the welfare of the family, should be within the man's domain. Camhi further explains:

> In the antisuffrage cosmology woman's influence did not stop in the home, but reached out through her lovingly indoctrinated citizen-sons to bring her message of love and fair play into the legislatures of the world. What was happening, in fact, was that woman's role was beginning to assume an almost mythic quality. It was only natural, therefore, that women who accepted the myths felt that they stood to lose considerably in the event of any basic rearrangement of the pyramid. The arguments used by the Antis reflected this basic fear.

For the Antis it was better to be the mother of a President than to be in Congress herself (it was unthinkable at the time that a woman could actually be President); better to "honor and obey" her protectors than to seek a career of her own; and better to know how to run a home than to have great education. A woman's knowledge of science, history, Greek – or politics – might in fact be dangerous and contrary to the smooth running of the home. And certainly it was better to be feminine than to be 'unsexed,' an association frequently made with suffragists.

There was within the Antis' assertions a strange contradiction. While woman was lauded and the role of domesticity, wife, and mother extolled as being all that women could (or should) ever desire, there was also within the Anti philosophy a not-so-hidden assertion of women's natural inferiority to men in every sphere except the home. Even renowned scientists of the day weighed in. For. example, it was contended that strenuous education, particularly higher education, would lead to damage to a woman's nervous system or to her physical well being. Dr. Edward H. Clarke, who once taught at Harvard Medical School, wrote *Sex in Education,* which asserted that "women who went to college were likely to suffer mental and physical breakdowns and possible sterility." In addition, a highly-educated woman, many claimed, somehow lost her charm.

The basic truth of the matter, according to the Antis, both male and female, was that women within man's realm were decidedly inferior. As Elilhu Root put it:

> One question to be determined in the discussion of the subject is whether the nature of woman is such that her taking upon her the performance of the functions implied in suffrage will leave her in the possession and the exercise of her highest powers or will be an abandonment of those powers and an entering upon a field in which, because of her differences from man, she is distinctly inferior.

Racism, sexism, fear, and xenophobia also became serious issues for the Antis. What if "negresses" voted? Or immigrant women? Bad, dirty, foreign, illiterate, different women? "Apathetic, ignorant, sordid women – poor or rich—as things now stand, are at worst a negative evil. But such women, with votes, become potential reinforcements to the forces of vice, and those forces are always prompt in rallying their re-enforcements."

The loss of power within the home, the break-down of the family…and the state, and the weakening of "good" women along with the strengthening of the bad, these were only a few of the inherent evils of woman suffrage expressed by the Antis in legislatures, pamphlets, newspapers, speeches, and literature. It is a curious fact that many women against suffrage did lobby, speak in public, and use other political measures to get their point across. Many believed that women suffrage would ultimately lead to a type of unfeminine woman/man and possibly even worse, to women who became bosses in employment, giving other women orders. Few had even considered the possibility of women bossing men in business and the professions. Woman suffrage was an evil plot foisted upon unwitting women. Perhaps it was even a socialist plot against the nation. No possible good could come of it – none at all. It was against God, the Bible, democracy, and justice, according to the Antis.

In light of such reasoning, it is no wonder that Rebecca, who well knew the claims of the Antis; who understood much better than most politicians the political climate of Georgia; who was the wife of a minister, and who promoted serious causes for women within her state and nation; would ignore the issue of woman suffrage in the 1880s and '90s. She took pains to present her ideas and issues as a loyal, loving wife and mother, feminine in every respect. As many photos and physical descriptions prove, Rebecca Felton aged well. Even major newspapers often described her beauty and intelligence. As the St. Louis *Globe Democrat* once said of her after a ball given by the British Minister, "A very lovely woman is Mrs. Felton, of Georgia; a sweet-voiced lady with soft black eyes, gray hair and a complexion as fine and pure as a roseleaf." She used her feminine attributes to her advantage and did not step out of the ideals of southern chivalry in this respect. Georgians may not have agreed with her, but they respected her and accorded the dignity and politeness granted to a Southern lady of the time. She often claimed that she was above all a practical woman, as her actions demonstrated.

Chapter Twelve

Rebecca, Age 80, the Suffragist

By the 1890s Rebecca began to grow weary of the pro-
nouncements of both men and women who foresaw so many dangers in permitting a woman to vote – problems so great that
woman suffrage could possibly lead to the destruction of the
American family. She particularly resented the following statements that had been published and shouted so often that it was
starting to become an assumed truth:

> Though woman is disbarred from voting, she brings into the world,
> and rocks the cradle of the nation's future citizens. She rears and
> molds the character of those who are to be the future rulers and
> statesmen; the heroes and benefactors of the country. Surely this is
> glory enough for her.

Although Rebecca fought for the betterment of women in their
primary domain, the home, as wives and mothers, and for the
rights of their progeny, she refused to accept the above generaliza-
tions. Around the turn of the century, in various speeches, such as
those given before the Mother's Congress (precursor of the P.T.A.)
in Washington, D.C. and the Atlanta Woman's Club, she said:

> We are told that the hand which "rocks the cradle rules the world."
> I have lived in the world for over half a century, but I find no evi-

dence of rulership in the act of cradle-rocking. If it had been recorded that the hand which rocks the cradle bears the burdens of
the world the connection between the truth and poetry would have
been self evident.

She deplored the age of consent for a "woman" to marry in Georgia, saying, "It is a crying shame that a little 10-year-old girl in
Georgia is deemed qualified to protect a woman's dearest posses-
sion from rapine and seduction. From my point of view maternity
would rank higher than anything in creation below our eternal salvation." Yet, she noted that marriage was often entered into by
both sexes with little thought and less preparation. She said that
business ventures would fail without serious planning, education
and preparation, as would farming. "But our present civilization
permits two children sometimes, who know no more about raising
a family than the loose straws in a last year's bird's nest, to enter
into marriage...."

Her points were clear and ringing: education – instruction –
that's what women need – as badly as men. She fiercely countered
the anti-intellectual sentiments, rampant among the Antis, who often viewed the suffragists as a "damned mob of scribbling women
who were swarming all over America." Rebecca countered such
notions by saying, "For the mother to do her duty she must be instructed. Ignorance is discounted, as it should be everywhere."
She played upon the sympathies of her audience, not berating men
for the state of things. "No honorable father ever looked in his
daughter's face and thought her inferior to anything that constituted excellence and high character."

It was hard for anyone to fault Rebecca's reasoning. If the
mother was the first instructor of the child, as nearly everyone asserted, then for the infant's well being, and ultimately the good of
the nation, the mother must be educated – instructed in her treasured role as mother. After all, as Rebecca so ably stated, "The
Lord was willing to trust the mother. He knew her loyalty to the
maternal instinct." She spoke as a mother herself who knew the
joys and sorrows of motherhood, who had lost four of her five
children, and whose only child had become a doctor, like his fa-

ther. Many have commented upon her voice, low and winning –
exciting, even thrilling – with a quality that held the attention of
her audience.

Sometimes she said things others had never before uttered,
even to themselves. "Better a thousand times be very lonely in
single blessedness than to be very unhappy in married misery."
Better to be single than married unhappily? A spinster – in the
South? Although many of Rebecca's assertions carried suffragist
implications, she did not at first allude to women and the right to
vote. She appealed to her audiences in a wise grandmotherly way.
People listened.

She wrote many magazine articles championing the rights of
women and the need for their education so that they could raise
children properly. She lobbied the state legislature, gave lectures
at women's clubs, and spoke on women's issues nearly everywhere
in Georgia. Until the end of her life, Rebecca addressed "the business and profession of home-making," demonstrating its importance and the need for qualified, educated members of this profession, as in any other career. In 1901 she was invited to speak before the Georgia legislature in November. There was some opposition within this body to her speaking. One legislator protested that,
"the time of the body was too precious and expensive to waste either, on permitting a woman to address the legislature." But Rebecca had never been one to shrink before criticism.

The President of the Senate, Clark Howell, introduced her:
"There is a great deal of discussion and contention as to who is the
smartest man in Georgia, but it is universally conceded that the
woman who is to address you today is the brightest and smartest
woman in the state."

She quickly responded to Senator Howell, "Old age is sus-
ceptible to compliments. I will gladly swallow the taffy just
handed to me." Many prominent politicians referred to Rebecca as
the most intelligent woman in the state. She accepted such praise
with wit and graciousness. Did she see that such a compliment
might serve a double purpose? By claiming that she was more intelligent than any other woman in the state, clever politicians were
able to set her apart, making her something of an anomaly. More

to the point, if she was not herself an ordinary Georgia woman, she could not truly represent their ideas and beliefs. With such continuing 'compliments' she was transformed (in the minds of many) into a gracious southern woman – with a man's brain.

But she had a few tricks up her sleeve, too. She made her point about the need for woman suffrage quite unobtrusively, almost in fact, as if she were not making one at all. She remarked to the state legislature, "As I speak to you, you will understand that I am a person without any political influence. I have no vote to give any one of you. I cannot occupy any public office, and it seems I am only a small taxpayer and nothing else, so far as I am estimated by law makers of Georgia."

Yet woman suffrage was not on her agenda in her speech in the state capitol. Informed, well-educated mothers and compulsory school attendance were. She favored compulsory education for everyone – black, white, rich or poor, male or female. At the time most poor white mountain children did not attend school, working the fields instead. And many children in factories and black children working in the fields did not attend either. Often parents refused to allow their children to attend school, preferring their field or factory work in lieu of education.

> The lash of compulsory taxation is laid upon the back of the man who has by thrift, economy and industry earned some property to tax, and no obligation whatever is laid upon the man, whose children are to be educated at public expense, and he fails to accept the benefit.

> The obligation should be mutual, gentlemen. The responsibility should be mutual.

Exactly when Rebecca first publicly espoused the need for woman suffrage is not clear. But she was active in the Georgia Woman Suffrage Association by the turn of the century. Always good with money and keeping the books, Rebecca became the GWSA's auditor. Her sister Mary McLendon served as State President of that organization from 1906 to 1921. From the beginning of the twentieth century, both sisters actively planned the meetings, agenda, and recruitment activities of this growing suffragist organization. The founder of the GWSA, H. Augusta Howard, often joined them. William Felton favored woman suffrage by 1907, and probably much earlier. When she helped her husband, whose palsy required aid in walking, to go to the poles that year to vote liquor out of the state of Georgia, he said to Rebecca, "I wish you had been allowed to vote it out."

Although she was becoming more actively involved in suffrage, much of her keen interest and speeches remained devoted to the ordinary woman. She wanted to put away forever the "old saw" that said, "A dog, a woman, and a walnut tree, the more you beat 'em the better they be." For Rebecca, "Tis home where the heart is, and I know enough of my own sex to say to you, the best investment a man ever put his money into was the satisfaction and happiness of his own wife, and the mother of his children." She also continued to encourage the farmer to allow his wife to have a part of the farm for her own business, a cotton patch, a hen house, a vegetable garden, and to permit his wife to have her own money and to use it as she saw fit.

In the fall of 1900 Rebecca began writing a column for the *Atlanta Journal,* entitled "The Country Home: Women on the Farm." She would continue to write for this semi-weekly journal for decades. It became one of her favorite ways to discuss any topic, whether education, politics, taxes – Czar Nicholas II of Russia, or a Senator from Georgia. Everything was fair game for her popular column. She frequently discussed women's issues – usually leaving favorite recipes and household tips to others. Women who would never think of attending a GWSA meeting, could now read Rebecca's column in the comfort – and privacy – of their homes.

In fact, it was getting easier for women to inform themselves about the activities and agendas of women's clubs, suffragist meetings, and temperance organizations, thanks to the *Constitution.* The editor of that Atlanta newspaper decided to separate women's club news from the Society Page. Suddenly, one newspaper page contained the activities and meetings of all the women's organizations: the Georgia Woman Suffrage Association, the Woman's

Christian Temperance Union, the Daughters of the American Revolution, United Daughters of the Confederacy, and the Woman's Club of Calhoun all found themselves together – at least in the newspaper. And each in its own way strived to better the community, whether in the restoration of an historical site, the creation of new playgrounds and parks, or obtaining civil rights for women. As for the Woman's Christian Temperance Union, it stood in near shambles in Georgia at the turn of the century, thanks in large part to Rebecca's nemesis, Bishop Warren A. Candler. He wanted no part of an organization that had a second agenda – women's rights – in addition to prohibition. He (along with other prominent members of his family) saw to it that funds dried up for the WCTU.

While Rebecca remained in robust health, her husband grew weaker, although his mental faculties remained unchanged. His palsy severely limited his movements, and he required aid in nearly everything he did. A serious undisclosed or unknown illness in the fall and early winter of 1907 left him even weaker. For eighteen months he was bedridden, sometimes suffering with great pain. Still his mind was alert. During this period Rebecca remained almost constantly at his side, read to him often, and took care of him faithfully. She was cheered by the visits of many friends to their Cartersville farm, and by even more letters often expressing admiration for the care and devotion that she bestowed upon her husband. Then William was stricken by what appeared to be an acute case of indigestion, according to his attending physicians, Dr. R. E. Adair, Dr. R. I Battle, and William's son, Dr. Howard Felton. Although the stated diagnosis was indigestion, everyone, including William, knew that he was dying.

He lingered peacefully throughout the day of September 24, 1909, surrounded by his beloved wife, his son, and other relatives. Rebecca read to him about the good service of the Western and Atlantic Railroad that he had once saved for Georgia. He listened quietly, a hint of pride upon his face. Then at about 6:30 P.M. he peacefully died. She later wrote, "Dr. Felton's death was the most beautiful going away that my eyes ever witnessed, calm, serene, conscious and at perfect peace with all mankind, and I ever thank God that he gave such beautiful evidence of a Christian's faith in leaving me."

The following day the *Atlanta Georgian* announced, "W. H. Felton Dies after Long Illness: Was Noted Orator and Statesman of Old School." In many respects, William Harrell Felton was not literally old school, but rather one of the most progressive men of the South. He saved countless soldiers' lives as a doctor in the Civil War. As a U.S. Congressman, he helped to improve rivers and harbors within the nation. He introduced a bill in Congress (and helped to pass it) that strengthened national quarantine. And he explained and helped to pass a revision which admitted quinine, a badly-needed drug for the treatment of malaria, into the United States without tariff. He worked diligently for the end of the convict lease, for better and less corrupt railroads within his state, for prison reform, monetary reform, for separate reformatories for youth, and for educational improvements at all levels.

At the age of sixteen he joined the Methodist Church and was a devout and active Methodist for the rest of his life, becoming a licensed preacher for that denomination in 1848. He served his and other counties faithfully for nearly a half century, preaching the first sermon ever in a Methodist Church in Cartersville. Before she died, Rebecca Latimer Felton saw to it that her husband's papers, including his sermons, would be preserved within the archives of the University of Georgia. This Preacher often spoke at Methodist camp meetings, religious rallies, and small country churches, and had a reputation for being able to hold his listeners spellbound. It would be logical to assume that his sermons evoked hell-fire and damnation with huge appeals to emotion, ranting, shouting, maybe even gimmicks – so characteristic of the old timey religion, popular in those times. But William Harrell Felton defied logic.

He wrote his sermons out in a clear, open, easy-to-read cursive. And he certainly did not whoop or speak down to his congregations. "It would be anomalous in the philosophy of morals, as it would be unwise in social life, to bestow an inheritance where there was not ability to retain and augment it," he said referring to the Bible parable of the talents given to men to use, to hoard, or to hide. He continued by eloquently explaining the parable and saying, "God never permits a gift to perish for want of power to sustain it. Advancement and increase are not demanded without 'motion power' sufficient to propel onward the entire man." His sermons were beautiful, wonderfully worded, his conclusions a profession of his faith: "There is the most complete harmony between the ability of the man and the gifts of God. The whole building is fitly framed together – all its parts, and even the furniture are in strict proportion with each other. If the design is frustrated and the symmetrical proportions disfigured 'an enemy hath done it' – not God."

He displayed a simple faith and honesty with intelligence and eloquence seldom found anywhere. Dr. Felton preached and conducted his religious duties for many decades in north Georgia, performing more marriages and probably more burials than any other man of his times in that part of the state. Yet he took no money for his religious work, believing that the best way for him to try to follow Christ was to work without salary.

William Harrell Felton was an honorable man, thoughtful, perceptive, and learned; a doctor who brought new ideas to the practice of medicine; a statesman at a time when crooked politicians ruled Georgia; a devout and able minister who took no money for his work; an orator who moved great crowds with his convictions; a progressive who looked forward to a better life for all Georgians and was willing to fight for this ideal; a father who dearly loved his son; and a loving and devoted husband who encouraged his wife to step out of corseted tradition. He was buried in Cartersville in the Oak Hill Cemetery. His neighbors carried his coffin. Every state legislator and congressman either attended the funeral or sent their condolences to Rebecca.

In March 1910 Rebecca put a marble slab over her husband's grave:

WILLIAM HARRELL FELTON
1822-1909
A HEROIC SOUL, EVER ENLISTED IN THE
CAUSE OF RIGHT

She later erected a monument in her husband's memory on the courthouse square in Cartersville. On it she wrote:

> Endowed with a magnificent mind, matchless
> eloquence and the commanding force which
> acknowledged integrity and lofty courage inspire;
> he gave to his country – effective, patriotic and unsullied
> service in state and national legislation.

> On his beloved home – he lavished tender care and
> affection – while for 50 years the best efforts of this
> superb intellect and noble heart were devoted to the
> continuous, zealous gratuitous and consecrated work of
> a minister of the Gospel.

Remarking about the fifty-seven-year marriage of William and Rebecca, biographer John Talmadge said, "A man's character is not entirely safe in the hands of feminists, even when one of them is his wife. They are usually too concerned with the interests of their sex to do him justice." Considering the life of this couple, their words, respect, and actions both toward others and each other, it is easy to believe that John Talmadge may have been mistaken.

The two men who had been the most important in the life of Rebecca Latimer Felton were now gone: her father Charles Latimer, and her husband, William H. Felton. Both men loved her deeply and encouraged her mind and spirit. It is impossible to imagine what she might have become had her father and husband not been so farsighted and progressive. Charles provided her, at considerable sacrifice to himself, with an excellent education, and William encouraged her to use it. Now, except for her son Howard and her step-daughter Ann, who was married and lived far away, she was alone. She had a six-hundred-acre farm to run, newspaper articles to write, and other affairs to look after. She was seventy-five and had already lived a full and eventful life. Anyone else might think of retirement at that age – but for Rebecca, her biggest achievements were yet to come.

Just as she had done to ease the pain of the loss of her children and the damage to her plantation following the Civil War, she threw herself into her work. And on top of everything else, woman suffrage began to take on a new urgency for Rebecca. It was becoming a hot issue, disputed by men and women...even in the South. Many women did not hesitate to disparage themselves regarding their fitness to assume the responsibility of the ballot. Men and women agreed with the conclusion of Californian, Annie Bock, when she spoke before the U.S. Senate Committee on Woman Suffrage and said, "Woman is impulsive; she does not inform herself; she does not study; she does not consider the consequences of a vote. In her haste to remedy one wrong she opens the way to many. The ballot in her hands is a dangerous thing."

Rebecca decided that it was time to do something about such beliefs. It was time for her to become a full-blown suffragist in every sense of the word. She spoke about woman suffrage, wrote about it, campaigned for it. Her words ultimately formed a lengthy article entitled, "Why I am a Suffragist?" It was first published in 1915, when she was eighty years old, and stands today as one of the most convincing and eloquent documents ever written on the subject.

Chapter Thirteen

Troubled Times

In 1915, the same year that Rebecca wrote her work explaining why she had become a suffragist, a failed minister, "Colonel" William Joseph Simmons, decided that he would found a group in Georgia, certainly not a suffragist organization, and become its leader. Along with other men who shared his sentiments, he petitioned the state of Georgia for a charter. He spent many hours planning for his group's inauguration, thought about it –even dreamed about it – for almost as long as Rebecca had considered becoming a suffragist. On Thanksgiving night, he and several other men climbed to the top of the huge granite rock a few miles from Atlanta, that loomed several hundred feet in the air: Stone Mountain. There in the moonlight they erected an altar, draped it in flags, and opened a Bible upon it, turning to Romans, Chapter 12. In that chapter one reads, "Vengeance is mine, I will repay, says the Lord." These men intended to become the servants of God by helping Him carry out his vengeance.

They put on white robes and hoods that masked their faces and came to a point at the top. Then they lit a huge cross, which could be seen all the way to Atlanta. At midnight, by the light of that burning cross, they performed a secret ceremony and reawakened the Ku Klux Klan, which had lain dormant for some fifty years.

"Colonel" Simmons, Founder of the 1915 KKK

If their activities atop Stone Mountain were not enough to reestablish the Klan, they had a powerful and convincing ally – one that would premiere in Atlanta the following week: a movie called *The Birth of a Nation.* This film, based upon a novel, *The Clansman,* by Thomas Dixon, a Baptist minister from North Carolina, glorifies the Ku Klux Klan, which ultimately saves the day in the film by rescuing "white civilization from a cowardly Negro militia." The personages in the movie are stereotypes of the darkest southern versions of Reconstruction, "replete with villainous Radicals, sinister mulattoes, blameless Southerners, and unfaithful darkies." Enormously popular, both in the North and the South, *Birth of a Nation* helped to pave the way for the re-establishment of the Klan. Grossing about eighteen million dollars, and running continuously in many Southern states for as long as fifteen years, its impact cannot be underestimated. This romanticized movie version of the Klan caused many people to join its ranks, or to look upon the KKK with sympathy and excitement.

"Colonel" Simmons, self-declared "Emperor of the Invisible Empire, Knights of the Ku Klux Klan" was himself a strange man with serious flaws and assets. A native of Alabama, Simmons had tried his hand at several occupations before becoming "Emperor." He decided to become a doctor, but dropped out of medical school. He became a Methodist minister, but was soon defrocked. Then he tried his hand at insurance, but was not overly successful. He drank. "Mints and cloves wrestled with the bourbon on his breath...." And he was always available for a game of poker. What he liked best was to join clubs. He belonged to fifteen other fraternal organizations and loved to bond with other men through celebration of "the united powers of our regal manhood." No one could glad hand, preach, pray, and present wonderful attention-getting images better than the self-appointed Emperor of the Invisible Empire.

It was, in fact, one of these images which allegedly reinstated the Klan – a dream Simmons claimed to have had, no, better yet, a *Vision*, of Klansmen united together gloriously riding their steeds across his bedroom wall. If Simmons could do anything, he could stir men's imaginations – and collect money. He knew the value of publicity. He saw to it that his first public announcement of his Invisible Empire appeared right next to the *Birth of a Nation* publicity in the Atlanta *Journal*. From the $10.00 "klecktoken," which all new members paid, $8.00 of it went for expenses and promotion. Publicity, marketing, expansion, speeches, articles – William Simmons was excellent in these arenas. As for genuine ideas, ideologies, philosophies, policy, Simmons didn't have any – except, of course, for the concept of hatred and intolerance. A Charleston editor once noted that what Simmons excelled in was "selling people their own prejudices." At that he showed a skill "almost equal to the old bunco game of selling a hick the Capitol."

He also knew how to wrap his message so cleverly as to make it sound as if joining the KKK were something akin to the expression of loyalty to God, country, and family. "Out of the chaos of unholy selfishness, up from the storm-tossed and all-encompassing sea of indifference, down throughout the ages of ignorance and bigotry, comes Light – faint and feeble in its infant beams, heralding the DAWN of a NEW DAY." Yes, the new day when the KKK is in control. Simmons continues, "Already we can hear the peals of laughter, the songs of gladness, the clasp of honest hands, the blending of hearts with Truth like emerald leaves and redolent golden flowers. Life's dark night is almost ended and the way lies open unto Eternal Day." Simmons didn't often speak in terms of hatred, lynching, and bigotry. Instead, he spoke of truth, freedom, good citizenship, sacred honor, and the protection of "virtuous womanhood." In his "I Will – A study in Practical Citizenship," he states that all KKK members should pledge, "I will strive, through the constituted authorities, to correct prevailing evils in my community, particularly vices tending to the destruction of the home, family, childhood and womanhood." He concludes, "I will in every way, try to live up to the high standards of Arian citizenship." Cloaking its true intentions in patriotism, honor, and the defense of the Protestant religion, the KKK appeared to many to be at first just another secret society, a fraternal organization ...one that brought some spice and excitement to lives that often lacked such elements.

While the KKK began to invade sleepy Georgia farms, villages, and towns, terrorizing those it perceived to be "different" – immigrants, blacks, Jews, Catholics, even those who did not attend church – there was another potentially devastating invasion of Georgia, not by man, but by a tiny bug. Coming from Mexico, and crossing into Texas about 1894, the boll weevil was an insect with a long snout that laid its eggs in the little leaves surrounding the cotton blossom. These eggs prevented the boll, where the cotton grew, from developing." By 1913 it had invaded southwest Georgia and was headed toward the rest of the state with as much determination as General Sherman.

In a sense, Rebecca in 1915 was also planning an invasion...into the most sanctified traditions and beliefs of the South regarding chivalry, the Southern Belle, and the traditional role of women. She begins "Why I am a Suffragist?" by citing some of the progress that women have made, along with needed improvements. "A woman in Georgia could not own her own wages – as late as 1897." ... "Before the Civil War, a married woman in Georgia could not own her own clothes." ... "A woman cannot practice law in Georgia today, no matter how well prepared by study and genius." ... "Georgia women have not had any jury opportunity." ... "It is said that women are represented by their husbands at the ballot box. This is not true...."

As for women who did not want to vote, Rebecca said, "To these I can only say if they prefer to hug their chains, I have no sort of objection. If they accept the position of inferiority, why try to impress them with repeated arguments against serfdom in mind, body or estate?" She hastened to add that while these "distinguished Georgia women" were telling their state legislature that they already had all the rights they could possibly need, other serious women begged that same legislature to raise the age of consent for women (girls), which was the lowest in the United States – ten years – and that women who were taxed needed to be represented. After all, the issue of taxation without representation was one of the major causes of the Revolutionary War.

As slavers had used the Bible to defend slavery, many Antis pointed to certain passages in the Bible to support their anti-suffragism. Along with other suffragists, Rebecca began to confront these issues. Responding to the Bible quotation, "Submit yourselves to your husbands," she claimed that that statement did not mean that a woman should "endure, suffer, forbear, obey and have no opportunity to do anything except as commanded or permited [sic] by a husband who can take her children from her – take her property away from her – and make life a torment to her with his infidelities, with drunken habits and horrid examples for his own sons and daughters!" Regarding chivalry, Rebecca wrote the following:

> It exploited itself in courting days, in bowing and scraping in public company, and in personal encounters, which were known as du-

els. An insult called for a challenge, and then pistols. Nevertheless, the law of Georgia allowed any sort of a man to beat his wife,
provided the switch was no bigger than his thumb. Glance down at
your thumb, my dear reader, and then we will proceed a little further.

Actually, Rebecca "proceeded" much further. In addition to equality at the voting poll, Rebecca called for equality in marriage.
"Marriage between a master and a slave was obliged to be debas-
ing to both. Marriage in its true meaning rests upon absolute
equality between the sexes as to rights and privileges – legal, political and social." In addition, she asked for equal pay for equal
work. She responded to those who claimed that women who favored suffrage were out of their sphere. "I have seen white women
on their all-fours, scrubbing the halls of the great Department in
Washington City, thirty years ago and nobody protested that these
child-bearing women were out of their sphere."

Her speech was a call for freedom and rights for everyone.
She reiterated the idea that she had previously stated that slavery
had been the curse of the South, and concluded that, "We are only
interested in human liberty." In her conclusion she stated, "The
call of the age is for partnership in the family, in the church, in the
State and National affairs, between men and women."

Yet even as she penned these powerful words, the boll
weevil munched its way though another sunny field of cotton,
leaving it destroyed, while the KKK rode through Georgia nights,
terrorizing, beating, burning, and often lynching those it deemed
deserving of such heinous acts.

Only one year earlier (1914), another secret organization
was gaining power in Europe: the Black Hand. The oath its members took was:

> I, in joining the organization "Union or Death," swear by the Sun
> that warms me, by the Earth that nourishes me, before God, by the
> blood of the ancestors, on my honour and on my life, that I will
> from this moment until my death be faithful to the laws of this or-
> ganization; and that I will always be ready to make any sacrifice
> for it.

I swear before God, on my honour and on my life, that I will take
all the secrets of this organization into my grave with me.

On June 28, 1914 the Black Hand assassinated Archduke Franz
Ferdinand, touching off what would soon become the largest war
ever known to date: World War I. At first the United States remained aloof, isolationist. After all, it was a European War; no
need to become involved. Rebecca eyed the European war with
grave concern, hoping the United States would refuse to enter the
fray. She continued to fight for better conditions within the state
of Georgia, and for national woman suffrage.

Rebecca soon encountered the KKK herself near Cartersville. Disliking the progressive ideas of William Felton, the Klan
desecrated a marker to this minister at Felton's Chapel, previously
donated by the Feltons to the North Georgia Methodist Synod.
The Klan hid the marker under the chapel steps. In another incident, the Klan paraded by the Felton memorial that she had erected
in her husband's memory, and then entered the Sam Jones Taber-
nacle where Jones was preaching. According to Rebecca, just as
the services were closing one evening, "...a hooded gang marched
down the middle aisle with pillow slips and bed sheets covering
them, and handed up an envelope to the preacher." According to
an eyewitness, there were at least twenty-five hooded men. In the
envelope was $25.00. KKK candidates won the election a few
days later by a landslide. Rebecca believed that her own church
had betrayed her, with its support of the Klan. In fact, Methodists,
Southern Baptists and other denominations, along with Masons
and other fraternal organizations and secret societies, and many
members of police departments and ministers (who were not required to pay the entrance fee, "Klecktoken") thronged to the Klan.

In the spring of the same year that the Black Hand assassinated Archduke Franz Ferdinand, another organization was
formed: the Georgia Chapter of the National Association Opposed
to Woman Suffrage. Within three months, 2,000 Georgia men and
women belonged to this association, led by two powerful women:
Mildred Lewis Rutherford, President of the United Daughters of

the Confederacy, and a mesmerizing speaker; and Dolly Blount Lamar of Macon, an author and also an excellent speaker.

Mary Latimer McLendon and Rebecca debated against these two anti-suffragists before a house committee of the state legislature, but this committee already favored the Antis and voted five to two against suffrage for the women of Georgia. Undeterred, pro-suffrage women held a rally in Atlanta in 1914; they gathered peacefully on the steps of Georgia's State Capitol in May 1915; and in November they marched in a parade in Atlanta, the Harvest Festival, wearing sashes, carrying banners, waving, smiling, with some in decorated vehicles. Mary McLendon was in the lead automobile, and Elanore Raoul, who founded the Fulton and DeKalb Equal Suffrage Party, was on horseback. It was quite a gathering. There was even a small pony cart filled with flowers on top of which was a sign: GEORGIA CATCHING UP. In 1916 the suffragists were the first non-labor group ever to march in the Labor Day Parade in Atlanta. Suffragists were making no headway within the state legislature, but they were being seen and heard – perhaps one might even say that they were becoming – almost respectable.

Looking at these spirited, determined women, young and old, marching proudly down Atlanta's streets, it is difficult to agree with Eugene Anderson, President of the Georgia-Alabama Business College (preparing young women to do office work) as he spoke in Macon, describing the suffragists as being part of an "attack of the demons of the underworld." He gave all the usual reasons for not giving women the vote – their weaker minds, their nervous, fragile systems, their unsexing, and their loss of identity. He believed that giving women the vote "would eventually lead to the ruin of American homelife; the destruction of our moral code; the lowering of woman's power and influence; and the final undoing of our government." Many Antis agreed with him.

Then Anderson went even farther than most Antis, claiming not only that there were evil women, but that women had been the cause of the fall of empires and civilizations. One must note, according to this speaker, that there were "wicked elements of womankind." He concluded his speech with a spirited and patriotic portrait of Uncle Sam and then declared him to be the "modern Sampson." He urged all men not to give "Delilah the shears with which to trim his locks and bring about the destruction of the temple."

The anti-suffragist movement occurred throughout the nation in all states that had not yet granted women the vote (by 1914, only eleven states, mostly in the West, had passed woman suffrage). Ignoring the insults of the Antis, Rebecca and the suffragists doggedly worked on. They hoped that soon, in the very near future, in fact, and in spite of all the shouted words to the contrary, the concept of woman suffrage would gain respect within the nation. The speeches and articles of Rebecca Felton helped to give woman suffrage respectability, even in the recalcitrant South.

Schoolhouse in Kirkland Georgia

Chapter Fourteen

New Suffragist Tactics

Susan B. Anthony had been right when she maintained that the lobbying effort was essential to the passage of a suffrage amendment. With her death on March 13, 1906, no one stepped in to take over the Washington lobbying duties she had so faithfully carried out each year. Important contacts were lost; no one curried favors for the woman's movement; and money supporting suffrage began to dry up. In fact, headquarters for the National American Woman Suffrage Association were now in New York, not Washington. And with the NAWSA Convention no longer held every year in Washington, legislators began to pay less attention to the movement. Besides, most governmental officials were much more interested in the situation across the Atlantic, which seemed to be getting bigger and more ominous every day. With little lobbying money, few significant and influential Washington contacts, and no real lobbyist to speak for the suffragists, the movement began to lose its momentum. Instead of trying for a Federal amendment, suffragists were now attempting to obtain the vote on a state-by-state basis.

During the second decade of the 1900s Rebecca and others worked hard to gain suffrage endorsements from significant women's clubs within Georgia. Although several groups did give some support, most of the major organizations failed to favor the suffragist agenda. The WCTU, which in much earlier years had worked for the goals of woman suffrage, now remained silent about the subject, having lost too many battles to the Antis, especially Bishop Candler, who had seen to it that they also lost much of their financial backing. The WCTU decided to work for temperance and to leave the hotter suffrage issue alone.

The suffragists thought that the Georgia Federation of Women's Clubs might endorse the cause of women suffrage. But their hopes were dashed in 1914 when the President of this Organization, Mrs. A. I. Fitzpatrick announced her firm opposition to woman suffrage, stating what had so often been repeated: "We are the power behind the throne now, and would lose, not gain, by a change. I am opposed to bringing the question with its attendant train of politics into the Federation. Politics means dissension." The D.A.R. generally agreed with Fitzpatrick's beliefs. The movement for a national suffrage amendment had stalled in Georgia, as it had in much of the rest of the nation.

President Woodrow Wilson

In addition to Rebecca, other suffragists, particularly in the North and East wrote articles and books in an attempt to revive and increase enthusiasm for a national woman suffrage amendment. One of the most effective of these women was a journalist for the *New York Tribune*, Alice Duer Miller. When President Wilson gave a speech extolling the right of all people and nations to decide their own forms of government, Miller retorted in her regular column, "Are Women People?" the following:

To President Wilson

> WISE and just man-for such I think you are-
> How can you see so burningly and clear
> Injustices and tyrannies afar,
> Yet blind your eyes to one that lies so near?
> How can you plead so earnestly for men
> Who fight their won fight with a bloody hand;
> How hold their cause so wildly dear, and then
> Forget the women of your native land?

Her competitor, *The New York Times,* wrote on February 7, 1915, "The grant of suffrage to women is repugnant to instincts that strike their roots deep in the order of nature. It runs counter to human reason, it flouts the teachings of experience and the admonitions of common sense." Miller wrote another poem entitled, "To the Times Editorials," in which she stated:

> LOVELY Antiques, breathing in every line
> The perfume of an age long passed away,
> Wafting us back to 1829,
> Museum pieces of a by-gone day,
> You should not languish in the public press,
> Where modern thought might reach and do you harm,
> And vulgar youth insult your hoariness,
> Missing the flavor of your old world charm;
> You should be locked, where rust cannot corrode
> In some old rosewood cabinet, dimmed by age,
> With silver-lustre, tortoise shell and Spode;
> And all would cry, who read your yellowing page;
> "Yes, that's the sort of thing that men believed
> Before the First Reform Bill was conceived!"

Yet even with Rebecca's powerful suffragist messages and the wit and rhyme of Alice Duer Miller, along with serious speeches and articles written by others, the movement languished. The situation did not really change until the highly-educated, intellectual, and charismatic Alice Paul, along with her friend Lucy Burns, asked the NAWSA to co-chair its tiny, flagging Congressional Committee in Washington D.C. Their request was gratefully accepted. Had the leaders of the NAWSA realized that the philosophy and tactics of these two women were so different from those of earlier suffragist lobbyists, they might have hesitated. Although both women were Americans, much of their suffragist experience came from England where they had been imprisoned for their suffrage work. In fact, they first met in a London police station, both arrested for demonstrating for woman suffrage before the Parliament building.

Unlike former suffragists, neither woman had a "beg and plead" philosophy regarding lobbying Washington legislators. Both were determined, highly capable, knowledgeable and experienced. Miss Paul, as she liked to be addressed, knew how to get her message across, obtain publicity, and perhaps throw a bit of spectacle into the mix, in spite of the fact that she was herself a demure Quaker, often seated stoically with her hands folded in her lap. No one guessed at first that behind that quiet façade lay a nimble mind and boldness as yet unheard of within suffragist ranks. At the very least, she was not one to make an appointment with a Congressman, politely enter his office and pleasantly request that he support her cause. "Demand," not "plead" was the mainstay of her thought.

Miss Paul knew how to take advantage of certain activities and celebrations, and the one she eyed was the Inauguration of Woodrow Wilson, set to take place on March 4, 1913. Tirelessly working, Paul and Burns organized the nation's pro-suffrage women within a period of two months and "staged a suffrage spectacle unequalled in the political annals of the nation's capital [sic.]." One day before Wilson's Inauguration, when every statesman was in Washington, and publicity and onlookers were at their height, the suffragists held a parade, and not just a little one either. Eight thousand women "in costumed marching units, each with its own banners" walked from the Capitol down Pennsylvania Avenue past the White House. There were also many floats, decorated with waving women and suffragist propaganda. Leading the whole procession was the then-famous lawyer and suffragist, Inez M. Boissevain, dressed in long white robes and sitting proudly astride a beautiful white horse. Eyes bugged everywhere. Some said the suffragist parade got more attention than the Inauguration itself.

Inez M. Boissevain Leading the
1913 Suffragist Parade

Other suffragists from all over the country soon followed suit, holding parades, and requesting audiences of state and national representatives. At first President Wilson, who was usually anti-suffragist, but could waffle on the suffrage question depending upon whom he was addressing, tried to ignore the suffragists. He even became engaged in efforts at 'hide-and-seek' regarding the reception of certain suffragist representatives in the White House. For example, two prominent Philadelphia suffragists had an appointment with Wilson to ask him to meet with a suffragist delegation when he went to Philadelphia to welcome 4,000 foreign men into citizenship (and suffrage). At first the women were informed that the President was so busy with foreign matters that he had no time to see anyone. After a phone call made by Senator Clapp, the suffragists learned that, "the President had left the White House for the day. At that moment the Philadelphia callers ascertained that the President was eating luncheon preparatory to going to the golf links for the afternoon."

Suffrage Parade in Washington, March 3, 1913

While Miss Paul and others were drawing attention to the suffrage movement and thereby increasing its growth, the anti-suffragist movement was growing, too. Although their conclusions about suffrage were quite different, both suffragists and anti-suffragists came from similar backgrounds. They were generally from the upper-middle to upper classes, but the Antis were more associated with the upper echelons of manufacturing and commerce, and therefore generally somewhat wealthier than their counterparts. Rebecca sometimes combated the anti-suffragists, with their own arguments. In her article, "Some Arguments against Woman Suffrage," she noted that many people claimed that women wouldn't vote if they could. While other anti-suffragists claimed "that women would forsake all of their domestic pursuits to be on hand at every election." Other anti-suffragists argued that women would always vote as their husbands wished, while others claimed that there would be such political disagreements between husband and wife as to destroy the household. Some said women were too good to vote, while others said they were too bad. Some men claimed that women couldn't understand politics, while others feared that women would take over politics. After pointing out many more contradictions among the anti-suffragists, Rebecca concluded that, "I have not in this symposium of able anti-suffrage arguments said a single thing in favor of the franchise for women!"

In 1914 a Georgia proposal for woman suffrage was placed before the state legislature for its consideration, along with eloquent speeches given by Georgia's suffragists and anti-suffragists. This scene was becoming a yearly production, always with the same outcome...the legislature siding with the Antis and defeating the proposal. In these sessions the Antis trotted out all the long-held notions and traditions of woman as queen exclusively of the home. To change this system would destroy everything. It was the same old song.

To further punctuate the Antis beliefs, many people, often led by their pastors, continued to claim that the role of men and women had been ordained by God. To attempt any changes in the roles of men and women within society would counter God's great Plan. As Bishop Candler said, "You wives must submit to your husband's leadership in the same way you submit to the Lord. ... So you wives must willingly obey your husbands in everything, just as the church obeys Christ." Candler concluded that, "the whole basis of the woman's suffrage movement is unscriptural and sinful." Most clerics and their congregations agreed with him. The Antis had a hand in the defeat of every suffrage referendum put before the states between 1896 and 1910.

Throughout the spring of 1915, Rebecca added more pro-suffragist material to her other lists of causes that she regularly espoused in Georgia newspapers. A few editors took exception to her frankness in some of her articles because she spoke of harlots, drunkenness, mulattoes, and other topics once taboo for a southern lady. For example, the vice president and managing editor of the *Richland News*, M. B. Brown, wrote to her on May 25 saying that he would not publish her article because children sometimes read his paper. He then stated, "Now mother Felton, in your feeble age, I fear that you are too easy to take exceptions and get offended. It seems that you get angered with me at every article I write when I do not mean offense at all." He further wrote, "Now listen, dear Mother Felton, we have an annual meeting of editors and newspaper men and women each year. This year we meet at Eastman, GA. Suppose you come down and lets make up and be friends. I would take the greatest sort of delight in letting you whip me slap my jaws and just have a grand jolly good time all the way through." How or if she responded to this letter is not known; it remains one of a great many patronizing and critical letters that she received...and saved. In spite of harsh criticisms, sly epithets, and outright name calling, Rebecca continued her suffrage crusade undaunted.

On May 7, 1915, only one week before Rebecca finished her major work advocating woman suffrage, nearly two thousand people heard something that sounded like a great crash of thunder, or as one person put it, "like a million-ton hammer hitting a steel boiler a hundred feet high and a hundred feet long." Of those that heard this noise, 1,201 had little more than twenty minutes left to live. The Germans had torpedoed the liner, *Lusitania*, on its way from New York (carrying many American passengers) to England. Most historians agree that this dramatic sinking by German submarines first caused the United States to give serious consideration to entering the Great War.

Although Rebecca viewed the European situation with serious concern and wrote about it often, hoping that the United States would remain isolationist, her main focus continued to be on her defense of woman suffrage, countering the attacks of the Antis. In the South at that time, the Antis had the upper hand, particularly with the legislature. But nationally the Antis didn't have the likes of Alice Paul on their side. In 1916 she founded the National Woman's Party, which believed that those in power should be held accountable for the lack of advancement of the woman suffrage amendment. The NWP did all that it could to oust the Antis from governmental positions, and demanded – *demanded* – the passage of the suffrage amendment, which Miss Paul named the Susan B. Anthony Amendment. Some of the more demonstrative members of the National Woman's Party found themselves imprisoned for their protests and demonstrations. Again Miss Paul turned this fact to the advantage of the movement. Formerly jailed suffragists were sent by train on a national speaking tour. Dressed in their prison garments, they addressed their audiences, explaining that they had been imprisoned, and for what? For wanting to go to the polls and vote – as men did. While these women "made their way across the country, they stopped in cities and towns along the route and secured the signatures of hundreds of thousands of women and men on suffrage petitions to be delivered to Congress."

Decades before the Civil Rights Movement, Paul used the tactics that Martin Luther King would later use. Her change from pleading to demanding, with the clout of so many petitions behind her, led to dramatic results. In nearly every part of the nation signs of the reawakening of the woman suffrage cause appeared under Paul's leadership and plans. "These included parades, demonstrations, mass meetings, picketing, suffrage watch fires, hunger strikes, deputations to the President, communication with the press, publication of a stylish weekly called the *Suffragist,* organizing women who had secured suffrage in western states, and lobbying."

President Wilson took a dim view of these protesting women who were now interfering with his second campaign, along with the campaigns of other elected officials who had shown themselves to be Antis, in spite of their sometimes soft-spoken words. It was simple in Miss Paul's opinion. If they refused to ratify the Susan B. Anthony Amendment, they should be thrown out of office, and the National Woman's Party did all that it could to accomplish that end...without voting, of course.

In spite of the efforts of the NWP, Wilson was re-elected in November, 1916. As the war in Europe flamed, the United States continued its isolationist policies, and Wilson took advantage of this sentiment. His campaign motto had been, "He kept us out of War." But he couldn't keep himself out of the aim of Miss Paul.

In January 1917 a group of protestors peacefully picketed in front of the White House. They were the first group of protesters ever to take such an action in the history of the nation. These quiet, well-behaved picketers were suffragists who called themselves the Silent Sentinels. They said nothing; they did nothing – except to hold up banners and signs that demanded (no longer asked for) the right to vote. Soon the police came and told them that they must leave, that they were not permitted to picket in front of the White House. But they did not leave. These picketers became "the first group in the United States to wage a nonviolent civil disobedience campaign." President Woodrow Wilson was furious. However, he had much more important concerns at that time than a few 'silly' women holding placards in front of the White House. His most important worry was that War.

In spite of diplomatic protests, the Germans, effectively blockaded by the Allies on the high seas, ignored maritime legalities and sank many neutral ships, frequently American ships. While American trade with Germany greatly declined, it increased dramatically with the Allies and went from $825,000,000 in 1916 to $3,200,000,000 by 1918. That trade with Europe was vital to America's economy. Isolationist sentiment persisted, and still those silent, solemn women stood before the White House, even on the coldest days of winter.

In early 1917 came the Zimmermann Telegram. It was not meant to be sent to the United States at all, but rather to Mexico. It was written by Germany's Foreign Minister Alfred Zimmermann. This telegram stated that if Mexico decided to help Germany against the United States, Mexico's reward would be the return, with Germany's help, of the so-called "lost territory" (New Mexico, Arizona, and Texas) to its 'rightful owner.' The British managed to decode the German telegram and promptly sent it to President Wilson. A few days later the American press – and the world – knew what had been written in the so-called Zimmerman Note. By April 6, 1917 the United States was at war. Although the Americans entered the war nearly three years after it had begun and soon discovered that the Allies "over there" were in even worse condition than had once been thought, America provided an influx of money, arms, machinery, and fresh soldiers, committed to the Allies of the Great War, later known as World War I.

Because of the war, it was no longer a question of whether women were competent to do a man's job. American men were entering the armed forces by the hundreds of thousands, and women were taking their positions in the workplace. Countless thousands of women left home for the first time in their lives to take the jobs left vacant by men who were becoming soldiers. Other women remained in the home, but sold War Bonds and worked actively for the Red Cross. They were determined to do whatever they could to help to win the war. Noting the work of the American woman for the war effort, one of the leaders of the Woman Suffrage League stated, "The Women of our State are devoting most of their energies on the Red Cross, army relief and work of various kinds in our camps. While this is not suffrage, it goes to strengthen our cause."

But even with this change of global conditions and with the United States now firmly entrenched in World War I, those Silent Sentinels did not quit their posts before the White House. Perhaps what most infuriated Wilson were those signs the stoic women held. While he was engaged in a World War to liberate all of Europe, while he was setting in motion the "War to end all Wars," these stubborn women held signs for everyone to see, signs that read, "Mr. president [sic], how long must women wait for liberty?" With each passing day, these signs became more pointed, calling the President a "hypocrite" and asking how he could battle for liberty abroad when women at home did not even have the right to vote. Some who passed these determined women now became angry, assaulting them, verbally abusing them, yelling, threatening. Just as the picketers themselves, the police did nothing. No attempt was made by anyone to stop or even soften their abuse.

An order went out. From whom? By whom? To this day exactly who gave the order is not clear, but if it was not directly given by the President, at least it was given with his complicit agreement. The Silent Sentinels were arrested for "obstructing traffic." That should show them. After a few hours in the police station, the charges were dropped. But the Silent Sentinels had not "learned their lesson." They went right back to picketing. Then they went to prison, at first for only a few days; then upon their return to their pickets after their release, their prison terms grew longer.

Hoping to put an end to this picketing once and for all, Alice Paul was tried and sentenced to seven months in jail. She spent the first two weeks in solitary confinement, with only bread and water,

Alice Paul, Suffragist Tortured Under the Wilson Presidency

after which she was taken to the prison hospital because she was too weak to walk alone. There she began a hunger strike, one which her followers also began. "It was the strongest weapon left with which to continue...our battle...."

The prison doctors transferred her to a psychiatric ward at the Occoquan Workhouse, and three times a day forced a tube down her throat and forced food into her stomach. They also threatened to place her in an insane asylum, but

still she wouldn't eat.

In all, Miss Paul served three prison terms in the US. During her imprisonment in the District of Columbia Jail in October 1917, weakened by her hunger strike, she was taken by stretcher to the prison hospital. There she was held incommunicado: no attorney, no member of her family, no friend was allowed to see her. Prison officials threatened her with transfer to the jail's psychopathic ward and St. Elizabeth's Hospital, the Government's institution for the insane, if she did not break her hunger strike. When she refused, she was taken by stretcher to a cell in the prison's psychopathic ward and treated like a mental patient. At night, she could not sleep for more than a few minutes at a time because an electric light was aimed at her face once every hour all through the night.

Hundreds of other women were also arrested, most sentenced to the Occoquan Workhouse in Virginia, while a few went to the District of Columbia Jail. Conditions at the Occoquan Workhouse were atrocious, with filth everywhere, worms in food, blankets washed only once a year, and open toilets that the prisoners could not flush. Several diaries still exist, describing the treatment of these women for their crime of silently standing before the White House, carrying signs: "No woman there will ever forget the shock and the hot resentment that rushed over her when she was told to undress before the entire company. We silenced our impulse to resist this indignity, which grew more poignant as each woman nakedly walked across the great vacant space to the doorless shower!" The sanitary conditions were vile. "The water they (the suffragists) drink is kept in an open pail, from which it is ladled into a drinking cup. The prisoners frequently dip the drinking cup directly into the pail. The same piece of soap is used for every prisoner. As the prisoners in Occoquan are sometimes afflicted with disease, this practice is appallingly negligent." Then came the night of November 15, 1917:

> Under orders from W. H. Whittaker, superintendent of the Occoquan Workhouse, as many as forty guards with clubs went on a rampage, brutalizing thirty-three jailed suffragists. They beat Lucy Burns, chained her hands to the cell bars above her head, and left her there for the night. They hurled Dora Lewis into a dark cell, smashed her head against an iron bed, and knocked her out cold. Her cellmate Alice Cosu, who believed Mrs. Lewis to be dead, suffered a heart attack. According to affidavits, other women were grabbed, dragged, beaten, choked, slammed, pinched, twisted, and kicked.

These wretched, tortured women, jailed in filthy and barbarous conditions, made their point. Wilson decided to begin to work not with Alice Paul and her group, but with the earlier suffragists, who were more willing to cooperate with the President instead of picketing the White House. Seeing that the nation needed women to do the work that American soldiers had left behind, Woodrow Wilson appointed the President of the NAWSA, Dr. Anna Howard Shaw, to a new position. Shaw had fought for woman suffrage for decades and was friends with both Rebecca and her sister, Mary. Now by order of the President of the United States, she became the National President of the Woman's Committee Council of National Defense. The purpose of this council was to oversee and coordinate the war activities of the nation's various women's clubs. They helped people plant, harvest, and preserve vegetable gardens, provided care packages for soldiers, chaperoned dances and parties for the military, found families willing to give a soldier a good home-cooked meal, looked after the health of children, provided libraries and reading material for those in the military, and knitted warm clothing for those going "over there."

At the age of eighty-two, and in spite of her original opposition to the War, Rebecca became part of Herbert Hoover's campaign to oversee and promote food production. In her position, she found herself putting into effect many of the ideas she had been promoting in her journal articles for decades: the diversification of crops, including the introduction of more grains; more and better food preserving and canning; and the teaching and development of women's so-called "kitchen gardens," long one of Rebecca's crusades. She realized that women were taking part in the war effort in every way that they could, and that this participation was making them prouder and more independent than they had been when they were confined to the duties of the house.

Women also demonstrated the benefits of mechanization in both time and labor. Female members of the Atlanta Equal Suffrage Party talked the ruling Democrats of the day into participating in a plowing contest in Atlanta. Governor Hugh M. Dorsey and Mayor Asa G. Candler (both ardent anti-suffragists) plowed with mules, while the women used tractors – and won handily. Many Georgia women now drove tractors – and often automobiles and ambulances. One woman who owned a huge estate and was considering employing women to do the farm work, asked how many men she would also be required to hire "to dig, plough and do all the hard work." She was told that the women did everything, all of the work. To that the worried woman replied, "But how about their corsets?" And to her astonishment came the response, "They don't wear any." Rebecca Latimer Felton had lived through an era when women, herself included, wore corsets laced so tightly that sometimes they fainted. And now she had come to a time when women wore no corsets at all so that the heavy work (once men's work only) could be more quickly and easily done.

Posters sprang up everywhere depicting women and the war. Pictures of women, often draped in flags were depicted working outside the home, with such mottos as: "Remember the Girl behind the Man behind the Gun;" and "Oh, Boy, that's the girl," (a woman providing food for soldiers); "Sow the seeds of Victory," (a woman dressed in a flag planting seeds); "Our boys need sox – knit your bit." There were pictures of women working in offices, as nurses, as telephone operators, in factories, even pictures of women in a Winchester factory making Browning machine guns.

At least one poster depicted a smiling woman holding a military rifle. The caption read, "If you want to fight, join the Marines." In fact, the Washington War Department didn't want any woman admitted into the military, although in 1901 and 1908 a few women had already been admitted into the Army and Navy Nurse Corps. As America joined in the battle of World War I, the War Department threw out miles of red tape and bureaucracy limiting or preventing women from joining the armed forces. The Army became so entangled in bureaucracy, it ceased to seek the enlistment of women. But the Navy and Marines and even the tiny Coast Guard ignored the War Department's red tape and did enlist women into its ranks, nearly 13,000 of them. Many of these women wore a uniform blouse with insignia; some even had the same status as men. Even the Army found ways to use women in their cause, especially as nurses, but also in the Signal Corp, and as Reconstruction Aids (providing occupational and physical therapy). American women could be found on troop ships, trains, and throughout most of the Allied countries of Europe. Countless thousands of American women honorably served the military cause both at home and abroad. Approximately thirty thousand American women, either directly in the military or associated with it, made significant contributions to the war effort. Some received the Distinguished Service Cross (the second highest military honor); others the Distinguished Service Medal (the highest non-combatant service award); while others serving in France received the distinguished French Croix de Guerre. Many were wounded – and some were killed, still buried somewhere in Europe.

Many newspapers in Georgia and throughout the nation echoed the sentiments of the Columbus, Georgia *Enquirer Sun* when it said, "The Women of the country have done most noble work; they are still doing it. This very fact is going to

WWI Poster Recruiting Women

give them such a hold upon the consideration of the men of the country that the latter will not think of withholding from them the ballot...." Before and during World War I, Rebecca spoke everywhere she was invited. Supposedly, she was to receive a fee, but a good fee for one of Rebecca's speeches was often not more than $25.00, and organizations often paid only her expenses. Still Rebecca continued her crusades, warming almost instantly to a crowd who had come to see and hear her. She was becoming famous in Georgia. And with women so involved in war work, serving in nearly every capacity, except for actually fighting, the idea of woman suffrage that Rebecca espoused did not seem unreasonable.

Yet everything changed when the war ended (officially on November 11, 1918) for those women who had served their country so admirably. In spite of ardent lobbying by women's organizations, especially the YWCA, educational groups, and even the Army itself, which wanted a woman's corps similar to Britain's WAAC units (where 80,000 British women had served), the War Department, which had never wanted all those women in the first place, officially discharged them. The possibility of a woman becoming an official part of the U.S. military would be closed for another twenty-three years.

On September 1918, a man made a speech before the United States Senate, which included these words:

> Are we alone to ask and take the utmost that our women can give, service and sacrifice of every kind, and still say we do not see what title that gives them to stand by our sides in the guidance of the affairs of their nations and ours? We have made partners of the women in this war; shall we admit them only to a partnership of suffering and sacrifice and toil and not to a partnership of privilege and right?

That speaker was the same man who may have sent those Silent Sentinels to be brutalized at the Occoquan Workhouse, the President of the United States, Woodrow Wilson. The time had come for woman suffrage, whether he approved of it or not. He was, after all, first and last a politician. With his pronouncement the process of the passage of the Nineteenth Amendment was begun in earnest. The ratification by the United States Congress was overwhelming, except for the Georgia delegation, which had before this period unanimously rejected any congressional proposal to grant woman suffrage. This time, U.S. Representative William D. Upshaw and Senator William J. Harris, both representing Georgia, voted for the amendment, with the rest of Georgia's congressional representation rejecting it. In June, 1919 what many now referred to as "The Susan B. Anthony Amendment," as Alice Paul had named it, was submitted to the states for ratification.

Chapter Fifteen

The Susan B. Anthony Amendment, Race, and Georgia

Now it was time for the states to ratify the Nineteenth Amendment. Knowing the state legislators' staunch opposition to woman suffrage in Georgia, the suffragists for that state hoped that the proposal would be delayed – that for at least some period of time the Georgia legislators would table their decision on woman suffrage. But the Georgia legislators had another idea. By the first of July nine states had ratified the Susan B. Anthony Amendment; none had rejected the proposal. Some Georgia legislators then decided, "Why not be the first to reject it?" Several others agreed with this idea. On July 7, 1919 U.S. Representative from Georgia, J. B. Jackson, recommended that the Anthony resolution be amended to read "rejects" instead of "ratifies" this Constitutional Amendment. "Thus a favorable report on the resolution, as amended, would be a report against ratification." There were many impassioned speeches for and against this action. One of the most eloquent came from Mrs. J. K. Ottley, representing the executive committee of the National Democratic Party. She pleaded, "Don't make Georgia the first state to reject the amendment. If you do the time will most certainly come when you will be

ashamed of your action." Rebecca Felton also tried to convince
her fellow Georgians and their legislators that this rejection of the
Nineteenth Amendment was wrong, to no avail.

In fact, most of the Georgia legislators wanted to be the
first state to reject the Nineteenth Amendment and thereby counter
the states that had already ratified the Woman Suffrage Constitutional Amendment by huge majorities. In spite of fierce lobbying
efforts on the part of the anti-suffragists, thirty-three states had
ratified the Amendment by the end of July 1920, with three more
added to the plus column in early August.

Wrangling, speeches, proposals for postponements, filibus-
tering, nearly everything but fistfights ensued for days in both the
Georgia State House and Senate. In the midst of the fray and making this inflammatory situation even worse, President Wilson sent
a telegram to Governor Hugh M. Dorsey asking that Georgia ratify
the amendment because it was, according to Wilson, "essential to
the fortunes of the Democratic Party." This unfortunate telegram
turned the Susan B. Anthony Amendment into a States' rights issue with more speeches and even greater fury on all sides.

Technically, the issue never came to a full vote in Georgia
since the House made a resolution that the Senate did not pass, and
the Senate made a different resolution that the House rejected. Yet
since both had overwhelmingly refused to pass any proposal to
amend the Constitution to permit woman suffrage, Georgia became
the first state in the nation to reject the Susan B. Anthony Amendment. But most other states did not follow Georgia's lead. The
thirty-sixth state, Tennessee, broke ranks with the anti-suffrage
South and ratified the proposed resolution in August 1920. A
southern state had cast the deciding vote making the Susan B. Anthony Amendment the Nineteenth Amendment of the United States
Constitution. Only a few days later the Nineteenth Amendment
became the law of the land.

In Columbus, where the cause of woman suffrage had begun in Georgia so many decades ago, suffragists requested that on
a certain day and time, all the mills, the churches and factories
blow their whistles and ring their bells in support of those gallant
Columbus suffragists, the first in Georgia, and women everywhere

who now had the right to vote. At the appointed time everyone waited expectantly.... There was total silence within the entire town. Not even one small whistle peeped in celebration. After the passage of the suffrage amendment, one Georgia politician lamented, "Next we will be giving our dogs the right to vote."

In spite of the generally cold reception of this Anthony Amendment in Georgia, suffragists throughout the state were ecstatic. Mary McLendon noted that this amendment had finally done what Georgia had failed so many times to do by state amendment. She said, "Thank God, the nineteenth Federal Amendment has knocked this foolishness higher than a kite...."

There was so much to do between the end of August when the amendment became law and November, when women would for the first time cast their votes in the national election, helping to decide who would become the nation's next President. The women suffrage societies, such as the Georgia Woman Suffrage Association now turned themselves into organizations that helped women to understand the voting process and learn about the qualifications of the candidates. In other words the GWSA and other such organizations gave birth to the League of Women Voters in the South.

But for the Antis all was still not lost. Bureaucratic changes had to be made in order to enable women to vote; they had to be registered, judged fit to vote; the polls must be readied (although no one seemed to know why); there was so little time before the election in November. No! It was impossible. Georgia women would just not be able to vote in the 1920 national election. The State was simply not prepared. With only two exceptions, all of the other states in the Union were ready and able to have women register and vote in the 1920 election. Georgia women were once again denied the ballot – for technical reasons, of course – as were the women of Mississippi, the only two states to deny the ballot to women in 1920.

One of the reasons that Georgia was so opposed to woman suffrage was the fact that ratifying the Nineteenth Amendment meant granting the vote to all women – even black women. What

would that mean to politics and control in the South? Most people
shuddered at the thought. For many southerners it was one thing to
permit upper-class white woman to vote, and quite another to grant

Making the Polls Attractive to the Antis

suffrage at the same time to black women. This problem found its
roots in slavery and had become even graver in the South with the
Civil War and Reconstruction.   Although there are no accurate
population figures immediately following the civil war, the popula-

tion in Georgia in 1860 consisted of 591,550 whites and 465,698 blacks. By the end of the War, considering the number of white Georgian soldiers killed, the number of blacks and whites in Georgia may have been nearly even. In most places it was against the law to teach a slave to read or write. Following the War nearly half of Georgia's population was freed from slavery – blacks who were illiterate, who had little or no technical skills, and usually no money or significant property or belongings. Furthermore, black men were then enfranchised by the federal government, while many white men who had supported the War were at the same time disenfranchised. The South had been turned upside-down.

After the Civil War no one knew what to expect. Would there be black insurrections? Riots? An overthrow of all that the South held dear? The fear of white southerners was palpable as theories, conjectures, and rumors multiplied almost exponentially, fanned by local newspapers. At the close of the Civil War Georgia was an occupied land, controlled by the Yankee now, who was intent, in the words of famed historian W. J. Cash, "to make over the South in the prevailing American image and to sweep it into the main current of the nation. To that end, he set himself to destroy the Southern world." For Georgian whites the Civil War resulted in an end to slavery (the mainstay of the plantation), the destruction of land and property, and the loss of economic, social and environmental control. And to the Yankee, the best way to continue to deny control to the defeated white Southern male was to give that control to the black man, in spite of his lack of preparation, or perhaps even because of it.

The election of unqualified blacks during Reconstruction and the blatant buying and manipulation of black votes by political rings, which lasted for decades, enraged many white people. Instead of trying to rid the state of white political corruption, they began to try to think about ways to abolish the black vote entirely – to disenfranchise them. But southern white men had to disenfranchise blacks in a way that would not alarm the Federal government. After all, denying a black his right to vote was against Federal law, violated a Constitutional Amendment, and brought back issues that were supposed to have been settled during the Civil

War. Although fear, intimidation, and special voting rules designed to make blacks ineligible to vote were frequently employed
in the late 1800s in the South, it was not until 1908, under the leadership of Governor Hoke Smith, that Georgia actually passed the
Disenfranchisement Act, which was similar to laws passed in various other southern states.

Although this Act did not mention race per se, its rules effectively ended black voting in Georgia. And even if a black person proved that he had served honorably in a war, that he could
read (the Constitutions of the state or nation) and that he owned
property assessed at five hundred dollars for taxation and had paid
all taxes since 1877 (as specified by the Disenfranchisement Act),
his white judges were required to assess "his character," and if they
found him lacking, he was denied the vote in spite of his qualifications. A primary election law, also of 1908, assured in addition
that no one could vote in primaries unless he qualified to vote in
the election. It also decided that the political party (and in Georgia
there was really only the Democratic Party) could make its own
rules and decide who would vote in the elections. Again as in the
Disenfranchisement Act, there was no mention of race in the law,
although both laws were designed specifically to disenfranchise the
black voter. These acts in effect served to nullify the Fourteenth
and the Fifteenth Amendments in Georgia.

Now the Susan B. Anthony Amendment, a name that struck
no joy in most Georgian hearts, would give the vote to all women,
of all races. Nearly everyone knew that if the Federal government
took a close look at these two Georgia laws, they would quickly
discern their true intent and have them declared unconstitutional.
Most historians agree that two themes dominate the rhetoric of the
Antis in Georgia: a feeling of terror that if women were allowed to
vote, it would lead to society's downfall; and the belief that woman
suffrage could result in a return of dominance in Georgia by the
Federal government, ultimately leading once again to the horrors
of Reconstruction.

As few people of the times did, Rebecca Latimer Felton
knew and understood these concerns. She had, after all, begun her
life on a large, rich Georgia plantation with slaves to serve her

every need. She had also been a slaveholder herself. She was a woman of her times. It would be impossible to maintain that she began her life believing in the equality of the races. However, she plunged on in her cause for the passage of the Susan B. Anthony Amendment and all that it implied. Yet the history of Rebecca Latimer Felton has a strange twist in it regarding the issue of race, causing some historians and others to believe that she was one of the worst of Georgia's racists. It all happened not because of her suffrage cause, but because of a speech she made at Tybee Island, off the coast of Georgia in 1897 – a speech that haunted her all of her life and taints her memory today.

Rebecca had lived through a time when her state was in ruins, when her plantation was practically destroyed, and when many young Georgian soldiers either lost their lives upon the killing fields or came home so physically disabled that they could not contribute to rebuilding. Furthermore, although the former slaves were now physically free, most had nothing with which to sustain themselves. It was a scary time for black and white.

As slaves, blacks were valued as expensive property, costing $500 or much more to their white masters. Burning or lynching them was almost unthinkable. With the abolition of slavery, with the Yankees giving blacks new powers, they lost their value to their former masters, becoming instead objects and symbols of the loss of the War and of a way of life. The need to lash out, to "show Negroes their place," to express the growing hatred and resentment directed against blacks soon led to acts of white violence – lynching, burning, and brutality designed to convince former slaves that their freedom was but an illusion.

The exaggerated and often illogical fear and dread of "the Negro" centered upon the concept of the fate of the white woman, symbol of southern refinement, tradition, the centerpiece of chivalry. What if "the worst" happened to her? What if she were raped – by a black man? This fear gripped the South. While the rape of a woman by a black man did occasionally occur, it was not at all common – about as rare as being struck by lightning. Yet men and women talked of it constantly, feared it out of all proportion, whipped up by lurid newspaper accounts of a helpless white

woman at the mercy of a savage, evil black. Some historians have
called this phenomenon the "Southerner rape complex." It extended even to the possibility of the willing commingling of white
women with black men – and perhaps to their marriage (all of
which somehow in the Southern white mind violated and degraded
all white women, society, and the whole South). "Thus, interracial
rape (of a white by a black) was judged a crime against all whites
for which all blacks were guilty. The actual violation of women
became, in a social and political context, secondary to the symbolic
meaning of the act. Allegations were as damaging as evidence,
and in many cases, the white man's fantasy substituted for fact."

Southern white women, believing the rampant stories and
newspaper accounts of brutal rapes by black men upon innocent
white women, became caught up in this rape hysteria, and in a
sense became unwitting accomplices in black lynching and sup-
pression. In part because of this rape hysteria, most white women,
particularly in the South, refused to recognize "racial oppression,
even though it was similar to discrimination that in many ways
held them [women] to an inferior status." In a sense this myth of
black men running wild and raping white woman kept both the female sex and the black race "in their place." As one historian of
this period has remarked, "It is even more ironic that 'white womanhood' was an excuse for racial violence in the postwar South.
White women became symbols to the defeated Rebels; they were
the unsullied, alabaster icons of Confederate myth-makers." This
myth kept women carefully locked behind the traditions of southern chivalry, who guarded their purity and especially their chastity;
it ignored black women; and furthermore it demonized the black
man. This myth was enlarged and elaborated by the press, owned
and controlled by white men. Most southerners apparently ignored
the irony of rampant misogyny before and after the Civil War – sex
between a white man and a black woman – even unwilling sex –
that was somehow different. But sex between a white woman and
a black man, willing or not, seemed in the southern mind to violate
all the offspring of Georgia, all of white womankind, and could
not, must not be condoned or permitted.

Southerners were especially concerned about the farm woman, isolated, often alone – who would protect her? Must the farmer move his family into the city for their protection? Would the "ravenous Negro" destroy the family farm in agricultural Georgia? Southern men and women of the time talked about black rape, worked themselves up and spread the terror through rumor, innuendo, false accusations, exaggerations, and inaccurate newspaper and magazine accounts. Nearly everyone in Georgia became caught up in this Southern rape complex. There is evidence that even Rebecca Latimer Felton, at least for a time, believed the stories and newspaper accounts of rampant black rape of white women.

Everyone knew that law and order under Reconstruction had been a sham. And nearly everyone knew that the courts still could not be trusted. By 1897 Rebecca had certainly had enough court experience to mistrust Georgia's legal system. William and Rebecca had themselves known several brushes with shady justice in the state, not to mention the virtually unpunished murder of their friend Alston. Their legal experiences were not unusual. As historian W. J. Cash points out:

> For ten years the courts of the South were in such hands that no loyal white man could hope to find justice in them as against any Negro or any white creature of the Yankee policy; for twenty years and longer they continued, in many quarters, to be in such hands that such justice was at least doubtful. Hence the traditional inclination to direct action found here the same justification it had found in the case of mob violence – the justification of necessity.

Generally in newspaper accounts of lynching at the time, the name of the black person is not given; instead, he is called "the black brute," the "wanton, murderous monster," the "evil black beast." No human characteristics are given. Furthermore, it is assumed by all that he is without doubt entirely guilty on all counts; he is cast in the role of monster; the victim is always helpless and totally innocent; and lurid details of the lynching, mutilation, and castration are printed. After all, if blacks were wantonly raping white women, if all of those gory, bloody stories of black violation against innocent womanhood – growing more lurid and numerous with the telling – were true, what should the people of Georgia do to avenge these heinous acts? Violence, that was the answer...and not simply causing the perpetrator to disappear in the middle of the night. Many Georgians believed that violence that could be seen and talked about by all – and printed in the newspaper – was the answer, public violence designed to teach a lesson, to show what happens to black rapists of white women: Lynching! Castration! Burning! All committed at a time and place where everyone could see.

Given the rape hysteria of the time, any wrongdoing by black men could be and was construed by white men as sexually motivated. At all costs the white southern woman must be protected. White Southern men justified their violence against the black man as a defense of the white woman, even if the alleged sins of the black victim had nothing to do with rape. Control of the black man by the white man, that was what really counted. Both black disenfranchisement and lynching served as ways for the white man to regain the upper hand. Black men and, in a sense, white women became the victims and pawns of this logic.

In most cases lynchings were held in a carnival atmosphere in public areas. Women and children sometimes witnessed the brutalities, as well as men. Hundreds (at least once, thousands) watched as some black man was stripped naked, brutally tortured, castrated, burned, and usually hanged. The lynchers generally were not masked or in any way concealed, but stood with their heads uncovered in spite of the fact that everyone there could have been a potential witness. The lynchers were often neighbors, friends of those who watched and cheered them on. Almost no one considered it a crime, or even briefly entertained the thought that the lynching was illegal or the person being lynched might be innocent. The black victim was automatically guilty, without benefit of lawyer, court, clergy, or words on his behalf. His life was taken in the most brutal manner, his remains often kept as souvenirs of the event, and his lynchers, instead of being brought to justice, were often praised for their fine work – all done in the name of protecting white women from the "ravenous beast."

In many respects the black scare was not unlike the red scare of the McCarthy era in America during the 1950s. It fed upon itself, strengthened by many voices and few facts, fanned by exciting and inciting newspaper accounts. But many Americans who once agreed with Joseph McCarthy could later turn away from his wild accusations in disgust when the truth came out, and not be further accused of McCarthyism, leaving ruined reputations, but not deaths in their wake.

In the midst of this rape hysteria in 1897 Rebecca gave a speech to the Agricultural Society's Convention at Tybee Island. She spoke about women's rights, the need for more educational opportunities, and touched on the subject of the violation of white women by black men. In this speech, she claimed that blacks who raped were usually uneducated and drunk at the time (providing an example of the need for her crusades for temperance and education). Then she stated that the whites who lynched them were also uneducated and were depraved. She castigated the Democratic political machine that lured blacks to vote for them, providing them with false friendship at election time, then scorned and reviled them after the election. She believed that this treatment was another reason for blacks to turn to rape and crime in revenge. She called for reform within the Democratic Party. She asked for the church to help uplift morality. She asked the courts to become more concerned with justice. If these and other reforms were made, and if temperance and education prevailed, then, according to Rebecca, black crime – indeed all crime – would greatly diminish.

Almost immediately the *Atlanta Journal* printed a front-page article stating that Rebecca Latimer Felton favored lynching. It was entitled, "'Lynch,' says Mrs. Felton: She Makes a Sensational Speech Before the Agricultural Society at Tybee." The article was quickly picked up by the *Boston Evening Transcript*. This northern paper attacked race relations in Georgia and Rebecca Latimer Felton in particular. Other newspapers soon joined in, representing the North and the South. All claimed that Rebecca had said that in order to stop the rape of white women the "ravening beasts" should be "lynched a thousand times a week if necessary."

Because Rebecca saved nearly everything, most items now housed within the confines of the University of Georgia, it is easy to confirm or deny her alleged statement that black men should be "lynched a thousand times a week if necessary" to defend a woman's honor. A careful search of her Tybee Island speech reveals no such statement. LeeAnn Whites, in her highly critical article of Rebecca's racism also could not locate the damning phrase. She says, "I cite the newspaper version of this speech because the various handwritten versions of the speech in her papers do not include the notorious sentence that made the speech so incendiary." She overlooks the possibility that the newspapers had distorted and inflamed her words.

Rebecca was horrified and angry at the *Atlanta's Constitution's* alleged misquotes and misinterpretation of her speech, which had by now been picked up by other northern papers. She wrote a letter expressing her outrage to the Atlanta newspaper's editor. It appeared (not on the front page as did the first article, but on page four) as an item entitled, "Mrs. Felton Not for Lynching: Her 'Ifs' Were Overlooked – Answers *The Boston Transcript.*" But the damage was done. To her dismay, many Georgians who favored lynching wrote congratulatory letters to her welcoming her to Georgia's true right wing. Many others even believed that the "ravaging beasts" that Rebecca supposedly cited in her speech referred to all black men, not just guilty black rapists. Even her biographer, John E. Talmadge, furthered the belief that Rebecca Latimer Felton was an extreme racist. Not only that, he claimed that she had a "strange antagonism towards all men." A close examination of her writings reveals the falsehood of both statements.

More than twenty years later Rebecca wrote about a Georgia judicial case involving a white man who raped a black woman in her home and in front of her children. He was let out on bond and received a sentence of one year on the chain gang. She then remarked that "It goes without saying that a crime of that sort committed by a negro on a white woman would have been finished by daylight, by Judge Lynch, and the negro would have been only 'charred remains.'" She claimed that "juries are pussyfooting" and shielding white crime against blacks. As for bringing the lynchers to justice, she said that "as a rule, the county officers cannot discern a lyncher. There is no such animal when he gets in sight or halting distance."

Rebecca in this article refers to that Tybee Island speech. It is clear that she believed that she had denounced lynching as a means to obtain justice then as she was doing now, and in both cases excoriating the system that permitted it. She said of that Tybee Island speech, "I warned the farmers that mob law would wreck law and order, so long as our politicians hugged the negro voter with one arm and slung a lynch-torch in the other...That speech went like fire in dead grass all over the United States. I was pictured as a fiend – all over the northern states – but nearly every man who listened to me rose to his feet and shouted for me at Tybee." When one reads her later statements about that Tybee Island speech, it is clear that she believed that her audience was cheering her demands for social progress, particularly court reform, not lynching. Essentially, in 1920 she was saying the same thing she had said at Tybee Island: "Painful it is to me that I now say to you, in all truth and soberness, that our courts will not deal out justice, that our judges pussyfoot around these lynching atrocities, that our county officials cannot be depended on to arrest criminals and stand by the truth and the facts in this case."

But Rebecca's "Lynch 1000 times a week" quotation taken out of context continued to haunt her, branding her as an extreme racist. Even in 1999 Mary A. Hess in her Master's thesis, describes Rebecca as a woman who helped "foster ... racial hostility" in the nation, which therefore, "negates her importance as an icon of women's history...." Hess makes no mention of all that Rebecca did to attempt to further black education and opportunity in Georgia. Nor does she write about the Feltons dangerous and continued opposition to the nearly all-black chain gang.

Rebecca's words at Tybee Island, and their later misquotations in newspapers caused great distress in another state. On August 18, 1898, about one year following the Tybee Island address, a young editor of the Wilmington, NC newspaper, *The Daily Re-*

cord, the state's only black daily, wrote a thoughtful editorial regarding Rebecca's Tybee Island speech. Although his reactions are based upon the lurid statements about her speech taken from the *The Boston Transcript* and other newspapers, and in spite of the fact that he appears to have known nothing of her crusades, particularly to end the Georgia chain-gang system, his editorial was far from incendiary. In fact, he agreed with Rebecca on many points, particularly regarding the need for better education for both poor blacks and whites. He states, "If the papers and speakers of the other race would condemn the commission of crime because it is a crime and not try to make it appear that the negroes were the only criminals, they would find their strongest allies in the intelligent negroes themselves, and together the whites and blacks would root the evil out of both races." Then he continues, "Every negro lynched is called a 'big burly, black brute,' when in fact many of those who have thus been dealt with had white men for their fathers, and were not only not 'black' and 'burly,' but were sufficiently attractive for white girls of culture and refinement to fall in love with them as is well known."

That did it! Alex Manly, a black (who could pass for white), had dared to insult a prominent white woman, Rebecca Latimer Felton, along with poor white women, or perhaps even all of white womanhood. The newspapers roared, claiming that white women had been slandered. Wilmington's black homes, black businesses, black churches were burned or damaged, and between eight and eleven blacks were killed and countless other blacks wounded. As for Alex Manley, his publishing establishment was wrecked and burned, and he escaped, later to be banished forever from the town. All of this was committed by whites on blacks. But the newspapers saw the incident differently: The Raleigh, NC *News and Observer's* headlines read: "A DAY OF BLOOD AT WILMINGTON Negroes Precipitate Conflict by Firing on the Whites – Manly, the Defamer of White Womanhood, Escapes – Building of His Slanderous Paper Gutted and Burned." The Wilmington, NC *Morning Star's* headlines were just as lurid and false: "BLOODY CONFLICT WITH NEGROES. White Men Forced to Take Up Arms for the Preservation of Law and Order."

"BLACKS PROVOKE TROUBLE. Negro Newspaper Plant Destroyed – The Whites Fired Upon by Negroes – The Firing Returned – The Killed and Wounded – State Guard Out – Many Exciting Incidents."

Just as Rebecca had claimed to have been misquoted and misunderstood regarding her views on lynching, Manly now stated that his words had also been distorted by the press. According to Manly, "Flaming mutilations of this article were published all through the South, and I was charged with slandering the virtue of white women. Such a thought never entered my head." Both had been used and misquoted, thereby inflaming their positions by the press.

Six days following the Wilmington affair, Rebecca, after reading the white accounts of this incident in the newspapers, wrote a signed letter to the press. She stated then:

> With due respect to Southern politics, I say that when you take the negro into your embraces on election day to control his vote and use liquor to befuddle his understanding and make him believe he is a man and your brother, when you honey-snuggle him at the polls and make him familiar with dirty tricks in politics, so long will lynchings prevail, because the cause will grow and increase with every election when there is not enough religion in the pulpit to organize a crusade against this sin, nor justice in the court-house to promptly punish the crime, nor manhood enough in the nation to put a sheltering arm about innocence and virtue.

> If it requires lynching to protect woman's dearest possession from ravening, drunken human beasts, then I say lynch a thousand negroes a week, if it is necessary. It is the unwritten law in Georgia that the black fiend who destroys a white woman in her home or on the highway, and is identified with proof positive, must die without clergy, judge, or jury. I know that tens of thousands of honorable colored men and women in Georgia will approve the verdict.

There it was, proof that Rebecca herself had gotten caught up in the "Southerner rape Complex" and made deeply racist comments, even advocating lynching under certain circumstances. But why did she keep harping about politics with regard to black rape? A closer examination of the results of the Wilmington incident may provide the answer.

Before the 1898 violence, Wilmington had been a good place for blacks to live, with a small but active group of black professionals, entrepreneurs and craftsmen. When the economic depression of 1893 put many white workers into financial difficulty, resentment grew against the approximately 150 middle-class blacks. At this time the normally Republican blacks had joined forces with the white Populists and were briefly in political control of the town. The ousted Democrats formed rallies and clubs that supported white supremacy. Then they began to insist, fueled by the white press, that blacks threatened the innocence of the white women of Wilmington. Although this story is much longer and more convoluted than this brief summary allows, during the "Race Riot," a white mob surrounded city hall. The Democrats, guns at hand, forcefully declared themselves the replacements of those then in power. According to Margaret M. Mulrooney, Ph.D., and scholar in this area, "This event may be the only coup d'état in the United States." Because of Alex Manly and the "rioting negroes," the so called "Fusionist Party" (made up mostly of Republican blacks and white Populists) was broken up. And supposedly in the name of their "fair womanhood," the Democrats took over their town's government with guns – by force. Similar wild stories of abuse to Georgia's white women circulated by the white, nearly totally Democratic press. Although there were no real coup d'états of town governments in Georgia, it is clear that both blacks and white women were used as pawns.

In reality the ideas of Alex Manly and Rebecca Felton were not greatly dissimilar in many areas regarding race and the society of the times, in spite of the scare tactics and incendiary words of the press. Rebecca was formidable, and she could be obnoxious, opinionated, stubborn, and rarely inclined to admit that she may have misspoken, or even that she had used words that could easily have been misconstrued, facts which sometimes got her into trouble regarding the race issue in Georgia. But she was also deeply intelligent, willing to change her mind, and above all, compassionate. It is no wonder that regarding the issue of race, Rebecca would sometimes appear to champion both sides. Yet a careful examination of her papers leads to a fascinating clarity in this complicated woman living in such turbulent times. Her philosophy was simple: everyone needs a fair shake, a fair chance to do what he wants in life: that was her creed, and the basis behind most of her actions.

She worked actively with black suffragists, African-American communities, and even some of the most radical northern suffragists to promote temperance, suffragist causes, and education. Just as she had espoused the need for more and better technical education for young cotton mill women, she stressed the importance of stronger technical education for blacks. In spite of her Tybee Island speech, she later vehemently denounced lynching in many speeches and articles. Many blacks praised her stances on race. For example a black American Legion Post Historian wrote to her saying:

> Dear Madam:
> This morning I went to a news stand in Philadelphia and bought the Atlanta Constitution for Tuesday, January 13th. I turned to the editorial page and to my surprise I found one of the strongest articles that I have read from the pen of any writer under capitation of "Crime of Violence Unpunished in Georgia," written by you.
>
> I want to congratulate you, Mrs. Felton, upon your womanly stand that you have taken in defense of the race to which I hold identity.

Her later stances promoting black education and standing firmly against lynching won strong praise from many prominent blacks, including Henry M. Turner, Bishop of the African Methodist Episcopal Church, Albion W. Holsey of the Tuskegee Institute, and Benjamin J. Davis, editor of the black newspaper, the *Atlanta Independent*.

Of course, she also fought. She countered the idea espoused by S. P. Richardson and many pastors of the time that blacks were the true descendents of Ham, who, according to the Bible, moved to Africa and was cursed by his father Noah for seeing him naked. The progeny of Ham was considered by some to be innately inferior, doomed to become slaves forever. Rebecca denounced this interpretation of the Bible. Bishop Turner and other blacks supported her stance. Rebecca believed that no race was marked for servitude, certainly not according to the New Testament.

Her words in 1898, even if unjustified or misunderstood, were spoken in a time and place of terror in the South, even if that terror was not based upon fact. There is no doubt that this fear of black rape was exaggerated all out of proportion by the press, and that it served the interests of the Democrats and others in control at the time. Looking at Rebecca's record, it is difficult to accuse her of extreme racism when she fought so valiantly for reforms and the ultimate end of the chain-gang system in Georgia, when nearly all (in 1886, 90%) of the prisoners she fought for were black. That crusade was fierce, bitter, and often dangerous. Yet for more than thirty-five years (the Georgia chain-gang system did not end until 1911), she continued her crusade to end the chain gang, or at the very least to provide for more humane working and living conditions for prisoners and to separate men from women on the gangs, and to keep children away from this barbaric system. For all those decades she put herself on the line, facing enormous and powerful political opposition, witnessing the results of her fellow crusader's attempt to end the system: Robert Alston, murdered in the state capitol for his exposure of the atrocities of the chain gang. She worked diligently with both blacks and whites for prison reform and for temperance.

She also fought for better opportunities for blacks and more and better education. She consulted prominent people on the race issue in the South, even Isabella Beecher Hooker, a Yankee from Connecticut who became one of the most ardent suffragists of the United States, who had also been, like Rebecca, a member of the Columbian Exposition. They began their correspondence in 1891. Hooker welcomed Felton's letters, encouraged her thoughts – and they discussed race and education for poor blacks and whites. And Rebecca's later articles denouncing the atrocity of lynching are many and famous. But perhaps Rebecca explains her ideas best on the very first page (in the "Preface") of her long treatise on Georgia politics, *My Memoirs of Georgia Politics,* when she says:

> The "Solid South," really meant antagonism to negroism. It was skillfully forked to perpetuate in office many of the men who urged on the war, and who now fanned this war prejudice into fury, for political success, regardless of progress or financial development.

> We could not obtain clear vision on either side of Mason and Dixon's line. The Northern politicians worked in a similar way to produce the same political effect – on fanatical negropolists.

> Demagogues in both the great parties discovered a rare opportunity and snatched it. The negro was the popular subject worked **ad nauseam.** At the North they professed false friendship for him. In the South they perpetually lambasted him, because it was popular to do so. Tens of thousands of Southern men had no other political platform, except "I'm a Democrat, because my daddy was a Democrat, and I'm g'wine to vote agin the nigger!"

> As a result Congress soon filled up with small men with large ambitions.

Her book, *My Memoirs of Georgia Politics,* is filled with defenses and positive statements of the southern black race. She cites incidents of unfair black trials (58-59). She says, "I do not attempt to tell you what evil results will, in my opinion, flow from this crusade against the colored race, and the honest Republicans in Georgia...." (380, and argument continued on 381). In 1875 she praised the only black then serving in the United States Senate as a man who refused to sell his vote to anyone, not "Jay Gould or Huntington, or the Real Estate Pool of Washington City, or the Whiskey Ring, or the Seneca Sandstone Co, or the Ship Subsidy or any other scheme that was pushed through Congress by the 'infernal force of gold!'" He was, according to Rebecca, not merely a credit to his race, but a credit to the Senate(164). Much later she states in her book:

> When this promising leader [Ben Hill] dares to charge me with trying to "Africanize the State," because I claim for every man, white

and colored, the right to vote a free ticket and to have that vote
counted – because I claim the right of every child to a plain English education at the expense of the State and federal governments
– because I claim protection for the poor wretched creatures who
are by the multitude being pushed into the convict camps of the
senator's political allies – the people will begin to understand the
true inwardness of Bourbon supremacy in Georgia. I hope every
poor man, white or colored – the mechanic, the day laborer, the
men of sweat and toil, may hear this political autocrat as he cracks
his lash over my back because I dared to become their humble
friend and advocate! (414-415)

The study of race relations in Georgia following the Civil War to
the present would take several volumes, and Rebecca's part in this
difficult period, a book in itself. She had an opinion on other important lynchings, race riots, and how to make Georgia better and
never hesitated to express herself. What is important to remember
in Rebecca's case is that *My Memoirs of Georgia Politics* was
written in 1911, and that unlike many people who, as they grow
older, become more conservative in their thinking, Rebecca grew
more liberal with each passing year. There can be no doubt that
Rebecca vehemently opposed lynching in her later speeches and
writing. Nor is there doubt that she was taking aim at the ineffec-
tiveness of Georgia's courts, education, and religious and social
mores in her Tybee Island speech. A good case could be made that
Rebecca, while sharing some of the race prejudices of her contem-
poraries in the South, was, in fact, well ahead of her time – a
woman who supported better education for blacks, more progressive churches, equal justice under the law, and a "fair shake for
everyone" as she was so fond of saying.

Chapter Sixteen

Georgia's Blues

Many people have cited the lowest period in Georgia's history as occurring during the Civil War – and/or the period of Reconstruction when Georgia was a vanquished land held in bondage by Carpetbaggers and Scalawags. While there is good reason to agree with this assessment, one could also argue that the lowest period of Georgia's history actually occurred in 1920. Even Rebecca, who had gone through so much sorrow and destruction during and after the Civil War, might have agreed that 1920, if not marking the lowest point in Georgia history, certainly came close. Rebecca watched helplessly as the boll weevil destroyed field after field of cotton on her 600-acre farm; as the KKK continued its lynchings and terror tactics against those it deemed to have stepped out of their place in society; as the economy of Georgia continued to drop; and as the population (both black and white) continued to leave in droves in search of better working and social conditions.

In that year the state of Georgia caught the eye of an urbane, witty, sarcastic and highly popular writer/journalist who lived at 1524 Hollins Street, Baltimore, Maryland. His name was H. L. Mencken. When he fist met Mencken, Alistair Cooke described him as having light blue eyes. He was "a small man so short in the thighs that when he stood up he seemed smaller than when he was sitting down. He had a plum pudding of a body and a square head stuck on it with no intervening neck. His brown hair was parted exactly in the middle, and the two cowlicks touched his eyebrows." He loved his large row house where he had lived since the age of two. It was probably in that home that he put the finishing touches on a work that he would soon publish. Mencken was a man who loved to stir things up, spark controversy, and criticize. His greatest talent may have been provoking others, and his new book would soon result in more mayhem than even he intended.

Mencken was a gifted, opinionated, bulldog of a man, age forty, nearly at the peak of his considerable fame, and his new work was entitled, *Prejudices: Second Series*. His most controversial chapter was not located at the beginning of this series, but rather buried in the middle. Even the chapter title was designed to infuriate. Deliberately misspelling and deforming his words, he wrote "Bozart" for the term, "beaux arts." He then entitled his chapter (one of the most-read, most-disputed, most-infuriating nineteen pages he would ever write), "The Sahara of the Bozart." It is easy to imagine Mencken leaning back in his chair, placing his hands behind his head and looking again with great satisfaction at his title and thinking: Yes, what better way to describe the South in 1920 than this?

From the title to the last paragraph, Mencken, with the deliberateness of a toreador or a determined general, prepared his attack. Speaking of the South in general, he said, "Down there a poet is now almost as rare as an oboe-player, a dry-point etcher or a metaphysician. It is, indeed, amazing to contemplate so vast a vacuity." He describes the South as a "stupendous region of fat farms, shoddy cities and paralyzed cerebrums." Then, again in that first paragraph, Mencken, always the journalist, states his thesis: "And yet, for all its size and all its wealth and all the 'progress' it babbles of, it is almost as sterile, artistically, intellectually, culturally, as the Sahara Desert. There are single acres in Europe that house more first-rate men than all the states south of the Potomac...."

Almost nothing in the South escaped his sweeping, scathing pen. Mencken made his stance quite clear: "In all that gargantuan paradise of the fourth-rate there is not a single picture gallery worth going into, or a single orchestra capable of playing the nine symphonies of Beethoven, or a single opera-house, or a single theater devoted to decent plays, or a single public monument (built since the war) that is worth looking at, or a single workshop devoted to the making of beautiful things." For Mencken, the South was totally devoid of artists, composers, historians, architects, scientists – there was not even a decent southern theologian, philosopher, or sociologist. As for writers, with the possible exception of James Branch Cabell, "you will not find a single southern prose writer who can actually write." And, according to Mencken, no southern poet could rise "above the rank of a neighborhood rhymester."

Yet while Mencken lumped the entire South into a vast ocean of mediocrity, he was gentler with some states than others. Virginia, for example, was saved from his most savage remarks. He reserved another state for his most virulent jabs: Georgia. "There the liberated lower orders of whites have borrowed the worst commercial bounderism of the Yankee and superimposed it upon a culture that, at bottom, is but little removed from savagery. Georgia is at once the home of the cotton-mill sweater and the most noisy and vapid sort of chamber of commerce, of the Methodist parson turned Savonarola and of the lynching bee." Referring to Georgia, Mencken further declares, "There is a state with more than half the area of Italy and more population than either Denmark or Norway, and yet in thirty years it has not produced a single idea." In Mencken's opinion, "Virginia is the best of the south to-day, and Georgia is perhaps the worst. The one is simply senile; the other is crass, gross, vulgar and obnoxious. Between lies a vast plain of mediocrity, stupidity, lethargy, almost of dead silence."

Mencken's book, and especially his chapter, "The Sahara of the Bozart," caused a sensation throughout the nation, encouraging arguments between the North and South, fights, and southern fury. Mencken, who was called all sorts of names and epithets, including being a damned Yankee, mild-manneredly corrected his would-be abusers, saying that after all, he, too, was a southerner –

a southerner from Baltimore. It was not so much the perception that Mencken was telling lies that so infuriated the South regarding Mencken's chapter, but that nagging thought, like a persistent little tickle in one's throat that just wouldn't go away, that maybe he was right. Although no one in the South would actually admit it...there was this fear, the sickening ongoing feeling about that chapter Mencken had written about the South. After all, to everyone's dismay, at first no southerner had read it. It took Georgia two years to even notice Mencken's publication. Even then, Mencken's accusations were seldom denied. Instead of refuting Mencken's assertions, many Southern journalists resorted to attacking Mencken. Wightman F. Melton of the *Atlanta Georgian* provides a typical journalistic example: "Personally, I should rather be a hill-billy [sic] of the Bible Belt than to have been born with a silver spoon in my mouth, and that spoon filled with galvanized gall."

Whether Mencken was correct or not in his depiction of Georgia in 1920, the fact remained that the state's economy, based mostly upon cotton, was collapsing. The damage the boll weevil had done in Georgia was staggering. Cotton was measured in 500-pound bales. In 1879 Georgia produced 2,794,295 bales of cotton, second only to Texas in cotton production in the entire nation. By 1918 production had dropped to 2,122,000. It would continue its decline well into the 1920s – 1920, 1,415,000; 1921, 787,000; 1922, 715,000; and 1923, 588,000.

Instead of Cotton, His Sack is Filled With Boll Weevils

By 1920 "Ma Rainey,"a black woman born

and raised in Columbus, Georgia, who became a famous jazz singer, created a song about that old boll weevil, that blacks sang often, and even some whites. It was called the "Bo-weevil Blues:"

> Hey, hey, bo-weevil, don't sing them blues no more
> Hey, hey bo-weevil, don't sing them blues no more
> Bo-weevils here, bo-weevils everywhere you go.
>
> I'm a lone bo-weevil, been out a great long time
> I'm a lone bo-weevil, been out a great long time
> I'm gonna sing these blues to ease the bo-weevil's lonesome mind.

But except for singing about it, there was little that anyone could do. Farmers, including Rebecca Felton, watched helplessly as the boll weevil relentlessly invaded field after field. Some farmers then turned to other crops – tobacco, livestock, peanuts – while others simply abandoned their farms and left. And why not leave?

FOR THE SUNNY SOUTH.
AN AIRSHIP WITH A "JIM CROW" TRAILER.

"An Airship with a 'Jim Crow' Trailer"

Why not go north where there were more jobs, more money, more promise – or to southern cities where there were jobs and money, too. That's what many Georgian farmers did, both black and white, some 375,000 of them between 1920 and 1925. In 1923 alone 100,000 farmers packed their bags and left their Georgia farms forever.

It is not difficult to imagine the fears of many Georgians in 1920, and not just of that little cotton bug. The KKK was perhaps even worse, often luring prominent citizens into its ranks.— policemen, clergymen. It had become popular and respectable. In many police stations in Georgia a scenario such as the following often occurred. A large black woman, let's call her Tillie, is sweeping out the station, softly humming to herself. As she approaches the desk of the chief of police, she grows quiet, taking on a more serious air. He ignores her. He is busy reading the paper, the *Enquirer-Sun.* His badge glistens softly in the fading early evening light. Quickly, she passes him, then finishes up and prepares to leave. He eyes her quietly as he turns the page, watching as she puts the broom in the back room and starts for the door. They exchange brief, friendly "'byes" as she closes the door behind her. He is alone now. He waits a few minutes, still looking at the paper, then puts his paper down, gets up and goes to the door, locks it, and returns to his desk. Seated again, he takes out a key from his pocket and unlocks the upper left-hand drawer and removes a pamphlet containing the by-laws and principles of the club he has joined. Many eminent Columbus citizens also belong…a great many. In 1920 there are between four and five hundred members of this particular club in Columbus alone. In fact, it is probably the most popular club in the entire town. Its meetings are held in the armory – right above the police station where he is sitting. They call themselves the Alaga Club.

Like many other organizations, the Alaga Club has secrets and elaborate rituals, even secret meetings. Its officers take on strange names, such as Klaliff, Kludd, Klokard, Kligrapp, and Klokan. And, of course, there are secret passwords—Akia, Kigy, Ayak, Sanbog—and a special secret saying that nobody really understands: "Non silba, sed anthar." There is also a "klecktoken," an initiation fee of $10.00, a considerable amount in a state whose per capita annual income in 1920 is only $244. But that "kleckto-ken" bought its members excitement, night rides, idealism, violence, and of course, those picnics in the park.

Qualifications for membership in this organization were quite specific: Jews, Catholics, "Negroes," anyone with a foreign appearance or foreign born need not apply. The membership of this club was reserved exclusively for whites, native-born Protestants. And then, of course, there was its symbol...its famous, infamous, terrifying symbol: the burning cross. In short, the organization that called itself the Alaga Club in Columbus was really the KKK, part of the Invisible Empire, one of a great many such clubs in Georgia in 1920 and in fact, all over the nation.

It is now evening at that police station in Columbus, Georgia. The Police Chief goes to the back room, where Tillie has put her broom, opens a storage closet and takes out a box, carefully hidden behind some other boxes. He sets the box on his desk, opens it and smiles contentedly at the contents within. Then he takes out the long white robe, brushes it gently with his hands, and puts it over his police uniform. He adjusts it, making certain that nothing but the robe itself shows. Then he puts on that hood, smoothing the front down over his face, adjusting the eye holes. He turns and goes to the gun rack and removes a shot gun. He does not leave by the front door. His replacement will be coming into that front door any minute now. No, the back door is preferable for such an occasion. He steps quietly out into the warm, still evening, then ghost-like vanishes into the shadows.

Rebecca Felton was eighty-five in 1920. She had seen many positive changes within the state that H. L. Mencken had disparaged with such relish: many prison reforms, including the end of that wretched chain gang; improvements in public education, for both blacks and whites; the strengthening of the University of Georgia; the passage of the Eighteenth Amendment to the Constitution in 1919, which prohibited the making, selling, or transporting of intoxicating liquors – thereby (supposedly) making the entire United States dry. She had helped to make these changes.

In 1919 something else happened for which Rebecca was very proud. She had been advocating the admittance of women to the University of Georgia since 1897. It became one of her major crusades, claiming that young women were as intelligent as young men and needed as much education – for the sake of the women as well as their offspring. Both she and her husband supported the University of Georgia throughout their lives, fighting for less state political intervention, better teachers, and more books. One can only imagine her joy when in 1919 the Board of Trustees at the University of Georgia passed a resolution admitting women to the College of Agriculture and Mechanic Arts as well as to the Peabody School of Education.

Only two years earlier she had helped to lobby the state legislature to turn Georgia Normal and Industrial Institute in Milledgeville into Georgia State College for Women. Rebecca had always advocated that the school not only have academic education for women, but technical training as well. And in spite of Candler's anti-woman bias, Eleanore Raoul became the first woman graduate of Emory's Law School in 1920. Then came the passage of the Susan B. Anthony Amendment. Although her state had not permitted her to vote in 1920, she knew that with that Constitutional Amendment, it was only a matter of time. In 1921 the women of Georgia did vote, along with the women of the rest of the nation.

Of course, Bishop Warren Aiken Candler had fought against woman suffrage right up to the passage of the amendment, and even after. He helped to withdraw financial support from any organization that supported woman suffrage, particularly the Georgia WCTU. He wrote anti-suffrage letters to others who shared his views throughout the nation, urging the rejection of this amendment; he fought Rebecca at every turn on this issue; he even helped those in Mississippi to postpone woman suffrage until after the Presidential election of 1920 – as he had done in Georgia. He believed that women would turn militant in what he deemed to be their fanaticism. He proclaimed that people would see "Howling mobs of women in a struggle to secure the ballot go through the streets of the metropolis of the greatest nation of the earth, smashing windows and Ten Commandments with equal recklessness."

And now the worst had happened for Candler, and women had the vote. At least he still had his wife, Nettie, his faithful, obedient wife who had been at his side throughout everything, who had even helped him in the cause of anti-suffrage. At least there was one sensible woman left in this land who would not vote if her husband forbid her. But there were some things that even Bishop Warren Candler did not know about his loving and usually dutiful wife. In spite of her husband's firm commands that she must never vote, Nettie Candler sneaked out of the house with one of her lady friends and went to the polls and voted. Perhaps the end of the world had truly come for Bishop Candler. His long-term companion, his wife and helpmate, his faithful Nettie had voted, and not only that, she sometimes smoked – Quebec cigarettes. The Victorian laces on ladies' corsets had lost some of their constraint even in the parlors of Georgia's Methodist Bishops.

Both Rebecca and her sister Mary McLendon had made several trips to Washington to represent the suffragists' point of view when that topic was debated before Congress. After making their pleas, both went to New York in 1917 where Rebecca celebrated her eighty-second Birthday. They were also in Washington when the Nineteenth Amendment passed the Congress. Joyful, excited, and not wishing their trip to end, they went again to New York where they saw Staten Island and the many troop and hospital ships. She later wrote of her visit, describing her wonder at riding the double-decker buses in New York City and the modern elevated train system. She concluded that Mary and she had had so much fun they behaved like "two school girls on a vacation." At the time Rebecca was eighty-four, and her sister was seventy-nine.

Energy, action, justice, compassion – these four words seem best to describe the activities and purpose of Rebecca Latimer Felton. Instead of becoming weaker and less influential, she seemed to grow stronger with each passing year. In 1918 she began to study the Alien-Sedition Bill, which required less free speech and more government control over the people, because of

the War. She wrote an eloquent letter to Senator Thomas Hardwick from Georgia, denouncing the bill, saying that it would give
the President too much control, that it would choke independent
thinking or differences of opinion, halting free speech. Hardwick
had her letter read to the Senate.

She worked with many prominent people to rid her state of
lynching and involuntary servitude. She continued to believe that
crackdowns on the courts that tended to be soft on lynchers, or
overlook the entire situation, were the best way to rid the state of
this curse. She also worked with many others to end the system of
peonage, involuntary servitude for minor infractions. This time
her allies were the United States District Attorney for North Georgia, Hooper Alexander, and the Governor himself, Hugh M. Dorsey.

Following Warren G. Harding's election, Rebecca was selected to be on the Woman's Advisory Committee of the State
Democratic Committee of Georgia. President Harding invited a
few prominent people from all parts of the nation to meet and con-
fer with him in St. Augustine, Florida. Nicknamed "the brains of
the nation" by the press, this group had only one woman and only
one person from the South: one and the same, Rebecca Latimer
Felton. Harding later complimented the octogenarian for her advice and inspiration. At about the same time she became good
friends with William Jennings Bryan.

Although she had many good friends, both male and female, her friendships with novelists, Corra Harris and Margaret
Mitchell, seem to be particularly unusual because Rebecca appears
to have many of the characteristics of two of these novelists' fictional heroines. Both Corra Harris and Rebecca Felton were intelligent, well-read, and complicated women from Bartow County in
north Georgia – and both were prominent writers. Curiously, both
had married men considerably older than they, and both of their
husbands were Methodist ministers.

The differences between these two women were also significant. Corra was unhappily married to a man who believed
much more in hell-fire, perdition, and damnation than God's love,
and who committed suicide in 1910. Corra did not approve of fe-

male politicians such as Rebecca. While Corra did not believe that men were more intelligent than women, she tended to be a much more introspective homebody than Rebecca. In theory, Corra supported the suffragist cause, but often her actions and even her own writings appear to contradict her supposed beliefs.

Harris authored more than twenty-five books, her most famous being the semi-autobiographical *A Circuit Rider's Wife.* She also wrote the novel, *Co-Citizens,* whose heroine seems to be based upon Rebecca. The plot deals with a woman suffragist and political activist, married to a sentimental old politician whom she can (and does) dominate. Reviews for *Co-Citizens* were mixed, some seeing it as supporting suffrage, while others saw anti-suffrage sentiment within its pages. Apparently Rebecca supported the book, not objecting to the fact that neither she nor her husband had been shown in positive roles. She supported her friend and took the whole novel as a fictional satire. Her biographer John Talmadge harshly criticized Rebecca for not correcting the unflattering portrait that Corra Harris had painted of the protagonist's husband in her book.

However, Rebecca was Corra's friend. The book was a novel – fiction, and the way that Corra earned her living, having been left a widow without much inheritance. Furthermore, *Co-Citizens* was published in 1915, six years after William's death. Rebecca had already commended her husband, given speeches that lauded him, and written a book of nearly seven hundred pages (*My Memoirs of Georgia Politics)* that praised, explained, and defended her husband's every action – not to mention the memorial to him that she erected in his honor in Cartersville. In addition, the Harris book had not sold well and was little noticed. If she had raised a furor over any possible similarities between the Feltons and the co-citizens of the book, her denunciations could have backfired, resulting not only in the loss of a friendship that was important to her, but also in more publicity and sales of the book.

Rebecca's other friend who was also a woman novelist portrayed her in a much different manner than the nagging suffragist of the Harris novel. Although Rebecca is not the protagonist of the famous Scarlett O'Hara, several incidents in Rebecca's life have striking similarities to those in *Gone with the Wind*. Both women lost nearly everything in the Civil War, but their homes, while nearly ruined, were not burned. Both hid their silver in the well, remarked about the chimneys darkened with soot pointing the way back home, had saved Confederate money which was now without value, had brushes with typhoid, and refugeed for a time in central Georgia. Both saved money carefully, kept accounts, vowed never to be hungry or poor again, and became extraordinarily shrewd businesswomen in a man's world. While both women knew terrible defeats, both got up to fight again – and again – seeming to become stronger with each defeat. Both were called names, gossiped about and accused of "unsexing" themselves. As stated earlier, both Rebecca and Scarlett had no material for new dresses that they needed. Rebecca tore down her curtains, dyed them, and made a dress for an important meeting. Scarlett did the same, except that she did not dye the material.

Having led such a long and colorful life, it is not surprising that Rebecca, or at least certain prototypes of her or parts of her life might appear in literature. How could she possibly have known that the most exciting part of her life was yet to come? She was already so busy. In addition to managing her 600 acre farm, she still did all of her own housekeeping, served on several boards, corresponded with just about every woman's organization in the country, bred and purchased horses, and gave countless speeches across the state – not to mention her newspaper work, which included regular columns in two newspapers plus many more articles in other newspapers on important issues of the day. Even Presidents had consulted her on serious topics. And when she wasn't doing all of that, she was fighting the tax collector, always agitating for less, local, state, and federal taxation. She abhorred government spending (she believed it to be squandering) of poor people's money. In fact, in many of her tax returns, she complained bitterly that her tax bills were far too high. For example, in a tax return sent on March 19, 1918, she stated, "I am an aged widow – trying to manage my farm lands, which are excessively taxed at #20 per acre – in Bartow Co – on worn out lands – and a large amount, not cultivated at all – as [illegible] as poorly cultivated farms. – I will reach my 83rd year in [illegible] 1918 - if I live to that period." Paying taxes was always one of Rebecca's greatest concerns and angers. Although she was a wealthy woman, she hated paying her hard-earned money to politicians, and then watching the taxpayers' money spent on boondoggles and corruption. It seemed to her that paying taxes, crusading for reform, writing, tending that farm, giving speeches, and visiting with friends would be all that she would do for the rest of her life. Then something totally unexpected happened in the life of this courageous and cantankerous old reluctant taxpayer, something that she had never even considered.

It all started with sorrow – the death of one of her dear friends, Senator Tom Watson. They had known each other for decades, worked together, disagreed, fought, and somewhere in between their politicking, they became friends, good friends. Watson's wife, Georgia Watson, also liked the feisty old lady. They exchanged letters, visited each other, and the Watsons praised Rebecca's honesty and courage in her newspaper articles. He gave her good advice, and she did the same for him. She even visited the Watsons in Washington for two weeks when he was Senator. No one dared say a word against Rebecca Felton in Tom Watson's presence. He even referred to her as "my dear old mother-in-law." But it was apparent that Watson was not well. Then on September 26, 1922 Senator Watson died at the age of sixty-six of a cerebral hemorrhage. Rebecca recounted what happened only a few days later:

I was in my home in Cartersville, and the telephone rang.

I answered it.

Thus far the incident was routine and commonplace, but soon after I took down the receiver I realized that it was a day I always would remember, and I noted that the date was October 3. The voice at the other end was speaking for Governor Thomas W. Hardwick. The Governor wanted to know whether I would accept an interim appointment as United States Senator.

I said I would. I added that I was grateful for the honor.

The conversation was over, and I was left to ponder the significance of it.

It meant that a woman reared in the sheltered security of an antebellum plantation was to be the first of her sex to sit in the United States Senate. It was hard to realize. I thought back through the years and decades, and remembered the first time a woman had lifted her voice in public at our little country church in my girlhood. What a stir that had caused! Who in that day would have had the hardihood to predict that the time would come when Georgia women would hold public office?

Almost immediately letters and telegrams started pouring into Rebecca's Cartersville farm. Some were reserved and dignified, such as the telegram from Alice Paul, who had been imprisoned and tortured for her suffrage beliefs, and was now vice-president of the National Woman's Party. She said, "Georgia has honored herself in being the first state to appoint a woman to represent her in the Senate of the United States, and especially in the appointment of one who has given herself as you consistently have in the cause of woman's advancement. Women, throughout the world will learn of your appointment with the deepest pleasure as a recognition of the new position of women and the new political importance of women as voters."

Others, even some prominent men and women, were less restrained in the expression of their delight at Rebecca's appointment. For example, Lucien Lamar Knight, State Historian and Director of Georgia's Department of Archives and History, stated in a letter to Rebecca, "Hurrah! I feel like hanging my hat on the horne of the moon. The first woman in the history of our government to wear the toga of the American House of Peers! What a distinction for Georgia to hand down to future generations and what a halo of honor for your own brow."

There was more to the story, of course. How many backhall conferences and smoky rooms filled with white men in earnest discussion no one knows. Apparently, there were even groups of politicians congregating here and there in the train cars coming back from Watson's funeral – the discussion was always the same.

Who should replace him? No one even knows exactly who first thought of the idea. What is certain, however, is that the motives of those in power might not have been entirely pure – that honoring Rebecca Felton, and thereby all of womankind, may not have been the motive for this choice. And what is absolutely certain is that everyone who had a hand in that decision had seriously underestimated the determination of the eighty-seven year-old woman they had just appointed.

In the first place, Rebecca Felton was not the Governor's first choice. He first asked Tom Watson's widow, Georgia, to fill the Senatorial seat left vacant by her late husband. She gave her poor health as the reason to turn down the offer. It was only after her refusal that Hardwick asked a friend to phone Rebecca with the same offer. But one must wonder why Governor Hardwick, an ardent-anti-suffragist would ever appoint any woman to serve for even one minute as a Senator of the United States. One of the answers to that question came the following day, October 4, 1922 when Governor Hardwick formally appointed Rebecca to fill the seat left vacant by Tom Watson. At the same time that he appointed her, he announced his intention to become a candidate for Watson's position in the United States Senate. He was, at the time of Watson's death, a lame-duck governor, having been badly beaten in his second gubernatorial election by Clifford Walker. Having already served in the Senate, Hardwick intended to run again for that Senate seat in the fall primary.

The *New York Times* and other newspapers noted sarcastically that the Felton appointment might serve Hardwick's purposes quite well. If he placed one of the able men of Georgia in that position, he might find himself facing a strong contender, and an incumbent at that, in the primary. Certainly, Rebecca was too old to run for Senator, and besides, in all likelihood no one in Georgia would vote for a woman Senator in any event. Now that there were women voters in Georgia, giving them a bone by honoring a woman wouldn't hurt. And Rebecca had actively supported Hardwick in his run for governor of the state. She wouldn't really do anything but accept a little plaque and give a little speech at Cartersville. She liked Georgia Watson, and was not offended in the least that this widow had been Hardwick's first pick. In addition, it wasn't as if she would really be a Senator and go to Washington. That was out of the question. In fact, appointing Rebecca Felton interim Senator seemed to help Hardwick on two counts. It would give him less serious competition for the Senate seat, and it just might send a few more women's votes his way.

Hardwick's appointment was just a token, an honor bestowed upon a very old woman – possibly for his personal political reasons – but definitely meant to be a local affair. Even the newspapers noted that her actually serving in the Senate was unlikely and her going to Washington quite doubtful. Most newspapers echoed the words of the *Indianapolis News* when it said, "Whether Mrs. Felton will actually have an opportunity to qualify and sit in the senate is doubtful, as her successor will have been elected before the expected special session of the congress in November." She was to be commissioned as Junior Senator of Georgia on October 7 at the Cartersville Courthouse. The ceremony was open to the public. Would anyone come? Or would it be like all those bells and factory whistles in Columbus, Georgia, stone silent instead of pealing in celebration at the passage of the Susan B. Anthony Amendment?

In addition, there was a pouring, drenching rain in Cartersville on the day of October 7. Governor Hardwick would present the commission personally. Rebecca was fearful that no one else would come, especially because it was chilly and dark, with rain sometimes blowing sideways with the wind. At least she was fairly certain the Governor would be there. Head down, she slowly climbed the steps and entered the courthouse…where hundreds of people joyfully waited for her. In spite of the bitter storm outside, the entire town had come to help her celebrate her honor. There were cheers, speeches, ancient friends and new, all smiling, all joyful at her entrance, all waiting for this old lady who had fought so long – so hard – so determinedly for the betterment of Georgia. Even the media, some from other states, had come. As Rebecca later wrote of that day and the following week, "The newsreel and newspaper photographers moved in like an invading army. Telegrams, letters and phone calls began to come from all over the United States, particularly from women's organizations."

There were many speeches. Corra Harris expressed her approval of the honor and distinction that had come to Rebecca Felton and felt certain that other Georgians shared her feelings. Governor Hardwick also gave a speech. When he presented Rebecca with her commission, he said, "She is splendidly fitted to adorn the highest public station in the land for she wields the gifted pen of a cogent and forceful writer, and has all the qualities of heart and head that equip one for broad and constructive statesmanship. She is wise even beyond her years, and is glorious in the sunset of a splendid and useful life."

Accepting her commission, she made a short speech. She said, "The biggest part of this brief Senatorial appointment lies in the recognition of women in the government of their country." She stated that the rest of her life would be short, and that such an honor really belonged to the women of the nation. "I am happy over it chiefly because it means, as far as I can see, that there are now no limitations upon the ambitions of women. They can be elected or appointed to any offices in the land. The word 'sex' had been obliterated entirely from the Constitution." She tried to continue, but tears welled up in her aged brown eyes and ran down the wrinkles in her cheeks. As her voice broke, it was replaced by a spontaneous ovation, sweeping the room, with people clapping, cheering and practically embracing this old lady who stood before them with head bowed and shoulders shaking. Finally she raised her tear-stained face to the crowd and said, "God has been wonderfully kind to me. The credit is all His."

Willie Snow Ethridge was in that Cartersville Courthouse the day that Rebecca became a Senator of the United States. He was working on an article about Rebecca for *Good Housekeeping,* entitled "Lady from Georgia," which would appear in its January, 1923 edition. In this article he wrote:

> There were other speeches – but I failed to hear them. Sitting near the door with the rain pattering outside, my mind became filled with the romance and novelty of the occasion. There before me

was an old lady, nearing her century mark, an achievement in itself, who had just received the highest honor ever tendered a
woman in the United States. Without one move on her part, the
senatorial toga had been placed upon her in the sunset of her life,
after she had spent more than sixty years fighting for the cause of
women and above all for the cause of mothers.

That should have been the end of it. Certainly Governor Hardwick
believed that it was. Perhaps even Rebecca that night believed that
there would be no more to this story. But the letters and telegrams
kept pouring in, congratulating her, praising her, and saying that
she represented women everywhere. She heard from prominent
and simple, humble people alike – all saying that somehow she
represented them. It was almost like those old days in Washington
when her husband was in Congress. Then she opened her door to
everyone, rich or poor – she believed she represented her state, especially Georgia's women. And now...and now as first woman
Senator of the United States, perhaps the women she symbolized,
she represented, deserved more than a simple ceremony in Cartersville, Georgia. Perhaps it wasn't all over now...it was only just
beginning.

Chapter Seventeen

From Cartersville to Washington?

Governor Hardwick had been correct to assume that Rebecca would support him in his run for Tom Watson's seat in the Senate. The gallant old lady Senator often stumped for her friend, Hardwick, supporting his senatorial election in every way she could. Writing to the people of her county regarding Hardwick, she said, "He has honored me, a citizen of Bartow County, by naming me U. S. Senator to succeed Hon. Thos. E. Watson. In paying me this great honor, he honors the people of Bartow County, and I ask the people of our county, and especially the ladies of the county, to honor him with their vote and support."

Although Rebecca's advice and support had helped Hardwick considerably in winning the governorship, he was defeated in the Senate race by a judge, who had once been a justice of the State Supreme Court, Walter George, of Vienna, Georgia. As Historian Josephine Floyd concluded, with the election of George as Senator on November 7, Felton's appointment legally became an "empty honor." She had done nothing but remain in Cartersville because the Senate was not in session, and now Georgia had a newly elected Senator. She would no longer be needed, especially not in Washington. When Hardwick had announced Rebecca's appointment, he emphasized that she could never actually serve in Congress and expressed his feelings of regret in this matter. Now with George elected, it seemed hopeless. Rebecca would have to settle for the honor her home town had paid her.

Still, hundreds of letters from women arrived at Rebecca's Cartersville home from all over the nation, even after her little ceremony. Nearly all of these letters expressed the same thing. They wanted her to be sworn in like every other Senator, by the Vice-President of the United States, in the Senate, in a real and traditional ceremony. And Rebecca wanted this too, for herself, but more importantly for women everywhere. It was not a good start to have the first woman Senator of the United States take the oath of office in a little backwoods town in North Georgia…and have no senatorial duties at all. And all of those letters, those hopeful people…was there nothing more that she could do? She no longer had Hardwick's support for a real swearing-in, and in fact, she realized that she had never had it. She didn't have any real political support in Georgia or in Washington, except for all of those letters, arriving ceaselessly at her home.

It would all be over when George presented his credentials to the Senate in November. Then the headstrong, spirited young widow of General James A. Longstreet, Helen Longstreet, long-time friend of Rebecca, had an idea. Why not have a special seating in Washington for the nation's first woman Senator? George had not yet been officially certified. Technically, Rebecca was still the Junior Senator from Georgia. Maybe it was possible, if enough pressure were exerted, to obtain that special seating. Although it is not clear that Rebecca knew all about the plans, Helen Longstreet and her friends wrote women's organizations throughout the nation, who in turn flooded Warren G. Harding with letters requesting a special seating for Rebecca. Harding replied that the whole affair would be too costly. But as the *Washington Star* reported, those efforts resulted in even more determined actions by nearly every woman's organization in the country, resulting in a "merry political row." Every seated Senator received wires from these women's groups asking them to come to Washington at their own expense and use the money saved for that special session to seat

Rebecca Latimer Felton. The Senators either politely refused or plainly ignored the women's suggestion. After all, Harding had already refused the special session. The proposal was shelved...but not the idea...at least not among the women of the nation, of Rebecca being seated in the tradition of the other Senators.

Although it is not clear who first came up with the idea, another possibility was soon considered. During the next session of the Senate, what would happen if Walter George waited just one day to present his credentials? What if – while George waited – Rebecca presented her credentials and was officially sworn-in, taking the Oath of Office and her Washington Senate seat for just one day? Could such a thing happen? Was it possible – legal?

The first person to consult was George himself. Would he be willing to wait one day to take his oath of office while Rebecca was seated first? George said he would be willing to do that ... but. It is important to remember that George was a lawyer and had been a judge. He knew his Constitution. And he also knew that there were legal difficulties, which he proceeded to explain. George responded that waiting one day would violate the conditions of the Seventeenth Amendment, which specified that "the term of an appointed Senator ended the day his successor was elected." George believed that it would take a special bill, passed by both Houses of Congress to permit Rebecca to take her seat in the Senate – even for one day. And that possibility was at best highly remote, if not impossible, and would take much longer than the time Rebecca needed. When that bit of news reached the public, the letters started to dwindle, and the newspapers went on to other topics. In addition, with all of the stress and excitement, Rebecca caught a cold which seemed to get worse and worse, leaving her recuperating in a hospital in Atlanta.

It was over...but. Rebecca never seemed to understand the words "over, finished, ended." Not even at the age of eighty-seven with no hope and no ideas, and having landed in the hospital, she refused to quit. Lying in a hospital bed, Rebecca did again what she had always done best. She wrote a letter. On November 8, 1922 she wrote to her friend, President Harding. Again, she asked if there were any possible way that he could call a special earlier session of Congress during which she could truly represent women by taking the oath of office in the Senate. Without saying yes, Harding acceded to the old lady's request. He called for a special session of Congress to meet earlier, on November 20, never mentioning Rebecca Felton. The alleged reason he gave was to speed up some legislation that he wanted passed. One step closer. But there were so many other steps, including those undeniable, specific lines prominently featured in the Seventeenth Amendment of the Constitution about the legal admission of Senators. Yet there was no time to think of that – at least not for Rebecca.

Six days before Congress was to open its special session, Rebecca Felton got another step closer, and this time, it was not of her doing...well, not exactly. The brother-in-law of Rebecca's sister Mary McLendon announced that all the credentials for the certification of Walter George could not possibly be prepared in time for that November 20th session. In addition to being distantly related to Rebecca, S. G. McLendon was the Secretary of State in Georgia, and Rebecca's good friend. He had found a Georgia law that circumvented while at the same time upheld the Seventeenth Amendment. According to that law, as McLendon announced, George could not officially be "declared elected until the Governor, the Secretary of State, and the Comptroller General had canvassed his election returns. This had not been done, and Hardwick would not return from a trip to New York until next week." So if George were not certified as elected and Rebecca was in the Senate on opening day....

Rebecca got out of her hospital bed, went to Cartersville and started packing. She didn't ask anyone's permission to do so. It didn't matter to her that nearly everyone was still insisting that she probably would not be permitted to take the Oath of Office, or that she was sick, or that she had no one to accompany her. She was going to Washington.

Then Governor Hardwick, who had never intended Rebecca to do anything more than accept the little ceremony in Cartersville, and who may not really have changed his mind about woman suffrage (except out of political expediency) as he had so loudly proclaimed when he sought the women's vote, blocked her once again. On Wednesday, November 15, 1922, Hardwick sent a wire to McLendon ordering him to hold the election return canvass in his absence. Immediately, McLendon wired him back saying that he could not legally do so. Another wire shot back to McLendon telling him to have all the others certify George's right to become Georgia's next Senator, and that he could make it back to Atlanta on Saturday, November 18, and would sign the canvass in time for Walter George to catch the Saturday afternoon train to Washington. Hardwick was determined that George would be there, and certified at the opening session on Monday. Packed, ready, and entirely alone (her only living son Howard was recuperating from an operation), Rebecca caught the Friday train for Washington. Hardwick may have blocked the pass, but she wasn't down yet.

However, before she left, she had heard from one of the most significant players in this drama that was still unfolding. Now realizing that Rebecca wouldn't quit, the women of Georgia started to flood George with letters and pleas to let Rebecca present her credentials first. George was an affable young man. He didn't want to arouse the ire of half of his constituency even before he had taken office. And besides, he liked Rebecca and was sympathetic to her cause. On November 16, 1922, the Wednesday before the opening of the Senate the following Monday, George telephoned Rebecca. Essentially, he told her he was willing to let the Senate decide what to do. He would be there, of course, but he told her he would let her present her credentials first, without objection, if the Senate permitted it. That way, the Senate could decide the matter. This solution solved two problems for George. First, he would not be deemed responsible for preventing Rebecca from taking her seat. And second, the women of his state would be placated. There may have even been a third reason. George may have silently been rooting for the plucky old lady.

While Rebecca, still recovering from her illness, tried to make her train trip as comfortable as possible, the Senators of the nation were in a major uproar. There were small gatherings everywhere, with as many different opinions as to what to do about this old lady slowly approaching the Capitol as there were meetings. One can only imagine .... "But the Seventeenth Amendment clearly states..." "But doesn't she have the right to be sworn in within these hallowed halls?" "What about the women...they're voting for – or against – us now. And they want her sworn in properly." "We have the law and precedent to consider." "Is it legal?" "Someone should make a motion. If only one Senator makes a motion NOT to seat her, she can't be seated." "Not me!" More arguments, more disagreements, discussions everywhere, as Rebecca left her beloved state, listening to the clickety-clack of the train as it moved closer and closer to her confrontation.

Opposing Rebecca were the Harding Administration's Vice-President, Calvin Cooledge, and the Senate Rules Committee member, Charles Curtis, both of whom cited the Seventeenth Amendment, saying that she had no right to take a seat, even for one minute, in the Senate. Even the Senate Disbursing Officer got into the fray, declaring that he could not carry three Senators from the same state on the payroll. Most Republican Senators were against her seating. Yet although grumbling among themselves, they did not take a strong united stand against Rebecca, seeing no political advantage to alienating so many women voters who supported her. They wanted someone to do it, of course, but no one volunteered to overlook the women voters of his state and block her entrance into the Senate in order to take the oath of office.

And then, of course, there was Walter George himself. He was not firing objections to his period in the Senate being shortened by one day. In spite of the fact that he believed that legally and technically Rebecca should not be seated, he did nothing to stop or even slightly hinder her. He seemed to be watching this hullabaloo rather than leading it – just as he had told Rebecca he would. Rebecca later wrote, "Some of the Old Guard in the Senate didn't know just what to make of it – the notion of a woman entering those protected precincts...." Her observation may have been an understatement. Allegedly, in her handbag, she carried a Texas newspaper cartoon showing a very old lady peeking into a great room of frowning men. The cartoon's caption read, "Will the gentlemen offer the lady a seat?"

She arrived in Washington on Saturday. To her surprise, there was no one there to meet her. She proceeded alone to the Lafayette Hotel to unpack and get some rest before her appearance in the Senate. Like everyone else that Saturday evening, she had no idea what was going to happen. But she was unable to rest. The phone soon began to ring; reporters began to trickle into the lobby asking if they might be able to speak with Rebecca Latimer Felton. It turned out that everyone expected her to arrive on a later train. Ignoring her fatigue, she answered every phone call, invited everyone up to her room and became, in spite of her recent illness and train trip, the gracious hostess she had always been, posing for pictures, answering questions, laughing, and seeing what she could do to make everyone comfortable. Soon she had won over the Washington press, clearly admiring this very old lady who chuckled, sometimes called them children, and warned them that their pictures of her would not be pretty. Many ladies came up, apologizing for their mistake in train information and offering her a limousine ride for her trip to Congress on Monday morning.

Several women had become very worried and expressed their sincere concerns when they spoke with Rebecca. They suggested that perhaps it might be more prudent to give up the notion of actually being seated in the Senate. So many important people had, after all, said that the Seventeenth Amendment prohibited it, and that any Senator could stop her, and wouldn't that be so terribly embarrassing to Rebecca, to women watching, to women everywhere? Just being appointed Senator and taking the oath of office in Cartersville, Georgia, that should be enough in light of all of the opposition she could face in that Senate chamber. Rebecca would be able to avoid any embarrassment by simply making a showing and not asking for her seat...which, after all, really wasn't her seat.

The ladies made perfect sense. But they were talking to Rebecca Latimer Felton, who had been denounced in some of the finest churches in Georgia; who had been called a disgrace to womanhood...and so much worse; who had been the first woman ever to dare set foot in an election campaign; who was one of the first women to give a speech in Georgia, to speak in church, to own and run a newspaper, to fight her own legislature, to fight her own

church, to sue a railroad in court – and win, and to stump for temperance. It would be fair to say that Rebecca was not easily embarrassed and had never spent much of her time worrying.

Throughout her long life, Rebecca held to the following philosophy: "People grow old because they think too much about
themselves and their little troubles. ... I am eighty-seven, and expect to live much longer. What you can't help, put behind you.
Needless worry is the bane of American life – and almost all worry
is the needless kind." She wasn't worried, and no matter what
happened, she had no intention of worrying about it. Furthermore,
she hadn't come all this way just to be some quaint oddity and to
wave at bystanders.

Just in case she was refused her seat in the Senate she wrote
two speeches – one gracious, triumphant, speaking to the hearts of
women (and men) throughout the nation. And in the other, which
she probably wrote on Sunday, she scolded the Senate, was crisp
and sharp with many irate objections tersely presented to them
(and to the nation) for refusing her this one simple request. After
all, while she may not have been quite as knowledgeable about the
law as was Walter George, she did know that win or lose, having
been a Senator, she had the right to give a speech on the Senate
floor – no matter what! And she intended to do just that

She was the first Senator to arrive in front of the United
States Capitol building on Monday morning. She had carefully
placed both speeches in her handbag, ready for whatever was going to happen. Although she had always been a small, slender
woman, her eighty-seven years made her look tiny, frail, and her
curved shoulders belied the strength and determination that lay
within. She later said she wasn't afraid. "I don't know why they
expected me to have stage fright in Washington,' she laughed.'
"when I have appeared on the speakers' platform – and before
some of the most hostile audiences – for years and years. The little
fling I had in the Senate didn't scare me a bit." After she saw
some of the lame-duck senators she said, "I even told some of the
boys who were defeated the other day not to worry. One defeat
doesn't mean anything, I told them, if you made a fair honest fight.
I said: 'You must stand firm, – that's all. Don't lower your self-

respect and the tide will come your way again after a while.'" Was the tide coming in – or going out? She didn't bother to consider her chances, concentrating on climbing all of those Capitol steps.

One of the first people to greet her was Theodore Tiller, a correspondent for the Atlanta *Journal.* He told her that she might not have a chance to be sworn-in that day, that there was other business to attend to for the Senate, and besides, the Republicans wanted to hold their own meeting that afternoon regarding Rebecca's seating. She nodded, still heading straight for the Senate. She took off her coat and hat and handed them to a page who delivered them to the Democratic cloak room; then she was greeted by former Senator Hoke Smith. She entered the Senate chamber amid cheers from the gallery. Looking up, she saw throngs of women filling the gallery, all wearing the colors of their various organizations, all smiling and cheering for her. She waved and blew them a kiss. Hoke Smith escorted the old lady to a couch on the Democratic side of the Senate, and there she sat…quietly waiting. It was not until noon that the meeting was called to order, a prayer offered, and business begun. It was clear that her admission to this body was not the subject of the day. Feeling tired and hungry, she went down to the Senate restaurant for some lunch. Many Senators both before the Senate session and during lunch warmly greeted her and discussed old times. By the time she returned to the Senate, it had adjourned. Officially, they adjourned early by tradition out of respect to the passing of Tom Watson. She remembered also that, still not sure what to do with her, the Republicans would meet that afternoon to discuss her future. She had said and done nothing official that day. She retrieved her wraps and left.

Outside, on the Capitol steps, she posed for pictures, some of which still exist, showing a very small, old lady, dressed all in black, with her dress to the floor and wearing a coat and big hat, with a large pocketbook slung over her left forearm. A purse that contained two speeches and allegedly still contained a political newspaper cartoon asking if the grimacing, frowning men would give the lady a seat. She stood alone on those steps as the only woman Senator. What would happen next, no one knew, but few were optimistic about her chances for a seat within that august body.

Rebecca Latimer Felton

Chapter Eighteen

The Decision

What she didn't quite realize when that newspaper photographer snapped her picture, standing alone on the Capitol steps after her first day in the Senate, was that she really wasn't alone. The eyes of the entire nation were on her, this tiny old lady with her important pocketbook. Women from across the nation were calling, writing, seeing their Senators. Women everywhere used every possible influence they had to see that Rebecca Latimer Felton found that seat, for the sake of all of them…for the sake of the nation. And they had a weapon more powerful than they had ever had before. Now, they had the power to make Senators quiver, maybe even shake in their boots. These women, all of them, even the ones from Georgia, they had the vote! And most of them had good, long memories and could in future elections vote out of office those who had stopped her, those who sneered at this old woman. While Rebecca Latimer Felton went back to her hotel for yet another night of waiting, these women's organizations got ready…while the nation watched.

Rebecca appeared in the Senate chambers the following morning, this time taking the seat left vacant by the death of Watson, her seat, she hoped. And again the gallery was filled with women urging her on. It had been announced the there would be a joint session of Congress in the House of Representatives at 12:30

to hear President Harding give a speech. In the meantime the credentials of the incoming Senators were presented and read...at least all the credentials except those of Rebecca Felton and Walter George. Those read were two sets of credentials from newly elected Pennsylvania Senators and one from Delaware.

Then the Senior Senator from Georgia, William Harris rose and presented Rebecca Latimer Felton to the Senate. He was nervous. He explained the situation, hemmed and hawed, said he hoped no one would object, said that she would serve for only one day, and repeated that he sincerely wished that no one would object. He said that Mr. George was also present and had agreed to wait to take his seat. Then he concluded, "This will not in any way prejudice Mr. George's claims to his seat in the Senate, to which the people of my State have elected him, and his credentials will be presented to-morrow." It was said that Rebecca's credentials should be presented to the Secretary of the Senate, but the Senate soon learned and affirmed that the Secretary already had those credentials. There was a pause. Was it going to be this easy? Was she in?

From an unexpected corner a voice was heard. The Democratic Senator from the State of Montana, Thomas Walsh, had something to say. Citing the Constitution and the Seventeenth Amendment in particular, Senator Walsh had some questions regarding the eligibility of Rebecca Latimer Felton to take her seat. Many wondered why a Democrat would be questioning her credentials, when more Republicans were privately objecting. And Walsh was a liberal Democrat at that. He spoke slowly, seriously, and at length about the problems of seating this woman, while the women in the gallery exchanged serious looks and whispered.

Before he could finish 12:30 came, and it was time for the President's speech. Rebecca filed out with the other Senators. Although how she might have paid attention to Harding's speech is hard to fathom, she later said that she was pleased with what the President had said. "I heartily agree with him about getting rid of our old ships and stopping the loss of $50,000,000 a year. When money doesn't buy anything, I think it is high time to stop spending it." Following the speech, the Senators returned to their chambers where Senator Lodge announced that all Senators whose "commissions will provoke no discussion, be duly sworn in." Again there were serious looks and whispers from the gallery.

After the new Senators (all but Felton – and George) had been sworn in and had duly taken their seats, Walsh was supposed to resume. But the Senator from Idaho had something to say. Senator Borah asked, 'Mr. President, will the Senator from Montana indulge me for just a moment?" At first Senator Walsh yielded, but Senator Borah had another topic in mind entirely. Instead of discussing Rebecca's qualifications to take her seat as Senator, he wanted to talk about and present a bill dealing with Indian Lands. An argument was about to follow, but was interrupted when the Senator from Oklahoma also had something to say. But this time the Senator of Montana would not yield the floor once again. Mr. Walsh was determined to finish his speech about Rebecca Felton's being seated in the Senate. And this time he held firm.

After several requests that Walsh yield the floor and many assurances that it was only for the purpose of introducing a bill and would only take a moment, Mr. Walsh of Montana said, "No; I object to the transaction of any business whatever until the pending matter shall have been disposed of. It is a question of high privilege."

The Vice-President of the United States being out of the city that day, the President pro tempore was the Senator of Iowa, Albert B. Cummins, who then said, "The Senator from Montana is entitled to the floor and will proceed."

Walsh got quickly got to the heart of the matter. Was it legal under the Constitution of the United States, and particularly under the words of the Seventeenth Amendment, which all of them had sworn to uphold, to seat this woman even for a moment in the Senate of the United States? He continued, "As very grave doubt has been cast upon her present right to take the oath by the public statement of the governor of her State, I venture to submit for the consideration of the Senate some reflections upon the subject as well as some precedents in relation to it." He proceeded to read the part of the Seventeenth Amendment that was the cause of the hesitation on the part of the Governor of Georgia and the Senate of the United States regarding the legitimacy of Rebecca's being seated. According to the Seventeenth Amendment, if a vacancy in office were to occur, "the legislature of any State may empower the executive thereof to make temporary appointment until the people fill the vacancies by election as the legislature may direct."

All of that seemed clear enough. The appointee's term of office ends following the election of a new candidate. But what exactly constitutes the ending of an election? Was November seventh, the day of the election in this case its official ending? What if Walter George died on November the eighth? Would Mrs. Felton still be the official appointee or would the governor have to appoint a new Senator? Did the election end when all the votes were counted? When they were canvassed? When the true victor was announced? When all officials signed his credentials? And in the case of a Senator, was his election officially over when he presented those credentials? Or was the election truly over and the candidate a true Senator only when he was officially sworn into office?

In his slow and deliberate way, he cited many cases, precedence, other Senators who had been appointed and who had served, for one reason or another, well beyond their specified appointments. He also stated that the law "abhors a vacancy," and said that Rebecca had filled it well. Then came his *coup de grâce.* He cited the decisions of the Senate judiciary committee itself. The decision put before them today had already been made in 1850, and cited in a volume called "Senate Election Cases," which states that the office of the appointee "terminates upon the presentation to the Senate, during the next session of such legislature, of the credentials of the Member elected to fill such vacancy. This is the position maintained in the report of the committee." He went on to cite many precedents supporting this decision. It was quite clear that Senator Walsh had done his homework.

The Senator from Montana concluded his speech with these words: "I have said this much because I did not like to have it appear if the lady is sworn in – as I have no doubt she is entitled to be sworn in – that the Senate had so far departed from its duty in the premises as to extend so grave a right to her as a favor, or as a mere matter of courtesy or being moved by a spirit of gallantry, but rather that the Senate, being fully advised about it, decided that she was entitled to take the oath."

Many Republicans, and even some Democrats, previously set to raise some sort of protest, now seemed satisfied, relieved, especially when they looked up into the gallery. Some of the most prominent women of the nation were sitting or standing there…silently watching. According to Rebecca, "There were delegations from every woman's organization with headquarters in Washington." All of them were wearing their organization's sashes, or pins, or ribbons to signify that they were but a small part, a representation of something much larger. Making them an enemy by refusing Rebecca her seat, especially when they had so much, well, so much clout, especially now that they had the vote – and after all it would be for only one day, to protest just didn't make any political sense anymore. And now Walsh had proven it was legal, and had cited many precedents.

Many newspapers later approved of the seriousness with which the Senate, and Walsh in particular, dealt with this issue. For example, *The World* noted, "Not a mere matter of courtesy but an issue of law was involved, and it would have been a slighting compliment to ignore in the case of a woman points of law which would be sharply scanned in the case of a man.

But still it wasn't over. Any Senator at this point could have prevented her seating or delayed it so long that George would be obliged to take the oath. All that had to happen was for one Senator to protest under the proscriptions of the Seventeenth Amendment and draw out a protracted battle, and it would be over. Only one voice was needed in front of all of those women and all of the clubs and states and organizations they represented – in front of all of those serious, determined feminine eyes that fixed themselves now upon these Senators. Walsh had finished his speech and made his points. Now was the time for any Senator in that room to rise and speak against her. Some had been asked to speak – and had declined, in spite of the fact that there were precedents one could also cite for not seating her – in front of all of those important women.

For a few moments – perhaps an eternity to one old woman – there was no sound at all within the hallowed halls of the Senate chamber. Not a cough, not a sneeze, not even a rustling of papers. There was total silence from the floor and the gallery. It was as if they were all frozen in time – like an old photograph. No one spoke; no one moved; no one even seemed to be breathing. Then a voice rang out. It was that of Senator Cummins. His clear, deep voice broke the silence with knife-like clarity: "The Secretary will read the certificate of the Junior Senator from Georgia." Perhaps the next movement in those solemn chambers was Rebecca's lips quickly forming into a broad smile. She knew what those words meant. She was in; she had won! It seemed as if everyone exhaled at once. The "Grand Old Lady of Georgia" would be seated.

Cummins, the President pro tempore then said, "Mrs. Felton, being present, will kindly present herself at the desk to receive the oath of office." After making certain that there was a quorum of Senators present, "Mrs. Felton was escorted by Mr. Harris to the Vice President's desk, and the oath prescribed by law having been administered to her, she took HER seat in the Senate." There was only one awkward moment before her swearing in. When Cummins raised his hand, she mistook it for a wave, or perhaps a handshake and offered her hand to him in return. This little faux pas is symbolic of the always gracious always hospitable and friendly Rebecca Latimer Felton. Some witnesses to this event smiled at her small gesture.

She wanted to give a brief speech, but according to her biographer, John Talmadge, was "too weary" to do so then, and requested that she be permitted to give her speech first-thing the following day. Although she had every reason to be tired, it is difficult to accept Talmadge's statement. Rebecca Latimer Felton was a consummate politician. It would certainly serve to her advantage if the media first carried her seating in the Senate, and then the following day when the entire nation knew the outcome of this drama, she made her speech.

She had carefully put away that second speech that she had prepared just in case she was refused her Senate seat, and which would probably have touched off a war within the Senate, particularly between those men on the floor, and those women in the gallery. She was happy that she would not need that speech. In it she had stated her simple request for her day in the Senate should be granted, "not as a favor or a compliment – not as a bequest to a charity patient; but as a tribute to the integrity, the patriotism, and the womanhood of the blessed wives and mothers of our common country."

Instead she was standing with her right hand raised, in the Senate, taking the oath of office. Following her swearing in, one reporter said of her accomplishments, "Mrs. Fenton for half a century has taken an active part in the political actions and passions of her times, with scathing pen and unfaltering courage flaying political trickery in whatever guise it happened to be clothed." And now she represented all women as their first woman Senator.

For her real speech the next day, the Senate was packed with Senators on the floor and mostly women in the gallery, all wearing the colors of their organizations, crammed into gallery seats and lining the walls. A reporter at the time recorded:

> Like a great-grandmother, Mrs. Felton stood up behind the aisle desks of the rear row of seats on the seats of the Democratic side. No woman before had addressed the presiding officer of the Senate. Yet there was no nervousness about her.

> A remarkable picture she made – standing there in her black dress, with a bit of antique lace about her neck, her head inclined, through weight of years, her white hair giving a silver touch to the Mahogany furniture and dark-clothed men.

> The gallery, male and female, mostly female, leaned over and every eye in the chamber was upon her.

> "Mr. President," she began in a voice firm, yet gentle.

> "The junior Senator from Georgia," said the President pro-tempore, Senator Cummins.

That is how it started that day of November 23, 1922. Although she had written out what she wanted to say, she looked directly at her audience and spoke directly. In her initial sentence, she spoke about her "very remarkable campaign in Georgia, which, contrary to precedent, all came along after I was selected...." Her statement was true. She was appointed, and then she campaigned, as she had done so many years before for her husband. But if she campaigned, to whom and for what was she campaigning? A careful study of her papers reveals that she was campaigning to the nation, in the name of its women, and especially the suffragists, some of whom dated even earlier than the time of Susan B. Anthony. She had worked hard for this moment, and now it was hers.

Many histories have dismissed Rebecca Latimer Felton – or forgotten her completely. After all she really only served in the Senate for one day. Furthermore, she was appointed, just appointed for a short time by a governor who had his own reasons for that appointment, and who had ardently opposed woman suffrage. In a personal letter to Rebecca, written on December 12, 1922, from that governor, he said, "I did not and do not believe that your title to a seat in the Senate extended beyond November 7th." And as in any campaign, certain people helped her in her struggle: Governor Hardwick for appointing her in the first place; Senator George for letting her go first and for permitting the Senate to decide her case; Senator Walsh, for his remarkable and studied legal attention to this matter; Senator Harris who introduced her to the Senate and warmly escorted her through the proceedings, and Senator Cummins, who served as President pro tempore that day, and allowed the process to reach its conclusion. But really, in a sense, Rebecca was elected, not by Georgia, and not by those Senators or that one Governor who helped her on her way; but rather by the women of the entire nation. They didn't go to the polls to elect her – but they elected her just the same, not with a vote, but with the power of the vote, their newly acquired power that they now had and would use in the future. In her first and last speech before the Senate, Rebecca Latimer Felton assured her nation that "when the women of this country come and sit with you, though there may be very few in the next few years, I pledge that you will get ability, you will get integrity of purpose, and you will get unstinted usefulness." She always claimed that she went to Washington to accept her Senate seat not for herself, but for the women of the nation. In many ways, they were her electorate and her constituency.

When her short speech was over, the entire hall exploded with cheers, applause, and the stomping of feet. No one tried to stop them. The colors of those sashes and ribbons, the smiles, the crowds, all wildly applauded this tiny feisty woman, all dressed in black, eighty-seven years old, who became the first woman Senator of the United States.

Rebecca, Seated with Her Constituents

Afterword

What happened to some of the principals of this work could make another book. Here are some of the highlights:

Warren Akin Candler:

Warren Akin Candler and his brother Asa, the wealthy founder of Coca-Cola, were largely responsible for the move of Emory College from Oxford to Atlanta (Druid Hills), with their donation of one million dollars for the project. This money came from the Candlers (primarily Asa) because of a 1910 lawsuit which caused a further split within Methodism regarding just how conservative or liberal it should be. With the money donated by the Candlers, Emory would become one of two significant colleges under the control of the conservative Southern Methodists (Southern Methodist University in Texas being the other). Candler became Chancellor of Emory in 1914, holding the university to conservative traditions and values, but also opening a law school, medical school and hospital and helping to establish the University as a significant institution of higher education – except, of course in the field of athletics which Candler refused to support, even denying the university a football team.

Like Rebecca Felton, Warren Candler wrote for the newspapers of the day, and had a column for decades in the *Atlanta Journal,* in which he promoted his ideals and ideas and often fought with Rebecca, particularly over women's rights. He was, however, a religious idealist and attempted to smooth over the difficulties between science and religion. Throughout his long life, he continued to believe that women's domain was solely in the home, as God had ordained – at least in his opinion. And just like Rebecca, he intended to work, and to promote his beliefs until he died. On September 19,1941 the revered Candler passed away, his loving, supportive wife Nettie (who voted in spite of her husband), died two years later. As for Emory, it has become one of the premier universities in the nation.

Augusta Howard:

It will be remembered that Augusta Howard was literally banished from her state, for life, instead of serving her sentence on the work farm, because of shooting and critically wounding a young boy. She spent the last twelve years of her life in a boarding house in New York City. Sherwood Hall, the mansion in which she lived for most of her life was torn down, allegedly at the insistence of her brother. Having no home to return to in Georgia may have further assured her absence from that state. She was visited in New York by family members and supported by her brother Richard. She returned to Georgia in a casket in June 1934 (having died in a hospital in the Bronx on June 10, 1934.) She was buried in Columbus, Georgia in Linwood Cemetery on June 13, 1934. The Columbus *Ledger* and the *Enquirer-Sun* both carried one paragraph about her death, each quite similar and equally short. The entire obituary of the *Ledger* states:

> The remains of Miss H. Augusta Howard, who died in New York City Tuesday, are due to arrive here via the Southern railway Thursday evening. Private services will be held later at the Striffler funeral chapel. No flowers.

Although she is mentioned briefly in various biographies and jour-
nals, she has never been credited with being the Mother of the
Woman Suffrage Movement in Georgia, nor is the shooting mentioned. Most biographical information ends in this manner: "She
spent the last twelve years of her life in New York city where she
died of cancer of the stomach at the age of sixty-nine."

H. L. Mencken:

The South and Georgia in particular were in a pitiful state in
1920. The destruction of the Civil War, crooked politicians during
Reconstruction and later; vigilante groups, such as the Ku Klux
Klan; serious racial strife, and the boll weevil had all left their
mark. Menken's "Sahara of the Bozart," should have made things
even worse. But in a strange way, it started to wake up the South
and end its tendency to look to the past, longing for the traditions
upheld by the "Lost Cause." The olden days were over; it was
time for change. Menken's article and others like it awakened
many Southerners to their own dilemma and to the realization that
much of what that smug man from Baltimore had said was true.
Southerners began to criticize themselves. Even some noted
Southerners, such as William Henry Skaggs, in his book *The
Southern Oligarchy,* began to note and write about the South in
most unflattering terms, as did Wilber J. Cash and Thomas Wolfe.
Then H. L. Mencken did something most unexpected. He
began to encourage the growth of a new Southern culture, especially regarding its writers, encouraging them, helping them to get
published – even publishing some himself. The year 1920 may
have been the lowest point for Georgia, but it also marked a turning point begun by the very man who had most disparaged that
state. He established southern friendships. For decades he wrote
to Julia Collier Harris, who lived in one of those "obnoxious cotton-mill towns" (Columbus, GA), and she in turn wrote books, and
helped to edit with her husband Julien a small newspaper, *The Enquirer Sun,* which began a major, fierce campaign to end the KKK.
Their battles led to terrible incidents, threats, beatings, bombings –
that ultimately began the decline of the KKK in the South as peo-

ple started to recognize its true nature and violence. Julien and Julia Harris won the *Pulitzer Prize* for this tiny newspaper because of its work against the Klan.

Mencken encouraged blacks and whites, male and female, to write, and he backed his words with publishing offers for good and great writing. Today Mencken is famous for having launched literary renaissances in both the South and Harlem. He helped good authors throughout the country, regardless of their sex or color, boosting the careers of Eugene O'Neill, F. Scott Fitzgerald, Sinclair Lewis, James Weldon Johnson, Langston Hughes, and Theodore Dreiser, to name only a few. Instead of being remembered as the South's major detractor, he is famous today as the man who showed southern writers that they could write better, that they were living in the midst of literary poverty, and that Mencken would help them to publish their good works...and did.

Mary Latimer McLendon:

Inaccurately known, even today, as Georgia's Mother of Woman Suffrage with a small fountain and statue dedicated to her at the State Capitol in Atlanta, bearing that title, she did work for many decades in the causes of women's civil rights, improvement of conditions for the poor, better schools, and most of all for temperance with her significant work in the Woman's Christian Temperance Union. In the early years the WCTU was larger than the suffrage movement in Georgia and much more diversified. Blacks, whites, the poor and the rich all participated in one way or another in the WCTU. As one of its major leaders in Georgia, she became, along with her sister, one of the most powerful and persuasive women within the state. In addition, McLendon was the founder of the second Georgia Woman Suffrage Association in Georgia and tirelessly worked for its goals. Following the passage of the Nineteenth Amendment, McLendon swiftly turned the GWSA into what would soon become the League of Women Voters, teaching women how to vote and informing them about the candidates' qualifications for office. Throughout her long life, she dedicated herself, as did her sister, to the rights of all and worked to improve the situation of the disadvantaged in Georgia. She died on November 20, 1921. As was said at the time of her death, "Mrs. McLendon was firm in her belief that the ballot in the hands of women would prove a power instrument for the protection of the home and the welfare of the nation; that God created both men and woman in his own Image, and, therefore, there should be one standard of purity for both men and women, and that they had equal rights to hold opinion and to express the same with equal freedom."

William Harrell Felton:

Many years after her husband's death, Rebecca Felton said of him: "He went to his reward in 1909, and while he left but small fortune to his survivors, he did have a name for honest public service, and a life untainted with political corruption or bribe money. He led a crusade that only a brave man could lead, and he served his country as a watchman on a high tower." To this day, and in spite of the fierce and often underhanded enemies that William Felton accumulated because of his political activities, no one ever pinned a dishonest action upon this man. Devout, honest to the core, an intelligent man and wonderful orator, devoted to good politics and prison and school reform within his state, and dearly loving and encouraging his wife throughout their marriage of more than half a century, William Harrell Felton has gone down in history as one of the good, possibly great, men of his state.

Rebecca Latimer Felton:

Senator Felton did not retire to become some sweet little old grandmother, stroking a cat and gently rocking on the porch. There was far too much left to do. She wanted to wear herself out working, rather than rusting away through inaction. After she became a Senator, she once said, "People grow old because they think too much about themselves and their little troubles...I get up every morning at six o'clock, eat a light breakfast (of raw eggs chiefly), do my writing and other work in the morning and the rest of the afternoon." Throughout her life she firmly believed, "What you can't help, put behind you."

She continued her battles on behalf of the less fortunate, whether black or white. She kept up with her newspaper columns and often wrote for other newspapers. She worked for the betterment of mothers, children, schools. On her ninety-second Birthday, the town of Cartersville gave her a giant Birthday party. She sat beside her granddaughter Annie Felton as she rode through the town, festooned with decorations and flags in her honor. "'Look Grandma," exclaimed her granddaughter, 'the flags are all out.' Mrs. Felton crisply replied, 'Well a little airing won't do them any harm.'" She began her speech that day by saying, "When I was born 92 years ago, The Cherokee Indians were here. They were forcibly removed by the United States Government in 1838, when I was only three years old. ... I noted they did not walk in the middle of the road. Forests were all spacious without undergrowth, and I could see the Indians as they tramped along in the open woods, never in the main road, a hard looking race."

So much had happened to her since those Indian times. She recalled the first building erected in Atlanta, and her first telephone call: "I listened over the first official telephone, reaching a mile, from the United States Capitol to the Government Printing Office." She remembered that even as a child she had loved political discussions and remembered when she was five the election of 1840, and its campaign motto, "Tippicanoe and Tyler, too." She recounted, "I saw the miniature log cabins and the one-horse wagons that contained big Georgia ginger cakes and kegs of cider, which were featured in these political jamborees, to be sold to the cheering voters." It sometimes seems that she remembered everything. She became a member by acclamation of the National Women's Party, founded by Alice Paul. Both Paul and Felton believed in the causes that would become part of the Equal Rights Amendment proposals, although Felton tended to promote more forcefully the rights of mothers and children than did Paul. Rebecca continued to write for the newspapers on just about any topic she wanted; she continued to fight the KKK, intolerance, injustice, graft and corruption, particularly in politics; she became the first woman ever to receive an honorary doctorate degree from the University of Georgia; she drove a car, rode in the Goodyear Blimp, and was heard on the radio and seen in newsreels; she campaigned and she gave speeches, even if they were a little shorter and softer than they had once been.

She maintained throughout her life that music was her "passion." taught to her when she was a young child. She continued to sing and play the piano, often accompanying herself. She also played a small guitar and sang old-time ballads and "Negro spirituals." She was a firm supporter of the Atlanta opera and attended as often as she could, at least once a year. She vigorously opposed the state legislature's attempt to tax the opera saying, "It seems to me that the legislature is penalizing a city for being large and cultured enough to support this great institution."

As a slight concession to her age, Rebecca had given up riding horses at the age of seventy – but she gave up little else. She had also changed her mind about one of her crusades: Prohibition. When she saw what it did to crime and bootlegging, she decided that Prohibition should be repealed. As she stated, "I never had but one slogan … and that was 'sober homes for mothers.' We still haven't got them. We ought to face conditions and realize that the bootlegger is in power today. The government has got to regulate liquor selling in some way. Today children can buy it."

Deeply religious all of her life, she was curious about death, seemed to think about it often, but did not fear it. In March of 1929 she was seriously injured in an automobile accident. Although the driver, her grandson, was not seriously injured, she had severed an artery and was bleeding heavily. When the doctors started to give her an anesthetic, she refused. She wanted to know what death feels like. "Don't put me to sleep,' she said. 'If I'm going to die I want to know about it."

She died a few months later, as she would have wanted, working nearly up to the very end. Ignoring a severe cold, she had gone to Atlanta on business regarding the Girls Training School (a compassionate reformatory which helped delinquent girls learn a trade and turn their lives around). She had founded this institution. She developed pneumonia and was hospitalized. She asked her pastor to pray for her. But she concluded that she was not afraid. "If my time has come,' she said, 'I'm ready." She died on January 24, 1930. People everywhere grieved her passing. Tributes were paid to her throughout the nation and, looking at the pictures of her funeral, it seems that nearly all of Georgia was there to mourn her passing. The Senate recessed for one day to honor her memory and Senator George, who had helped her to be able to take the oath of office said that she was one of the "Greatest Women of her time."

But in spite of the speeches and tributes paid by some of the most notable people in the nation regarding the passing of this old woman, it was really Cartersville who brought her home. Nearly everyone in Cartersville dressed up in their Sunday clothes and marched to her home where she lay-in-state to pay their respects to "Grandma Felton" and say good-bye for one last time. Her neighbors bore her coffin; her pastor conducted a very personal funeral, and her many friends and neighbors sang "Abide with Me," and "Rock of Ages," in the old-timey doleful way so common of small church Methodist funerals in the South. Her friends placed her in the Georgia clay that she had so loved.

Mayor Ragsdale of Atlanta stated, "In the death of Mrs. Rebecca Felton the state of Georgia has lost one of her leading citizens. She was one of the most dominant figures of leadership and progress that the state has ever produced."

A little Georgian boy was only six years old when she died. He would become a farmer, then Governor of Georgia, then President of the United States, and finally one of the greatest humanitarians of our time. A small black Georgia baby who had "a dream" that would profoundly influence and change the entire nation was only one when she died. Georgia – Rebecca – The New South. Georgia even got around to officially ratifying the Susan B. Anthony Amendment. It did so in 1970.

Acknowledgements

As I have indicated earlier, it seems that nearly all of Georgia has helped me with this book: researchers, historians, relatives of the principal characters, courthouse clerks, and many others with an interest in the fascinating history of the South. I am particularly grateful to the University of Georgia, who accepted Rebecca Latimer Felton's papers and scrapbooks and conserved them on microfilm. These papers provide not only a priceless picture of William and Rebecca Felton, but also of the times in which they lived. I would also especially like to thank the staff of the Macon State Library for their wonderful help with my work. Research librarian at Macon State, Mary Morris, was invaluable to the research of this book. The Georgia State Archives, The Library of Congress, the Courthouse at Columbus, GA, the Hatcher Library of the University of Michigan, the Hargrett Rare Books Library of the University of Georgia, Georgia State University, and Emory University also provided significant information for this book.

I would also like to thank Ann Collins, a direct descendant of the Feltons, for her information; Betty Lane Phillips (of the Howard linage) and Carolyn Mitchell Howard for their information on Augusta Howard and her family, and particularly Rita Hale,

227

also a Howard descendant, for her introductions to other members of the Howard family and for her large genealogy of this fascinating family. My husband Dr. E. Michael Staman has provided me with invaluable support and technical assistance. I am also grateful to Pat Gallant in New York, Henri Thyssens in Belgium, and Karen Staman in Raleigh for their great editing suggestions and advice, along with Dr. Catherine O. Badura for her information on Corra Harris and race relations of the time. Others who have helped me considerably include Laura Staman and Gloria Adams for their encouragement and enthusiasm, along with Cathy Clark for her promotion. Although there are too many others to mention, who have also helped, I would like to name in particular Joey Nichols, Jeanne Campbell, Judy West, and Fran and Don Eckert.

NOTES

1: Out of the Embers

1   "(then age four)": According to the Cass County Census of 1850, in which Ann's age was listed as age one.
2   "awaits us all": Kennett, *Marching Through Georgia,* 37.
3   "not far from Macon": Handwritten document by Rebecca Felton in Rebecca Latimer Felton Papers, hereafter known as RLF papers, reel 1. and Felton, *My Memoirs of Georgia Politics,* 60.
4   "had loved her son": Talmadge, *Rebecca Latimer Felton,* 22.
5   "in which I was quartered": Sherman, *Memoirs,* 654.
5   "dreadful to look upon": Davis, *Sherman's March,* 6.
5   "make Georgia howl!": Davis, *Sherman's March,* 23.
5   "over the ruined city": Sherman, *Memoirs,* 655.
5   "the houses left standing": Davis, *Sherman's March,* 13.
6   "of a crazy fool": Davis, *Sherman's March.* 10.
6   "despite the guards": Davis, *Sherman's March,* 19.
6   "cheery look and swinging pace": Sherman, *Memoirs,* 655.
6   "of time and place": Sherman, *Memoirs,* 655-656.
7   "friend on the road": Davis, *Sherman's March,* 29.
7   "maybe I'll follow": Davis, *Sherman's March,* 30.
8   "Christianity and civilization": All three quotes in this paragraph come from Felton, *Country Life in Georgia,* 86.
8   "body as we rolled away": Felton, *Country Life in Georgia,* 86.
9   "Georgia was prostrate": Felton, *Country Life in Georgia,* 85.
9   "one side was nearly as bad as the other": Felton, *Country Life in Georgia,* 89.
10   "always plentiful at that": Handwritten speech by Rebecca Felton in RLF papers, reel 16.
10   "defended to the last": Jones, "Wilson's Raiders Reach Georgia," 316.
10   "Go to the left." "Look out": Jones, "Wilson's Raiders Reach Georgia," 321.

11   "no account could be taken": Martin, "Report of General Wilson," in
      Columbus, Georgia, part II, 185.
11   "military forces of the State of Georgia": Felton, *Country Life in Geor-*
      gia, 90.
11   "little horse was slow": Felton, *Country Life in Georgia,* 91.
12   "Yankee soldier like one of the family": Felton, *The Romantic Story of*
      Georgia's Women, 22.
12   "was not around": Felton, *The Romantic Story of Georgia's Women,* 22.
12   "horrors I suffered there": Talmadge, *Rebecca Latimer Felton,* 24.
12   "chilling off and on for months": Handwritten R. Felton speech, in RLF
      papers, reel 16.
12   "reason was not fatally dethroned": Handwritten R. Felton speech, in
      RLF papers, reel 16.
13   "slaves all gone, money also": Felton, *Country Life in Georgia,* 89.

2: Starting Over

14   "struggle to live, to exist": Handwritten speech by Rebecca Felton in
      RLF papers, reel 16.
15   "on borrowed money": Handwritten speech by Rebecca Felton in RLF
      papers, reel 16.
15   "promptly named him Zeb": That Rebecca loved her mules and helped to
      capture them following the war is a fact, although exactly what she
      named her mules is unknown.
15   "starvation in many places": Felton, *Country Life in Georgia,* 73.
16   "strenuous time": Handwritten speech by Rebecca Felton in RLF papers,
      reel 16.
16   "alone to manage for myself: Felton, *Country Life in Georgia,* 35.
16   "to her first day of school": Talmadge, *Rebecca Latimer Felton,* 4.
17   "cities to the north": Felton, *My Memoirs of Georgia Politics,* 18.
17   "mail bag to be opened": Felton, *My Memoirs of Georgia Politics,* 17.
17   "molasses, and kit mackerel": Felton, *The Romantic Story of Georgia's*
      Women, 15.
18   "freight car and engine": Felton, *My Memoirs of Georgia Politics,* 20.
18   "in the outside, busy world": Felton, *My Memoirs of Georgia Politics,*
      18.
18   "know so much and write so well": Felton, *My Memoirs of Georgia Poli-*
      tics, 18.
18   "life-long friend to Rebecca": A son was also born to the Latimers but
      died either in infancy or quite young.
18   "a big time for everybody": Felton, *Country Life in Georgia,* 52.
19   "afoot, others on horseback": Felton, *Country Life in Georgia,* 53.
19   "love at first sight": According to a letter sent to the author by Rebecca's
      granddaughter, Ann F. Collins, May 27, 2003.

20   "its ashes and poverty": Felton, *The Romantic Story of Georgia's Women,* 23.
20   "and the crop fails": Felton, *Country Life in Georgia,* 58.
22   "devouring flocks and droves": Felton, *My Memoirs of Georgia Politics,* 71.

3: Politics?

24   "The Bourbons": The enemies of the Georgia Democrats called them Bourbons, named after the conservative and effete, regal French rulers.
25   "and his way of speaking": Talmadge, *Rebecca Latimer Felton,* 36.
26   "Because he is *(W)right*": Newspaper clippings from RLF papers, reel 17.
26   "Favored Dr. Felton*":* Felton, *My Memoirs of Georgia Politics,* 160.
26   "Indians of that region": Talmadge, *Rebecca Latimer Felton,* 38.
27   "flung hand grenades": Felton, *Country Life in Georgia,* 120.
27   "a campaign manager does": Felton, *The Romantic Story of Georgia's Women,* 25.
28   "the heels of his boots": Felton, *My Memoirs of Georgia Politics,* 146.
28   "continue William's campaign": Felton, *My Memoirs of Georgia Politics,* 146.
28   "describe or pen portray": Felton, *My Memoirs of Georgia Politics,* 145.
28   "The Bloody Seventh": Felton, *My Memoirs of Georgia Politics,* 13.
28   "Echoed with their shouts": Felton, *My Memoirs of Georgia Politics,* 159.
29   "Negroes and Republicans": The accusations against Dr. Felton's campaign are found in Talmadge, *Rebecca Latimer Felton,* 36-37.
29   "loved his life": Felton, *My Memoirs of Georgia Politics,* 147.
30   "bite the dust": Felton, *My Memoirs of Georgia Politics,* 146.
31   "no use to try": Newspaper clipping, "The Political Truth," September 26, 1874, from correspondence in *Atlanta News,* in RLF papers, reel 17.
31   "strapped to his back...": Felton, *My Memoirs of Georgia Politics,* 147-148.
31   "ripe today for revolt": Felton, *My Memoirs of Georgia Politics,* 150.
32   "get up and write": Interview with Hon. W. H. Felton, *Chicago Tribune,* in RLF papers, reel 2.
33   "few other Felton supporters": Stevens, *The Road is Still Rough,* 67.
33   "nothing but skin and bones": Felton, *My Memoirs of Georgia Politics,* 154.
33   "no matter how the election went ": Felton, *My Memoirs of Georgia Politics,* 154.
33   "Dabney must have it": Felton, *My Memoirs of Georgia Politics,* 157.
34   "regret or reproach ourselves for": Felton, *My Memoirs of Georgia Politics,* 155.

34   "dropping from its mouth": Felton, *My Memoirs of Georgia Politics,* 156.

34   "eighty-two votes": Felton, *The Romantic Story of Georgia's Women,* 25.

4: From the Hills of North Georgia to Washington

37   "Medicine 75 cents: $208.92": Personal Hotel Bill in RLF papers, reel 1.

37   "always in their way": Felton, *My Memoirs of Georgia Politics,* 163.

38   "was particularly interested": Felton, *The Romantic Story of Georgia's Women,* 30.

38   "What is it, mother?": Felton, *My Memoirs of Georgia Politics,* 169.

38   "beyond all expectation": Felton, *My Memoirs of Georgia Politics,* 168.

39   "an impress on their times": Felton, *The Romantic Story of Georgia's Women,* 30.

39   "in return for $2,500": Hunter, *Rebecca Latimer Felton,* 19.

40   "killing escaped convicts": Talmadge, *Rebecca Latimer Felton,* 98-99.

40   "Cartersville's 'second representative'": Talmadge, *Rebecca Latimer Felton,* 45.

41   "Rev. O. B. Frothingham": *The Case Against Woman Suffrage: A Manuel,* 17.

41   "Archbishop of Baltimore": *The Case Against Woman Suffrage: A Manuel,* 18.

41   "New York Women's Press Club": *The Case Against Woman Suffrage: A Manuel,* 21.

41   "Goldwin Smith, D.C.I": *The Case Against Woman Suffrage: A Manuel,* 23.

41   "Rev. Theodore L. Cuyler, D. D.": *The Case Against Woman Suffrage: A Manuel,* 13.

41   "Dr. Charles L Dana, 'eminent' neurologist": *The Case Against Woman Suffrage: A Manuel,* 15.

42   "Daniel Webster": *The Case Against Woman suffrage: A Manuel,* 29.

42   "Demon Rum and drunkenness": Tyler, *Where Prayer and Purpose Meet,* 14-15.

43   "women could be voting members": Mattingly, *Well-Tempered Women,* 40.

43   "ugly sexless demeanor": Mattingly, *Well-Tempered Women,* 42.

44   "admiration they had won": Mattingly, *Well-Tempered Women,* 55.

44   "reliant and self-supporting women": Mattingly, *Well-Tempered Women,* 168.

45   "to change the same": Scott, *Natural Allies,* 103.

45   "reconstructing the ideal of womanhood": Scott, *Natural Allies,* 103.

5: Into the Battle Again

46   "rough and tumble rally": Talmadge, *Rebecca Latimer Felton,* 47.

47   "attacked the Bourbons": Talmadge, *Rebecca Latimer Felton,* 48.

47   "He hides behind his wife": Felton, *My Memoirs of Georgia Politics,* 489.

47   "collect a few voters": Felton, *The Romantic Story of Georgia's Women,* 27.

47   "it was far from unpleasant": Felton, *My Memoirs of Georgia Politics,* 176.

48   "I was out and going": Felton, *My Memoirs of Georgia Politics,* 173.

48   "host of the organized": Giles, "The Grand Old Lady of Georgia," 61.

49   "ears of the astonished lady": Felton, *My Memoirs of Georgia Politics,* 174.

49   "previous Friday night": Felton, *My Memoirs of Georgia Politics,* 200.

49   "people in later life": Felton, *My Memoirs of Georgia Politics,* 192.

51   "after he had died": Report of the Georgia State Investigation Committee, p. 51, no date, RLF papers, reel 1.

52   "and so did that man": "Bathed in Blood," The account of this entire murder, cited above, comes from this source, probably from the *Constitution,* March 12, 1879, appearing in the RLF papers, reel 19.

55   "in search of an outlet": This endnote marks the end of the "*Constitution's* lengthy description, including verbatim reports from the Coroner's Inquest, as found in "Bathed in Blood," RLF papers, reel 19.

55   "but to humanity": "The Latest Georgia Murder," *New York Times,* no date, found in RLF papers, reel 19.

55   "in their condemnation": Stevens, *The Road is Still Rough,* 78.

56   "life safe who attacks it?": Document hand-written by Rebecca Latimer Felton, RLF papers, reel 11.

56   "Alston, himself": Stevens, *The Road is Still Rough,* 80.

56   "dismissed from the force": Felton, *My Memoirs of Georgia Politics,* 491.

Chapter 6: Defeats and Wins

58   "of her native section": Document handwritten by Rebecca Latimer Felton, undated, p. 6, in RLF papers, reel 9.

58   "robust anatomy": Document handwritten by Rebecca Latimer Felton, undated, p. 7, in RLF papers, reel 9.

58   "outen her mouth inter thern": Document handwritten by Rebecca Latimer Felton, undated, pp. 8-11, in RLF papers, reel 9.

59   "wanted to ensure their rights": Stevens, *The Road is Still Rough,* 83.

60   "years in the penitentiary": Felton, *My Memoirs of Georgia Politics,* 444.

61   "was sent up for five?": Felton, *My Memoirs of Georgia Politics,* 444.

61   "taken her out and shot her": Felton, *My Memoirs of Georgia Politics,* 448.

63   "Rebecca later wrote": Felton, *My Memoirs of Georgia Politics,* 547.

63   "of the State of Georgia": Felton, *My Memoirs of Georgia Politics,* 548.

63   "injure him in the State": Felton, *My Memoirs of Georgia Politics,* 548.

64   "United States Senate": Felton, *My Memoirs of Georgia Politics,* 548.

65   "reviling Dr. Felton": Gordon letter (dated October 24, 1874) to Rebecca L. Felton with her personal comment are on Reel 1, of the RLF papers.

65   "Manassas or Chickamauga": Talmadge, *Rebecca Latimer Felton,* 51.

66   "unhappiest woman in Georgia": This incident is related in Talmadge's *Rebecca Latimer Felton,* 66-67.

67   "any man in Georgia": Felton, *My Memoirs of Georgia Politics,* 549.

7: Battles and Humiliations

69   "to their carnal desires": Felton, *My Memoirs of Georgia Politics,* 582.

70   "highest offices in the State": Felton Reminiscent Letter in Ansley's *History of the Georgia Woman's Christian Temperance Union,* 105-106.

70   "fell to the floor": Felton, *My Memoirs of Georgia Politics,* 590.

72   "Georgia is responsible for him": Felton, *My Memoirs of Georgia Politics,* 582-583.

72   "Felton's reformatory bill": Talmadge, *Rebecca Latimer Felton,* 80.

72   " John Howard of Georgia": Felton, *My Memoirs of Georgia Politics,* 602.

72   "aged, tottering frame": Felton, *My Memoirs of Georgia Politics,* 583.

72   : willing to undertake": Untitled article in the *Augusta Chronicle, 1887,* RLF papers, reel 8.

73   "She of Georgia": Stevens, *The Road is Still Rough,* 145.

73   "or else she would destroy": Felton, *My Memoirs of Georgia Politics,* 583.

74   "him in due time": "A Wild Scene," Atlanta *Journal,* August 10, 1887, no page, reel 20, RLF papers.

74   "Standing room only": "A Wild Scene," Atlanta *Journal,* August 10, 1887, no page, reel 20, RLF papers.

75   "frightful as a murder": Felton, *My Memoirs of Georgia Politics,* 612-613.

75   "applause and laughter": Felton, *My Memoirs of Georgia Politics,* 613-614.

75   "the family of another": Felton, *My Memoirs of Georgia Politics,* 614-615.

75   "the Father in Heaven": Felton, *My Memoirs of Georgia Politics,* 615-616.

76   "me from this world": Felton, *My Memoirs of Georgia Politics,* 616.

76   "fate that can befall him": "Waking Up an Old Lion," Dana, in *New York Sun,* no date or page, in RLF papers, reel 20.

76   "him upon his triumph":   "Simmons Replies," unnamed newspaper
        (probably in Atlanta) in the RLF papers, reel 20.
77   "home is by the fireside…": Stevens, *The Road is Still Rough,* 71.
77   "with slow torture added": Tallmadge, *Rebecca Latimer Felton,* 98.
77   "Epitomized Hell": Felton, *My Memoirs of Georgia Politics,* 587.

8: Feminine Awakening

79   "and nearly killed him": "Woman Shoots Small Boy for Climbing Tree,"
        Columbus Enquirer-Sun, May 21, 1920, 1.
80   "on the State Farm": "Summary of Court Cases Regarding Howard v. the
        State" August 5 1920 to December 14, 1921 found in Columbus County
        Courthouse, unpublished.
80   "mansion was torn down": Worsley, *Columbus on the Chattahoochee,* p.
        250. According to family members of the Howard family, the staircase of
        this incredibly beautiful mansion is presently located in one of the local
        restaurants.
80   "and other rare shrubs": Worsley, *Columbus on the Chattahoochee,* 250.
81   "that graced this home": Mill, *The Subjection of Women,* 233.
82   "control of others": Mill, *The Subjection of Women,* 262-263.
82   "as a wife is": Mill, *The Subjection of Women,* 269.
82   "of the legal penalty": Mill, *The Subjection of Women,* 306.
82   "swells to a great length": Taylor, "Origin of Woman Suffrage Move-
        ment," 3.
83   "Constitution of Georgia": Howard, "Progress of the Woman Suffrage
        Movement in Georgia," p. 82.
83   "working independently": Howard, "Origin of Woman Suffrage Move-
        ment," 3.
83   "being born a woman": Felton, *My Memoirs of Georgia Politics,* 666.
84   "Commonwealth of Georgia": Felton, *My Memoirs of Georgia Politics,*
        667.
84   "with judicial authority": "Before Congress. Mrs. Felton to Conduct Her
        Husband's Contests." *Rome Tribune,* 11 February 1896 in Rebecca Fel-
        ton Papers, reel 8.
85   "argue for her husband": Felton, *My Memoirs of Georgia Politics,* 667.
85   **"give it up"**: Felton, *My Memoirs of Georgia Politics,* 667.
85   "relieve me of the paper": Felton, *My Memoirs of Georgia Politics,* 668.
85   "within the courtroom": Talmadge, *Rebecca Latimer Felton,* 88-89.
85   "evidence to the contrary": Felton, *Country Life in Georgia,* 107-108.
86   "to represent her state": Felton, *Country Life in Georgia,* 108.
86   "in my hand": Felton, *Country Life in Georgia,* 110.
87   "before this great nation": Scott, *Natural Allies,* 129.
89   "success – and it was": Eaton, *The Waning of the Old South Civilization,*
        45.

90   "honor of their region": Eaton, *The Waning of the Old South Civilization,*
      29.

90   "advocated women's rights": Lewis, "Negro Slavery Throws Dark
      Shadow Across the South to Keep Southern Women from Securing their
      Freedom," 6.

90   "goodness and love": Lewis, "Negro Slavery Throws Dark Shadow…,"
      6.

90   "for her worshippers": Taylor, *Cavalier and Yankee,* 174.

91   "subordination of the heart": Olsen, *Chronology of Woman's History,*
      129.

91   "South bore eight": Taylor, *Cavalier and Yankee,* 167.

92   "would not demand more": Howard, "Progress of the Woman Suffrage
      Movement in Georgia," 82.

92   "compliance with his request": Olsen, *Chronology of Woman's History,*
      143.

93   "practical and comfortable": Mattingly, *Well-Tempered Women,* 105.
      The newspaper clipping comes from the 1853 *Utica Telegraph.* Olsen,
      Chronology of Woman's History, 143.

93   "wiped her spectacles": Mattingly, *Well-Tempered Women,* 105. The
      newspaper clipping comes from the 1853 *Utica Telegraph.*

9: New Obstructions

94   "business and home": The evidence that Sherman burned or destroyed
      the McLendons' Atlanta home is circumstantial. Before Sherman, they
      lived in a large home on Williams Street. Following the war, they lived
      at 139 Washington Street in Atlanta. Stevens, *The Road is Still Rough,*
      37.

96   "*WOMEN ARE PEOPLE*": Taylor, "The Origin of the Woman Suffrage
      Movement in Georgia," 67.

98   "place for them to go!": Bauman, *Warren Akin Candler,* 54.

98   "devil are you doing there!": Bauman, *Warren Akin Candler,* 56.

98   "laughing at my mishap": Bauman, *Warren Akin Candler,* 63.

99   "call her to labor": Bauman, *Warren Akin Candler,* 126.

100   "Church South in Georgia": Bauman, *Warren Akin Candler,* 135.

100   "pretensions and extravagance": Stevens, *The Road is Still Rough,* 166.

101   "lead man to ruin": Bauman, *Warren Akin Candler,* 138.

101   "in the house of God": Bauman, *Warren Akin Candler,* 107-108.

102   "not allowed to answer": Bauman, *Warren Akin Candler,* 108.

103   "who brought it to them": Felton, "The Pandora Incident," 1, handwritten
      document, RLF papers, reel 11.

103   "more easily located": Felton, "The Pandora Incident," 1-2, handwritten
      document, RLF papers, reel 11.

103   "be held for nothing": Felton "The Pandora Incident," 1, handwritten document, RLF papers, reel 11.

103   "decidedly the best of it": "Dr. Hawthorne Will not Bandy Words of Controversy with Mrs. Felton," *Atlanta Constitution,* January 13, 1893, 3.

103   "and no rebuttal allowed": Unidentified clipping (probably from the *Atlanta Constitution)* no date, RLF papers, reel 11.

103   "rescuing and perishing": "Mrs. Felton," *Atlanta Constitution,* January 13, 1893, 3.

104   "in politics as well as religion": Felton, "The Pandora Incident," 3 handwritten document, RLF papers, reel 11.

10: Susan B. Anthony's March Through Georgia

106   "until the crack of doom": Katharine Anthony, *Susan B. Anthony,* 375-376.

107   "of our national convention": Katherine Anthony, *Susan B. Anthony,* 412.

107   "of the majority": Katherine Anthony, *Susan B. Anthony*, 413.

107   "to attend this convention": Taylor, "The Origin of the Woman Suffrage Movement in Georgia," 6.

108   "North and the South": Taylor, "The Origin of the Woman Suffrage Movement in Georgia," 6.

109   "ready to help Atlanta": *Proceedings of the Twenty-sixth Annual Convention of the National American Woman Suffrage Association,* 103.

109   "to give the people news": *Proceedings of the Twenty-sixth Annual Convention,* 103.

109   "increase their membership": Taylor, "Origin of the Woman Suffrage Movement in Georgia," 7.

109   "a friend to woman suffrage": Taylor, "Origin of the Woman Suffrage Movement in Georgia," 8.

110   "without their consent": Taylor, "Origin of the Woman Suffrage Movement in Georgia," 8

110   "taken in with such affection": Taylor, "Origin of the Woman Suffrage Movement in Georgia," 8.

110   "and pardoned criminals": Taylor, "Origin of the Woman Suffrage Movement in Georgia," 9.

111   "their own children": Anthony, "Call to NAWSA, 27th Annual Convention" Susan B. Anthony Scrapbook 23, n.d.

111   "and suffering of war": "Woman's Rights in Dixie," *New York Sun,* January 27, 1895, no p., Susan B. Anthony Papers.

112   "of Susan B. Anthony": Katherine Anthony, *Susan B. Anthony,* 417.

112   "in the year 1895": Felton, *Country Life in Georgia,* 111.

112   "in men's work": Felton, *Country Life in Georgia,* 112.

112   "man was the only one": Felton, *Country Life in Georgia,* 113.

113 "thought and public opinion": Felton, *Country Life in Georgia,* 122.

113 "with a splendid audience": Anthony, Diary entry, Thursday, January 31 1895, Susan B. Anthony Papers.

113 "to greater power": Anthony, Diary entry, Sunday, February 3, 1895, Susan B. Anthony Papers.

114 "feeble-minded men": Harper, *History of Woman Suffrage,* vol. 6, 237.

114 "holders [sic] mansion": Anthony, Diary entry, Wednesday, February 6, 1895, Susan B. Anthony Papers.

114 "a cordial welcome": Anthony, Diary entry, Thursday, February 7, 1895, Susan B. Anthony Papers.

114 "Linsly's [sic.] slaves": Anthony, Diary entry, Friday, February 8, 1895, Susan B. Anthony Papers.

114 "woman suffrage to light": *Minutes of the Twenty-Seventh Annual Convention of the National-American Woman Suffrage Association,* p. 60.

11: The Pros vs. the Antis

115 "live with and endure him": Felton, *Country Life in Georgia,* 211.

115 "leave us defenseless": Felton, *Country Life in Georgia,* 213.

116 "continued through life": Felton, *My Memoirs of Georgia Politics,* 180.

117 "of a political opponent": Felton, *My Memoirs of Georgia Politics,* 484-485.

117 "those who suffer by it": Handwritten draft of article on temperance in RLF papers, reel 15.

118 "and ordained of God": Felton, *Country Life in Georgia,* 79.

118 "years of bloody war": Felton, *Country Life in Georgia,* 79.

118 "slavery contention": Felton, *Country Life in Georgia,* 85.

118 "a glorious cause": Felton, *Country Life in Georgia,* 92.

119 "both black and white": Felton, *Country Life in Georgia,* 96-97.

119 "have no fires": Letter from R. L. Felton to her husband, December 10, 1892, in RLF Papers, reel 19.

120 "a civilized country": Letter from R.L. Felton to her family, April 27, 1893, in RLF Papers, reel 19.

120 "its way to the front": Letter from R. L. Felton to her husband, May 3, 1893, in RLF Papers, reel 19.

120 "final count, not clothes": Letter from R. L. Felton to her husband, March 20, 1893, in RLF Papers, reel 19.

120 "over 3000 pieces": Written on the envelope of Mrs. Palmer's thank-you note, December 29, 1893, RLF Papers, reel 19.

120 "of the present generation": Letter from Bertha Honoré Palmer to R.L.Felton, December 29, 1893, RLF Papers, reel 19.

121 "in her dealings": Talmadge, *Rebecca Latimer Felton,* 94-95.

121 "need or want to vote": Talmadge, *Rebecca Latimer Felton,* 103

121 "right to vote": Felton, *Country Life in Georgia,* 297.

121   "man's world of politics": Talmadge, *Rebecca Latimer Felton,* 103.

122   "within the man's domain": Cambi, *Women Against Women,* 7.

122   "reflected this basic fear": Cambi, *Women Against Women,* 10.

123   "smooth running of the home": Cambi, *Women Against Women,* 24.

123   "possible sterility": Cambi, *Women Against Women,* 24.

123   "she is distinctly inferior": Cambi, *Women Against Women,* 40.

123   "rallying their re-enforcements": Cambi, *Women Against Women,* 55.

124   "pure as a rose-leaf": Felton, *My Memoirs of Georgia Politics,* 391.

12: Rebecca, Age 80, the Suffragist

125   "glory enough for her": Camhi, *Women against Women,* 8.

126   "been self evident": Felton, *Country Life in Georgia,* 265.

126   "eternal salvation": Felton, *Country Life in Georgia,* 154.

126   "to enter into marriage": Felton, *Country Life in Georgia,* 154.

126   "all over America": Benjamin, *A. History of the Anti-Suffrage Movement,* 80.

126   "should be everywhere": Felton, *Country Life in Georgia,* 148.

126   "and high character": Felton, *Country Life in Georgia,* 148.

126   "maternal instinct": Felton, *Country Life in Georgia,* 148.

127   "unhappy in married misery": Felton, *Country Life in Georgia,* 149.

127   "address the legislature": Felton, *Country Life in Georgia,* 170.

127   "woman in the state": Felton, *"Country Life in Georgia,* 171.

127   "handed to me": Felton, *Country Life in Georgia,* 171.

128   "law makers of Georgia": Felton, *Country Life in Georgia,* 171.

128   "should be mutual": Felton, *Country Life in Georgia,* 179.

129   "allowed to vote it out": Talmadge, *Rebecca Latimer Felton,* 95.

129   "mother of his children": Handwritten document by Rebecca L. Felton, in RLF Papers, reel 15.

129   "as she saw fit": Handwritten document by Rebecca L. Felton, in RLF Papers, reel 15.

130   "rights for women": Stevens, *The Road is Still Rough,* 317-318.

130   "Dr. Howard Felton": "W. H. Felton Dies after Long Illness," *Atlanta Georgian,* September 25 1909, in RLF Papers, reel 11.

131   "faith in leaving me": Felton, *My Memoirs of Georgia Politics,* p. 401.

131   "of Old School": "W..H. Felton Dies after Long Illness," *Atlanta Georgian,* September 25, 1909, in RLF Papers, reel 11.

132   "hath done it' – not God": William Felton sermon, from RLF papers, reel 9.

132   "work without salary": Felton, *My Memoirs of Georgia Politics,* 12.

133   "a minister of the Gospel": "Beautiful Tribute Paid to Late Dr. WM. H. Felton," untitled newspaper clipping, March, 1910, in RLF papers, reel 11.

133   "to do him justice": Talmadge, *Rebecca Latimer Felton,* 96.

134   "is a dangerous thing": Benjamin, *A History of the Anti-Suffrage Movement,* 71.

13: Troubled Times

136   "unfaithful darkies": MacLean, *Behind the Mask of Chivalry,* 5.
137   "bourbon on his breath": Tindall, *Emergence of the New South,* 186.
137   "regal manhood": Bartley, *Creation of Modern Georgia,* 170.
137   "the Atlanta *Journal*": MacLean, *Behind the Mask of Chivalry,* 6.
137   "expenses and promotion": Tindall, *Emergence of the New South,* 187.
137   "hick the Capitol": Tindall, *Emergence of the New South,* 189.
138   "unto Eternal Day": Tindall, *Emergence of the New South,* 189-190.
138   "Arian citizenship": Simmons, *ABC of the Invisible Empire,* 6.
138   "grew, from developing": Simmons, *ABC of the Invisible Empire,* 38.
139   "This is not true": Hepburn, *Contemporary Georgia,* 25.
139   "body or estate?": Felton, *Country Life in Georgia,* 248-252.
139   "sons and daughters!": Felton, *Country Life in Georgia,* 255.
140   "proceed a little further": Felton, *Country Life in Georgia,* 252.
140   "political and social": Felton, *Country Life in Georgia,* 249.
140   "pay for equal work": Felton, *Country Life in Georgia,* 257
140   "out of their sphere": Felton, *Country Life in Georgia,* 251.
140   "in human liberty": Felton, *Country Life in Georgia,* 251.
140   "men and women": Felton, *Country Life in Georgia,* 260.
141   "my grave with me": "Black Hand: 191," National Archives (Internet).
141   "envelope to the preacher": Hunter, *The Road is Still Rough,* 330.
142   "demons of the underworld": Anderson, "Unchaining the Demons of the Lower World," 2 (unnumbered).
142   : undoing of our government": Anderson. "Unchaining the Demons of the Lower World,"1 (unnumbered).
143   "of womankind": Anderson, "Unchaining the Demons of the Lower World," 9 (unnumbered).
143   "of the temple": Anderson, "Unchaining the Demons of the Lower World," 11 (unnumbered).

14: New Suffragist Tactics

145   "Politics means dissension": Taylor, "The Last Phase of the Woman Suffrage Movement in Georgia," 15.
146   "native land?": Miller, "To President Wilson," "Are Women People?" in *New York Tribune,* n.p.
146   "of common sense": *New York Times, February 7, 1915,* n.p.
146   "Reform Bill was conceived": Miller, "To the Times Editorials," "Are Women People?", in *New York Tribune,* n.p.

147 "the Parliament building": Fuentes, "Alice Paul" in *Three Legendary Feminists,* Internet citation in Bibliography.

147 "nation's capital [sic.]": Feuntes, "Alice Paul," Internet citation in Bibliography.

148 "beautiful white horse": Fuentes, "Alice Paul," Internet citation in Bibliography.

149 "links for the afternoon": "Press Copy from Headquarters of the Congressional Union for Woman Suffrage," 1, in RLF papers, reel 15.

149 "than their counterparts": Scott, *Natural Allies,* 139.

149 "at every election": Felton, "Some Arguments against Woman Suffrage," *Frost's Magazine,* May, 1900s, 18, in RLF papers, reel 20.

150 "franchise for women": Felton, "Some Arguments against woman Suffrage," *Frost's Magazine,* May, 19??, 18, in RLF papers, reel 20.

150 "church obeys Christ": Kelly, *Antisuffrage Arguments in Georgia,* 16.

150 "unscriptural and sinful": Kelly, *Antisuffrage Arguments in Georgia,* 17.

150 "between 1896 and 1910": Scott, *Natural Allies,* 140.

150 "offense at all": M. B. Brown, letter to Rebecca Felton, dated May 25, 1915, in RLF papers reel five, 1.

151 "all the way through": M. B. Brown, letter to Rebecca Felton, dated May 25, 1915, in RLF papers reel five, 3.

151 "hundred feet long": Hickey and Smith, *Seven Days to Disaster, 184-185.*

151 "twenty minutes left to live": Simpson, *The Lusitania,* 9.

152 "delivered to Congress": Fuentes, "Alice Paul," Internet citation in Bibliography.

152 "states, and lobbying": Fuentes, "Alice Paul," Internet citation in Bibliography.

153 "civil disobedience campaign": Fuentes, "Alice Paul," Internet citation in Bibliography.

153 "$3,200,000,000 by 1918": "The United States Enters the War (1914-1917)," 1. www.42explore2.comww1.htm.

154 "strengthen our cause": Taylor, "The Last Phase of the Woman Suffrage Movement in Georgia,"

154 "wait for liberty?": "Alice Paul's Fight for Suffrage," http://pbskids.org/wayback/civilrights/features_fsuffrage.thml n.p.

155 "continue…our battle…": "Alice Paul's Fight for Suffrage," see above.

156 "all through the night": Fuentes, "Alice Paul," end note 7.

156 "doorless shower": Fuentes, "Alice Paul," end note 3.

156 "appallingly negligent": Fuentes, "Alice Paul," end note 5.

156 "twisted, and kicked" Fuentes, "Alice Paul," end note 6.

158 "don't wear any": Blatch, *Mobilizing Woman-Power,* 91

158 "that's the girl": P & P Online Catalog, Internet, seen above, 17.

158 "Browning machine guns": These posters can be seen on the Internet. Search engine Google, for example, P &P Online Catalog.

158 "same status as men": "Thirty Thousand Women Were There," *World War I,* www.42explore2.comww1.htm , 1.

159 "somewhere in Europe": "Thirty Thousand Women Were There," 2.

159 "from them the ballot": Taylor, "The Last Phase of the Woman Suffrage Movement in Georgia.," 15-16.

160 "another twenty-three years": Thirty Thousand Women Were There," 2.

160 "privilege and right?": "Thirty Thousand Women Were There," 3.

160 "representation rejecting it": Taylor, "The Last Phase of the Woman Suffrage Movement in Georgia," 24.

15: The Susan B. Anthony Amendment, Race, and Georgia

161 "report against ratification": Taylor, "The Last Phase of the Woman Suffrage Movement in Georgia," 24.

162 "ashamed of your action": Taylor, "The Last Phase of the Woman Suffrage Movement in Georgia," 24

162 "the Democratic Party": Taylor, "The Last Phase of the Woman Suffrage Movement in Georgia," 26.

163 "peeped in celebration": Hyatt, "Georgia Suffrage Began Here," *Columbus Ledger-Enquirer,* August 27, 1995, A8.

163 "the right to vote": Hyatt, "Georgia Suffrage Began Here," *Columbus-Ledge-Enquirer,* August 27, 1995,A7.

163 "higher than a kite…": Stevens, *The Road is Still Rough,* 392.

163 "women in 1920": Causey, "For Decades Elections were for (White) Men Only," F2.

165 "465,698 blacks": Coleman, *History of Georgia,* 148.

165 "the Southern world": Cash, *The Mind of the South,* 103.

166 "vote in the election": Kelly, *Antisuffrage Arguments in Georgia,* 38-39.

166 "the black voter": Kelly, *Antisuffrage Arguments in Georgia,* 59.

167 "of Reconstruction": Kelly, *Antisuffrage Arguments in Georgia,* 76.

168 "struck by lightning": Cash, *The Mind of the South,* 115.

168 "Southerner rape complex": Cash, *The Mind of the South,* 115.

168 "substituted for fact": Clinton, *The Other Civil War,* 197.

168 "to an inferior status": Clinton, *The Other Civil War,* 196.

168 "Confederate myth-makers": Clinton, *The Other Civil War,* 196.

169 "justification of necessity": Cash, *The Mind of the South,* 119.

170 "nothing to do with rape": Cash, *The Mind of the South,* 117.

172 "week if necessary": "Lynch," says Mrs. Felton," *Atlanta Journal,* August 12, 1897, 1.

172 "speech so incendiary": Whites, "Love, Hate, Rape, Lynching," *Democracy Betrayed,* 171.

172 "Answers *The Boston Transcript*": Felton, "Mrs. Felton Not for Lynching…," *Atlanta Constitution,* August 20, 1897, 4.

172 "towards all men": Talmadge, *Rebecca Latimer Felton,* 113.

173 "charred remains": Felton, "Crime of Mob Violence Unpunished in Georgia, Declares Mrs. Felton," *Atlanta Constitution,* 1/13/20, n.p.

173 "halting distance" Felton, "Crime of Mob Violence Unpunished...," *Atlanta Constitution,* 1/13/20, n.p.

173 "for me at Tybee": Felton, "Crime of Mob Violence Unpunished...." See above.

173 "facts in this case": Felton, "Crime of Mob Violence Unpunished...," *Atlanta Constitution* 1/13/20, n.p.

173 "icon of women's history...": Hess, "*A Call to Honor*", 83.

174 "as is well known": Manly, "Editorial," *The Daily Record,* August 18, 1898, (P.C.1401.1 OS MSS , NC Archives, Raleigh).

175 "Gutted and Burned": "A DAY OF BLOOD AT WILMINGTON, *The News and Observer,* 11/11/1898, 1.

175 "Exciting Incidents": "BLOODY CONFLICT WITH NEGROES," *The Morning Star,* 11/10/1898, 1.

175 "entered my head": "Mrs. Felton vs. Manly, in RLF papers reel 13.

175 "will approve the verdict R. Felton, letter to the press, written in Cartersville, 11/15/1898, RLF papers, reel 13.

176 "in the United States": Mulrooney, *The 1898 Coup and Violence* (abridged), 3-4, on Internet.

177 which I hold identity" Coles, letter from Ardmore, PA, January 21, 1920, in RLF Papers, reel 5..

177 "the *Atlanta Independent*": Hunter, *The Road is Still Rough,* 240.

178 "to the New Testament": Hunter, *The Road is Still Rough,* 246.

179 "poor blacks and whites": Hunter, *The Road is Still Rough,* 242.

179 "men with large ambitions": Felton, *My Memoirs of Georgia Politics,* 5.

16: Georgia's Blues

182 "cowlicks touched his eyebrows": Cooke, *Six Men,* 90.

182 "so vast a vacuity": Mencken, *Prejudices,* 136.

182 "paralyzed cerebrums": Mencken, *Prejudices,* 136.

182 "south of the Potomac...": Mencken, *Prejudices,* 136.

183 "making of beautiful things": Mencken, *Prejudices,* 138.

183 "neighborhood rhymester": Both short quotes are found in Mencken's *Prejudices,* 138.

183 "the lynching bee": Mencken, *Prejudices,* 141.

183 "produced a single idea": Mencken, *Prejudices ,*141.

183 "almost of dead silence": Mencken, *Prejudices,* 142

184 "galvanized gall": Mencken, *Menckeniana,* 13.

184 "in the entire nation": Hepburn, *Contemporary Georgia,* 23.

184 "1923, 588,000": Bartley, *The Creation of Modern Georgia,*169.

185 "lonesome mind": Ma Rainey's lyrics in Davis, *Blues Legacies and Black Feminism,* 208.

185   "Georgia farms forever": Hepburn, *Contemporary Georgia, 25.*

185   "popular and respectable": Editor of the Columbus *Enquirer Sun* , Julian
      Harris and hi wife, Julia, discovered that the Chief of Police in their town
      was a member of the KKK. Muggleston, *Fruitful and disastrous Years,*
      137.

186   "the Alaga Club": Muggleston.. *Fruitful and Disastrous Years,* 136.

186   "Non silba, sed anthar": Tindall, *The Emergence of the New South,* 188.

186   "fee of $10.00": Tindall, *The Emergence of the New South,* 189.

186   "1920 is only $244": Bryan, *The Catalogue of the Georgia Society, 22.*

187   "Peabody School of Education": Hunter, *Rebecca Latimer Felton,* 79.

188   "Law School in 1920": Hunter, *Rebecca Latimer Felton,* 386.

188   "done in Georgia": Bauman, *Warren Akin Candler,* 288.

188   "with equal recklessness": Bauman, *Warren Akin Candler,* 288.

188   "the polls and voted": Bauman, *Warren Akin Candler,* 288-289.

188   "Quebec cigarettes": Bauman, *Warren Akin Candler,* 289.

189   "girls on a vacation": Hunter, *Rebecca Latimer Felton,* 108.

189   "read to the Senate": Hunter, *Rebecca Latimer Felton,* 109.

190   "advice and inspiration": Hunter, *Rebecca Latimer Felton,* 110.

191   "husband in her book": Talmadge, *Rebecca Latimer Felton,* 96.

191   "in central Georgia": See, for example, Mitchell, *Gone With the Wind,*
      632, 423, 404, 405, 418, 419, 421, 322, 430, 607. paperback edition.

191   "in a man's world": See, for example, Mitchell, *Gone with the Wind,*
      628-629.

191   "unsexing themselves": Mitchell, *Gone With the Wind,* 632.

191   "an important meeting": This dress can still be seen in Cartersville at the
      Roselawn Museum, 224 West Cherokee Avenue. Although Rebecca was
      an excellent seamstress, a close examination of the material that she used
      to make her dress reveals that it was originally used for curtains.

192   "live to that period": Felton, Tax Return for 1917, reel 15 of RLF papers.

193   "dear old mother-in-law": Hunter, *Rebecca Latimer Felton,* 111.

193   "would hold public office?": Felton, *The Romantic Story of Georgia's
      Women,* 44.

194   "of women as voters": Floyd, "Rebecca Latimer Felton, Champion of
      Women's Rights," 99.

194   "for your own brow": Lucian Lamar Knight, State Historian, letter from
      the Department of Archives and History, State of Georgia in Atlanta to
      Rebecca Felton, in Cartersville, GA, October 3, 1922 in RLF papers reel
      5.

195   "in the fall primary": Floyd, "Rebecca Latimer Felton, Champion of
      Women's Rights," 99.

195   "purposes quite well": Floyd, "Rebecca Latimer Felton, Champion of
      Women's Rights," 99.

196   "congress in November": "First Woman Senator Comes from Georgia,"
      The Indianapolis News, October 3, 1922, no page, in RLF Papers, reel 5.

196 "from women's organizations": Felton, *Romantic Story of Georgia's Women,* 44.

196 "splendid and useful life": Floyd, "Rebecca Latimer Felton, Champion of Women's Rights," 99.

196 "from the Constitution": Hunter, *Rebecca Latimer Felton,* 112-113.

196 "The credit is all His": Hunter, *Rebecca Latimer Felton,* 113.

196 "the cause of mothers": Ethridge, "Lady from Georgia," 27.

17: From Cartersville to Washington?

199 "vote and support": Draft of a letter written by Rebecca Felton to the citizens of Bartow County, not dated, but obviously written in October, 1922 in RLF Papers, reel 7.

199 "empty honor": Floyd, "Rebecca Latimer Felton, Champion of Women's Rights, 100.

200 "regret in this matter": Talmadge, *Rebecca Latimer Felton,* 140-141.

200 "merry political row": "Effort for Woman Senator Stirs Row," *Washington Star,* October 15, 1922, n. p. in RLF papers. reel 11.

201 "seat Rebecca Latimer Felton": "Effort for Woman Senator Stirs Row," *Washington Star,* October, 22, 1922, in RLF papers, reel 11.

201 "successor was elected": Talmadge, *Rebecca Latimer Felton,* 143.

202 "until next week": Talmadge, *Rebecca Latimer Felton,* 143.

203 "wasn't down yet": Talmadge, *Rebecca Latimer Felton,* 143-144.

203 "decide the matter": Floyd, "Rebecca Latimer Felton, Champion of Women's Rights,*"* 100.

204 "one minute, in the Senate": Floyd, "Rebecca Latimer Felton, Champion of Women's Rights," 101.

204 "on the payroll": Talmadge, "*Rebecca Latimer Felton,* 144.

204 "those protected precincts...": Felton, "*Romantic Story of Georgia's Women,* 45.

205 "the lady a seat?": Talmadge, *Rebecca Latimer Felton,* 144.

206 "what was going to happen": Felton, "*Romantic Story of Georgia's Women,* 44.

206 "is the needless kind": Giles, "The Grand Old Lady of Georgia," 1922, 62.

206 "scare me a bit": Giles, "The Grand Old Lady of Georgia," 1922, 62.

207 "again after a while": "Mrs. W. H. Felton's Own Story," *Atlanta Georgian,* n.p., probably page 1 in RLF papers, reel 11.

207 "for the Senate": Talmadge, *Rebecca Latimer Felton,* 145.

207 "Senator Hoke Smith": "Seating Mrs. Felton," *Atlanta Journal,* November 20, 1922, n.p., in RLF papers, reel 11.

18: The Decision

210   "presented to-morrow": *Congressional Record,* Sixty-Seventh Congress, Third Session, Tuesday, November 21, 1922.

211   "to stop spending it": "Mrs. W. H. Felton's Own Story," *Atlanta Georgian,* 11/22/22, n.p. in RLF papers, reel 11.

211   "be duly sworn in": "Talmadge, *Rebecca Latimer Felton,* 147.

211   "question of high privilege": *Congressional Record,* November 21, 1922, third page of that day.

211   "floor and will proceed": *Congressional Record,* November 21, 1922, third page of that day.

212   "precedents in relation to it": *Congressional Record,* November 21, 1922, 4th page of that day.

212   "legislature may direct": *Congressional Record,* November 21, 1922, 4th page of that day.

212   "sworn into office": *Congressional Record,* November 21. 1922, 5th page of that day.

212   "report of the committee": *Congressional Record,* November 21, 1922, 5th page of that day.

213   "entitled to take the oath": Talmadge, *Rebecca Latimer Felton,* 148.

213   "headquarters in Washington": *Congressional Record,* November 21, 1922, 6th page of that day.

213   "in the case of a man": Felton, *The Romantic Story of Georgia's Women,* 45.

214   "Senator from Georgia": *The World,* November 22, 1922, n. p., in RLF papers reel 11.

214   "HER seat in the Senate": Talmadge, *Rebecca Latimer Felton,*147. He also refers on that same page to Rebecca's smile coming next.

214   "first-thing the following day": *Congressional Record,* November 21, 1922, fifth page of that day.   In RLF papers, reel 19.

215   "of our common country": Talmadge, *Rebecca Latimer Felton,* 149.

215   "happened to be clothed": Giles, "The Grand Old Lady of Georgia," 62.

215   "voice firm, yet gentle.": "Senator for Day, Mrs. Felton Says 'Howdy and Good-By, '" *The Sun Bureau,* November 23, 1922, 1-3.

216   "after I was selected: *Atlanta Georgian,* November 24, `1922, in RLF papers reel 11.

216   "beyond November 7th": Hardwick, personal letter to Rebecca Felton, December 12, 1922, in RLF papers, reel 6.

217   "unstinted usefulness": Talmadge, *Rebecca Latimer Felton,* 148.

Afterword

219 "absence from that state": Much of this information comes from her descendants, who wish to remain anonymous.

219 "June 10, 1934": Certificate of Death for Augusta H. Howard, Department of Health of the City of New York, #AA35245, Register no. 5317.

220 "age of sixty-nine": *Dictionary of Georgia Biography*, Volume I, 483.

221 "qualifications for office": "Georgia Suffragist Association to Keep Up Work," January 16, 1921, newspaper and page missing, in RLF Papers, reel 11.

222 "with equal freedom": Boifeuillet, John T. "Mrs. Mary McLendon As I Knew Her," *Macon News*, November 20, 1921, 6. in RLF Papers, reel 5.

222 "on a high tower": Unnamed or dated newspaper clipping in RLF Papers, reel 11.

223 "put behind you": Claire Giles, "The Grand old Lady of Georgia," in *The Business Woman,* 1922, 37, 61- 62.

223 "them any harm": "Many Sides to Personality Shown in Felton Anecdotes," *Atlanta Constitution?* January, 1930, in RLF papers, reel 22.

223 "a hard looking race": "Body of Mrs. Rebecca Latimer Felton Lies in State at Cartersville Home," *Atlanta Journal.* January 25, 1930, 1, cont. in RLF papers, reel 22.

223 "Government Printing Office "Body of Mrs. Rebecca Latimer Felton Lies in State at Cartersville Home," RLF papers, reel 22.

223 "sold to the cheering voters": "Body of Mrs. Rebecca Latimer Felton Lies in State at Cartersville Home," RLF papers, reel 22.

224 "support this great institution": "Body of Mrs. Rebecca Latimer Felton…" RLF papers, reel 22.

224 "children can buy it": "Give U.S. People Good Liquor, Says Woman ex-Stnator, 92" unnamed newspaper clipping in RLF papers, reel 17.

224 "to know about it": Talmadge. *Rebecca Latimer Felton,* 158

225 "Women of her time": "One of Greatest Women of Time,' George Declares," unnamed newspaper clipping January 1930 in RLF papers, reel 22.

225 "state has ever produced": "Ragsdale's Statement" in unnamed newspaper account of Felton death, January 1930, in RLF papers, reel 22.

Bibliography

Anderson, Eugene. *Unchaining the Demons of the Lower World, or a petition of ninety-nine per cent against suffrage.* Macon, GA: Georgia Association Opposed to Woman Suffrage, n.d.

Anonymous. *The Case Against Woman Suffrage: A Manual for Speakers, Debaters, Lecturers, Writers, and Anyone Who Wants the Facts,* Intro by Hon Everett P. Wheeler, publication no 12 of the Man-Suffrage Association (no date).

Ansley, J. J. *History of the Georgia Woman's Christian Temperance Union from its Organization, 1883 to 1907.* Columbus, GA: Gilbert Printing Co., 1914.

Anthony, Katherine. *Susan B. Anthony: Her History and Her Era.* Garden City, New York: Doubleday & Company, Inc. 1954.

Anthony, Susan B. "Call to NAWSA, 27th Annual Convention" Susan B. Anthony Scrapbook 23, n.d. Susan B. Anthony Papers, 1895, DLC.

_____. unpublished *Excelsior Diary 1895.* describing trip to Atlanta and to Howard Home, Susan B. Anthony Papers, 1895, DLC.

Anthony, Susan B. and Ida Husted Harper, ed. *History of Woman Suffrage.* Vol. 4, New York: Arno & The New York Times, 1969.

Bartley, Numan V. *The Creation of Modern Georgia.* Athens, GA: The University of Georgia Press, 1983.

Bauman, Mark Keith. *Warren Akin Candler: Conservative Amidst Change.* Unpublished dissertation, Warren Akin Candler Collection, Emory University, 1975.

Benjamin, Anne Myra Goodman. *A History of the Anti-suffrage Movement in the United States from 1895 to 1920.* Lewiston, New York: Edwin Mellen Press, Ltd. 1992.

Blatch, Harriot Stanton. *Mobilizing Woman-Power.* Foreword by Theodore Roosevelt, New York: The Woman's Press, 1918.

"Bloody Conflict with Negroes: White Men Forced to Take Up Arms for the Preservation of Law and Order." *Morning Star* (Wilmington, NC), November 10, 1898, 1.

Bryan, Mary Givens. *The Catalogue of the Georgia Society.* Atlanta: DAR, 1955.

Cambi, Jane J. *Women against Women: American Anti-Suffragism, 1880-1920.* Brooklyn, NY: Carlson Publishing, 1994.

Cash, W. J. *The Mind of the South.* New York: Vintage Books, 1991.

Cass County Census of 1850.

Causey, Virginia. "For Decades Elections were for (White) Men Only," in "Viewpoint," *Columbus Ledger-Enquirer,* March 26, 2000, F 1-2.

Chalmers, David M. *Hooded Americanism: The History of the Ku Klux Klan.* Durham, Duke University Press, 1968.

Clinton, Catherine. *The Other Civil War: American Women in the Nineteenth Century.* New York: Hill and Wang, 1999.

Coleman, Kenneth, ed. *A History of Georgia.* Athens, GA: University of Georgia Press, 1977.

Collins, Ann F. Letter sent to A. Louise Staman (Collins is a direct descendant of Rebecca Latimer Felton).

Congressional Record, Sixty-Seventh Congress, Third Session, Vo. 63, no. 2, Washington, November 1922, in RLF Papers, reel 19.

Cooke, Alistair. *Six Men: Charles Chaplin, H.L. Mencken, Humphrey Bogart, Adlai Stevenson, Bertrand Russell, Edward VIII.* New York: Berkley, 1977.

Cunyus, Lucy Josephine. *The History of Bartow County, Formerly Cass.* Cartersville, GA: Tribune Publishing Co., 1933.

Davis, Angela Y. *Blues Legacies and Black Feminism: Gertrude "Ma" Rainey, Bessie Smith, and Billie Holiday.* New York: Vintage Books (Random House), 1998.

Davis, Burke. *Sherman's March.* New York: Random House, 1980.

"A Day of Blood at Wilmington." *The News and Observer* (Raleigh, NC), November 11, 1898, 1.

"Dr. Hawthorne Will not Bandy Words of Controversy with Mrs. Felton," *Atlanta Constitution,* January 14, 1893, 3.

Eaton, Clement. *The Waning of the Old South Civilization: 1860-1880's.* Athens: University of Georgia Press, 1968.

Ethridge, Willie Snow, "The *Lady* from Georgia," *Good Housekeeping,* January 23, 1923, 27, 122-125.

Evans, Sara M. *Born for Liberty: A History of Women in America.* New York: The Free Press (division of Macmillan, Inc.), 1989.

Felton, Rebecca Latimer. *Collection.* Personal papers for Rebecca Latimer and William Harrell Felton donated to the University of Georgia at Athens shortly before and after Rebecca Felton's death. Includes her scrapbooks containing newspaper clippings, handwritten speeches, letters to Rebecca Latimer Felton, some bills, Christmas cards, some typed speeches, and various miscellaneous papers. Part of Hargrett Rare Book Library. Now contained on twenty-two microfilm reels.

_____. *Country Life in Georgia in the Days of my Youth.* Reprint. New York: Arno Press, 1980.
_____. "Crime of Mob Violence Unpunished in Georgia, Declares Mrs. Felton," *Atlanta Constitution,* 1/13/20, n.p.

_____. *My Memoirs of Georgia Politics.* Atlanta: Index Printing Company, 1911.

_____. *The Romantic Story of Georgia's Women.* As told to Carter Brooke Jones in *The Atlanta Georgian.* Atlanta: Atlanta Georgian and Sunday American, 1930.

Floyd, Josephine Bone. "Rebecca Latimer Felton, Champion of Women's Rights," *The Georgia Historical Quarterly.* Vol. 30, June 1946, Athens, GA, 81-104.

Foster, Gaines M. *Ghosts of the Confederacy: Defeat, the Lost Cause, and the Emergence of the New South 1865 to 1913.* New York: Oxford University Press, 1987.

Fuentes, Sonia Pressman. "Alice Paul," *Three Legendary Feminists.* Moondance
http://www.moondance.org/1998/winter98/nonfiction/sonia.html

Giles, Claire. "The Grand Old Lady of Georgia." *The Business Woman*, 1922, 37, 61, 62.

Harper, Ida Husted. *History of Woman Suffrage.* Vol. 6, New York: Arno, The New York Times, 1969.

Hepburn, Lawrence R., Editor. *Contemporary Georgia.* Athens, GA: The University of Georgia Press, 1992.

Hess, Mary A. *"A Call to Honor": Rebecca Latimer Felton and White Supremacy.* Unpublished thesis for Master of Arts in history from Michigan State University, 1999.

Hickey, Des and Gus Smith. *Seven Days to Disaster: The Sinking of the Lusitania*, New York: Collins, 1981.

Hobson, Fred. *Mencken: A Life.* Baltimore: The Johns Hopkins University Press, 1994.

Howard, H. Augusta. "Progress of the Woman Suffrage Movement in Georgia," in *Woman's Progress* (Philadelphia, 1893-1896) II, no. 2.

Hunter, Joan Connery. *Rebecca Latimer Felton.* Unpublished thesis, University of Georgia, 1944.

Hyatt, Richard. "Georgia Suffrage Began Here," *Columbus Ledger-Enquirer,* August 7, 1995, A7.

Johnson, Gerald W. "Southern Image-Breakers." *Virginia Quarterly Review,* IV (October, 1928), 508-19.

Jones, James P. "Wilson's Raiders Reach Georgia: The Fall of Columbus, 1865." *Georgia Historical Quarterly,* vol. 59, no. 3 (1975), 313-327.

Kelly, Mary Kathryn. *Antisuffrage Arguments in Georgia: 1890-1920.* Unpublished thesis for M.A. at Emory University, 1973.

Kennett, Lee. *Marching through Georgia: The Story of Soldiers and Civilians during Sherman's Campaign.* New York, NY: Harper Collins, 1995.

Lane, Mills. *Georgia: History Written by Those Who Lived It.* Savannah: Beehive Press, 1995.

Lewis, Nell Battle. "Negro Slavery Throws Dark Shadow Across the South to Keep Southern Women from Securing Their Freedom," *News and Observer, Raleigh, N. C.,* May 3, 1925, 6.

"Love for Magnolias May Cost Willie Lee His Life," *Columbus Ledger,* May 21, 1920, headline.

"'Lynch,' says Mrs. Felton," *Atlanta Journal,* August 12, 1897, 1.

MacLean, Nancy. *Behind the Mask of Chivalry: The Making of the Second Ku Klux Klan.* New York: Oxford University Press, 1994.

Manly, "Editorial," *The Daily Record,* August 18, 1898, (P.C.1401.1 OS MSS , NC Archives, Raleigh, On Internet.

Martin, John H., ed. *Columbus, Geo., from its Selection as a "Trading Town" in 1827 to its Partial Destruction by Wilson's Raid, in 1865,* Columbus, GA: Thos. Gilbert, 1874.

Mattingly, Carol. *Well-Tempered Women: Nineteenth-Century Rhetoric.* Carbondale and Edwardsville: Southern Illinois University Press, 1998.

Mencken, H. L. *Prejudices: Second Series.* New York: Alfred A. Knopf, 1924.

Mill, John Stuart. *On Liberty* and *The Subjection of Women.* New York: Henry Holt and Company, 1898.

Miller, Alice Duer. *Are Women People?* 1915. http://womenshistory.about.com/library/etext/bl_awp_about.htm

"Mrs. Felton," *Atlanta Constitution,* January 13, 1893, 3.

"Mrs. Felton not for Lynching...." *Atlanta Constitution.* August 20, 1897, 4.

Milestone, William Frederick. *Fruitful and Disastrous Years" The Life of Julian Larose Harris.* Unpublished Dissertation for University of GA, Athens, GA, 1972.

Mulrooney, Margaret M. "The 1898 Coup and Violence," (Abridged) http://www.spinnc.org/1898/resources/history.htm from 1898 Foundation, Inc., Wilmington, N.C.

Olsen, Kirstin. *Chronology of Woman's History.* Westport, CN: Greenwood Press, 1994.

Pierce, Alfred M. *Giant Against the Sky: The Life of Bishop Warren Akin Candler.* Nashville: Abingdon-Cokesbury Press, 1948.

"Prints and Photographs Online Catalog," The Library of Congress (Women in World War I) http://www.loc.gov/rr/print/catalog.html

Proceedings of the Twenty-sixth Annual Convention of the National American Woman Suffrage Association. published by the National American Woman Suffrage Association, 1894.

Scott, Anne Firor. *Natural Allies: Women's Associations in American History.* Urbana: University of Illinois Press, 1991.

"Senator for Day, Mrs. Felton Says 'Howdy And Goodbye,'" *The Sun Bureau,* November 23, 1922, 1-3.

Shavin, Norman. *Atlanta Then, Atlanta Now.* Atlanta: Capricorn Corporation, 1978.

Sherman, W. T. *William Tecumseh Sherman: Memoirs of General W. T. Sherman,* Three volumes. New York: The Library of America, 1990.

Sibley, Celestine. *Peachtree Street, U.S.A.: An Affectionate Portrait of Atlanta.* Garden City, New York: Doubleday & Company, Inc., 1963.

Simmons, W. J. *ABC of the Invisible Empire: Knights of the Ku Klux Klan.* Atlanta: Knights of the Ku Klux Klan, 1917.

Simpson, Colin. *The Lusitania.* Boston: Little, Brown and Company, 1972.

Stevens, Carole A. *The Road is Still Rough: The Contribution of the Latimer Sisters to Georgia's Temperance and Suffrage work, 1880-1921.* Unpublished thesis. Georgia State University Special Collections, 1994.

"Summary of Court Cases Regarding Howard v. the State" August 5, 1920 to December 14, 1921, unpublished. Columbus County Courthouse.

Talmadge, John E. *Rebecca Latimer Felton: Nine Stormy Decades.* Athens, GA: University of Georgia Press, 1960.

Tankersley, Allen P., *John B. Gordon: A Study in Gallantry.* Atlanta: Whitehall Press, 1955.

Taylor, A. Elizabeth. "The Last Phase of the Woman Suffrage Movement in Georgia," *Georgia Historical Quarterly*, Vol. 43. No. 1, 11-28.

_____ "The Origin of the Woman Suffrage Movement in Georgia." *Georgia Historical Quarterly.* Vol. 28, No. 2, 1-17.

_____ "Revival and Development of the Woman Suffrage Movement in Georgia." *Georgia Historical Quarterly,* Vol. 42, No. 4, 339-354.

Taylor, William R. *Cavalier and Yankee: The Old South and American National Character.* New York: George Braziller, 1961.

Telfair, Nancy. *A History of Columbus, Georgia, 1828-1928.* Columbus, Georgia: The Historical Publishing Company, 1929.

"Thirty Thousand Women Were There." *World War I,* www.42explore2.comww1.htm , 1.

Tindall, George Brown. *The Emergence of the New South:1913-1945*, in vol. X of *A History of the South,* edited by Wendell Holmes Stephenson and E. Merton Coulter. Baton Rouge: Louisiana State University Press, 1967.

Tyler, Helen E. *Where Prayer and Purpose Meet: 1874 – The WCTU Story – 1949.* Evanston, Illinois: The Signal Press, 1949.

Unknown Author. "Alice Paul's Fight for Suffrage," http://opbskids.org/wayback/cicilrights/features_fsuffrage.thmll

256 Bibliography

Whites, LeeAnn. "Love, Hate, Rape, Lynching: Rebecca Latimer Felton and the Gender Politics of Racial Violence," in *Democracy Betrayed: the Wilmington Race Riot of 1898 and its Legacy.* Ed. David S. Cecelski and Timothy B. Tyson: Chapel Hill: University of North Carolina Press, 1998.

"Woman Shoots Small Boy for Climbing Tree." *Columbus Enquirer-Sun,* May 21, 1920, p. 1.

"Woman's Rights in Dixie," *New York Sun,* January 27, 1895, no p., Susan B. Anthony Papers.

Writers' Program of the Work Projects in the State of Georgia. *Atlanta: A City of the Modern South.* St. Clair Shores, MI: Smith & Durrell, 1973.

Worsley, Etta Blanchard. *Columbus on the Chattahoochee.* Columbus: Columbus Office Supply Company, 1951.

Index

257

Questions for Discussion

1. What surprised you most about Rebecca?
2. What qualities do you most admire in her?
3. What do you think people can learn from Rebecca?
4. Why do you think she became more liberal as she grew older?
5. Why did she become interested in politics decades before she could vote?
6. What, if anything, did you dislike about this woman?
7. Although women's lives have changed significantly since Rebecca's time, modern women still find that many attitudes and customs have been passed from generation to generation that remain unchanged. What has changed, and what remains unchanged?
8. How did the men in Rebecca's life influence her actions? What were the positive influences? The negative?
9. Did you identify with Rebecca and her battles?
10. Why do you think that she is nearly forgotten today?
11. How do you think she managed to enter into the wealthy circles of a Bertha Honoré Palmer and the powerful echelons of Presidents when she had almost no power and comparatively little wealth of her own?

12.   To what other woman in American history can she be compared?
13.   Could you call her a woman who was formed by the Civil War?
14.   Is her being seated in the Senate in Washington D.C. important? Why?
15.   Before you read the book, did you know what problems women faced within this country, and particularly in the South, a century or more ago?